American Cooking: Southern Style

TIME
LIFE
BOOKS ®

Foods of the World

American Cooking: Southern Style

by

Eugene Walter

and the Editors of

TIME-LIFE BOOKS

studio photographs by

Mark Kauffman

TIME-LIFE BOOKS, NEW YORK

THE AUTHOR: Eugene Walter *(far left),* a native of Mobile, Alabama, who lives in Rome, is a neo-Renaissance man. To wit: During World War II he served as a cryptographer in the United States Army. Later he organized a chamber orchestra in Mobile, then moved to Paris and wrote his first novel, *The Untidy Pilgrim,* which was awarded the Lippincott Prize. His first book of verse, *Monkey Poems,* won him a Sewanee-Rockefeller fellowship. He has served as associate editor to 10 different literary magazines, is a designer of magazine covers and illustrations, made his operatic debut in Hans Werner Henze's *The Young Lord* at the Rome opera, and has written for and appeared in numerous motion pictures, including Federico Fellini's *8½* and *Fellini Satyricon.*

THE STUDIO PHOTOGRAPHER: Mark Kauffman is a former LIFE staff photographer. His other books in the FOODS OF THE WORLD Library include *The Cooking of Provincial France, American Cooking* and *Classic French Cooking.* Still-life materials for his pictures were chosen by Yvonne McHarg.

THE CONSULTANT: James A. Beard *(far left),* special adviser on American regional foods, is a noted authority—and prolific author—on the culinary arts.

THE CONSULTING EDITOR: The late Michael Field *(left)* supervised the adapting and writing of recipes for this book. One of America's foremost food experts and culinary teachers, he wrote many articles for leading magazines. His books include *Michael Field's Cooking School* and *All Manner of Food.*

THE COVER: Fried chicken and crisp corn sticks are two of the South's most distinctive dishes. Both are listed in the Recipe Index.

TIME-LIFE BOOKS

EDITOR: Jerry Korn
Executive Editor: A. B. C. Whipple
Planning Director: Oliver E. Allen
Text Director: Martin Mann
Art Director: Sheldon Cotler
Chief of Research: Beatrice T. Dobie
Director of Photography: Melvin L. Scott
Associate Planning Director: Byron Dobell
Assistant Text Directors: Ogden Tanner, Diana Hirsh
Assistant Art Director: Arnold C. Holeywell
Assistant Chief of Research: Martha T. Goolrick

PUBLISHER: Joan D. Manley
General Manager: John D. McSweeney
Business Manager: John Steven Maxwell
Sales Director: Carl G. Jaeger
Promotion Director: Paul R. Stewart
Public Relations Director: Nicholas Benton

FOODS OF THE WORLD

SERIES EDITOR: Richard L. Williams
EDITORIAL STAFF FOR AMERICAN COOKING: SOUTHERN STYLE:
Associate Editor: William K. Goolrick
Picture Editor: Kaye Neil
Designer: Albert Sherman
Staff Writers: Helen I. Barer, Gerry Schremp
Chief Researcher: Sarah B. Brash
Researchers: Barbara Ensrud, Clara Nicolai, Diana Sweeney, Timberlake Wertenbaker
Test Kitchen Chef: John W. Clancy
Test Kitchen Staff: Fifi Bergman, Tina Cassel, Leola Spencer
Design Assistant: Anne B. Landry

EDITORIAL PRODUCTION
Production Editor: Douglas B. Graham
Quality Director: Robert L. Young
Assistant: James J. Cox
Copy Staff: Rosalind Stubenberg, Grace Hawthorne, Florence Keith
Picture Department: Dolores A. Littles, Joan Lynch, Barbara S. Simon
Studio: Gloria duBouchet

The text for this book was written by Eugene Walter, the recipe instructions by Michael Field, Gerry Schremp and Helen I. Barer, and other material by the staff. Valuable assistance was given by these individuals and departments of Time Inc.: Editorial Production, Norman Airey, Margaret T. Fischer; Library, Peter Draz; Picture Collection, Doris O'Neil; Photographic Laboratory, George Karas; TIME-LIFE News Service, Murray J. Gart; Correspondents Ann Natanson (Rome), Jack Bass (Columbia), Jim Bready (Baltimore), Sandra Hinson (Orlando), Jack Kestner (Norfolk), James Latimer (Richmond), Joyce Leviton (Atlanta), William Peterson (Louisville), Jane Rieker (Miami) and Wayne Whitt (Nashville).

Contents

The Recipe Booklet that accompanies this volume has been designed for use in the kitchen. It contains all of the 60 recipes printed in this book and 90 more. It also has a wipe-clean cover and a spiral binding so that it can either stand up or lie flat when open.

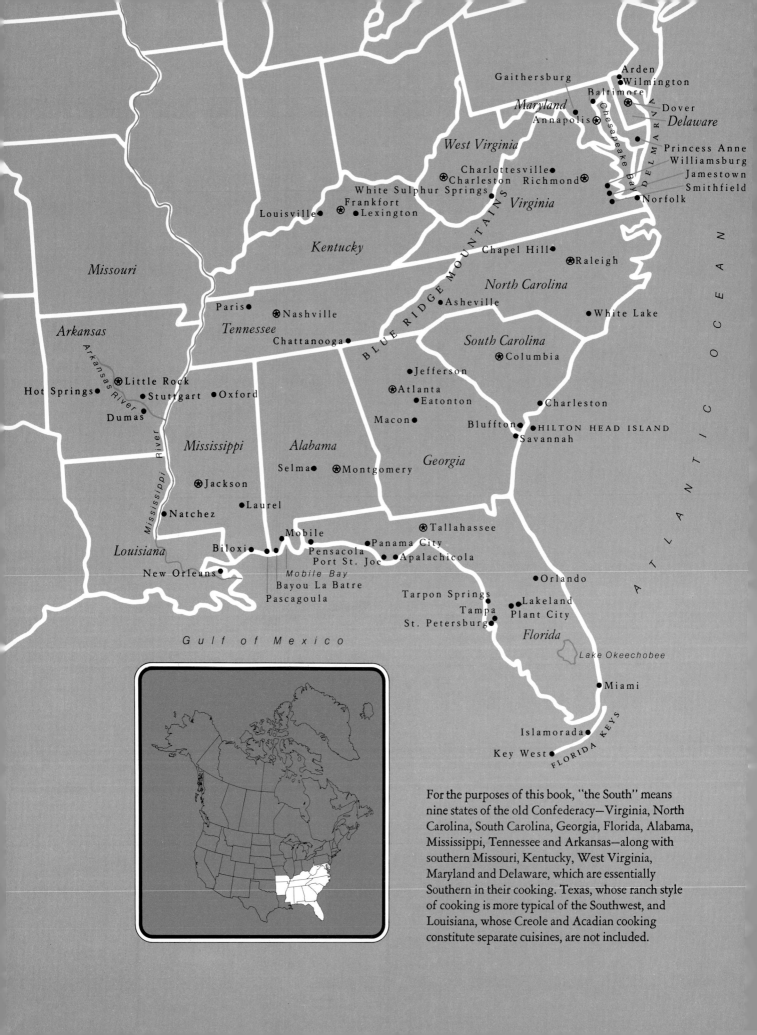

Gaithersburg

Arden
Wilmington
Baltimore
Dover
Maryland
Annapolis
Delaware

West Virginia

Charlottesville
Charleston Richmond
White Sulphur Springs
Virginia
Frankfort
Louisville Lexington

Princess Anne
Williamsburg
Jamestown
Smithfield
Norfolk

Kentucky

Chapel Hill
Raleigh

Missouri

North Carolina

Paris
Nashville
Tennessee
Chattanooga

Asheville

White Lake

Arkansas

Hot Springs
Little Rock
Stuttgart Oxford
Dumas

South Carolina

Columbia

Jefferson
Atlanta
Eatonton
Macon

Charleston

Bluffton
Savannah
HILTON HEAD ISLAND

Mississippi
Alabama

Jackson

Selma Montgomery

Georgia

Laurel
Natchez

Mobile

Louisiana
Biloxi
Pensacola
Port St. Joe
Panama City
Apalachicola

Tallahassee

New Orleans
Mobile Bay
Bayou La Batre
Pascagoula

Orlando

Tarpon Springs
Tampa
St. Petersburg
Lakeland
Plant City

Florida

Gulf of Mexico

Lake Okeechobee

ATLANTIC OCEAN

Miami

Islamorada
FLORIDA KEYS
Key West

Arkansas River

Mississippi River

Chesapeake Bay

DELMARVA

BLUE RIDGE MOUNTAINS

For the purposes of this book, "the South" means nine states of the old Confederacy—Virginia, North Carolina, South Carolina, Georgia, Florida, Alabama, Mississippi, Tennessee and Arkansas—along with southern Missouri, Kentucky, West Virginia, Maryland and Delaware, which are essentially Southern in their cooking. Texas, whose ranch style of cooking is more typical of the Southwest, and Louisiana, whose Creole and Acadian cooking constitute separate cuisines, are not included.

A Rediscovery of the South

While this book was in preparation I flew to Rome to talk with the author, Eugene Walter. I called on him at his apartment on the Corso Vittorio Emanuele, and we spent some hours going over our plans for the book. Then he took me out on the terrace to show me his garden.

As we stepped into the bright sunlight, Eugene pointed up the street and said, "That's the church of Sant' Andrea della Valle, where the first act of *Tosca* takes place." Then he turned and pointed in the opposite direction. "That's the church of Jesus," he said. "There's a legend that the devil and the wind came around the corner down there one day, and the devil said, 'You stay here. I'll be right back.' Then he went into the church and he never did come out. The wind has been waiting there ever since. It's the windiest corner in Rome—sometimes it blows so hard it knocks my flowerpots over."

On the terrace above the busy street, there were green things growing everywhere: passion fruit, Oswego tea, miniature red tomatoes, onions, chives, ribbon chervil, wormwood ("I don't make absinthe, but I could," Eugene said), rue, green bay, pomegranates, rosemary, sweet marjoram and an avocado whose blossoms had been scattered by the wind blowing up from the corner down the street. Eugene showed me a pair of strawberry plants and apologized for their condition. "I'm sorry I can't show you some strawberries," he said; "we had 10 ripe ones today, but I ate them all for lunch." He pointed out a pot of the familiar dark green mint used in juleps in the South, and he pinched off a leaf of a variegated white-edged mint from another plant and held it out for me to sniff. "It's too strong for juleps," he explained. "I use it to decorate the trays that I serve juleps on."

Eugene Walter has the greenest thumb I have ever seen, and he is also uniquely qualified to write this book. He was born and raised in the deepest part of the South—Mobile, Alabama. Although he left home not long after World War II to study and work in Europe, his enthusiasm for Southern food has never diminished. He is, in fact, so fond of it that he regularly prepares and serves Southern dishes in Rome. "I like rice, or grits, or spoon bread every day," he told me. "I just feel better if I have had one of them."

Along with his zest for Southern food, Eugene brings another special qualification to this book; in a sense, he is a Southern Rip van Winkle. When he traveled through the South to gather his research, it was the first time in more than 20 years that he had been in that region. His trip was a journey of rediscovery and the result is an informative, affectionate, highly entertaining report.

—*William K. Goolrick*
Associate Editor

I

The Southland I Remember

Fine cooking and gracious dining are as much a part of the South as colonnaded plantation houses. This lawn-party collation in Mobile, Alabama, offers a variety of classic Southern dishes. Going clockwise from the fried chicken at the top are cold roast turkey, baking-powder biscuits, Georgia ham ringed with fruit, and pecan pie.

W hen people ask where I come from I always reply, "I'm Southern." Even though I have lived in Rome and Paris for more than 20 years, the words come automatically. My nationality is *Southern* before it is American. When people say *America* I am tempted to whip out pencil and paper and ask them to draw me a little map of what they mean: do they include Tierra del Fuego and Hudson Bay or does the name symbolize for them something roughly corresponding to the continental limits of the United States? Or does *America* mean instead a fine clutch of abstract ideas including "Washington," "red-white-and-blue" and "the pursuit of happiness"? There are no such doubts when I say, "I'm Southern"—most people, even in Europe, know what is signified. They know I come from that country within a country, recognized as such although having no definable boundary (Mason-Dixon is useful as a conversational shortcut, but doesn't really work) and generally understood to have something special about it. The region called "the South" has little real unity whether in terms of geography, historical development, linguistic or cultural tradition, yet people from the area are Southerners first and Georgians, Mississippians or whatever after that.

More than anything, Southerners are bound by a shared attitude. In the years that followed the Civil War (known in the South as the War between the States) this attitude was epitomized by Joseph Cain, a clerk in the Mobile market, who rallied his friends on Shrove Tuesday, 1866, to revive the Carnival, the Mardi Gras, which had not been celebrated since the war began. Cain and his cohorts assembled in Wragg Swamp, where

Mississippi River steamboats were a colorful part of the Southern scene in the 19th Century. As depicted in this Currier & Ives lithograph, floating palaces such as the *Queen of the West* set forth on their river voyages with fireworks and fanfare. And one of the principal pleasures on these boats was their gastronomic delights: from sautéed robins and teal ducks to brightly hued ices and blancmange, a fancy confection with almonds and sugar.

they rubbed their faces with red clay and soot, decked themselves with Spanish moss and dead leaves, and rode into Mobile in a decorated charcoal wagon, making an infernal din on abandoned Yankee military band instruments. They called themselves "Chief Slackabamirimico and His Lost Cause Minstrels." It is this role that the South elected to play after the war—lost cause minstrel, wearing a mask to hide the hurt of defeat.

Even today, the South is quirky, quick to take offense, fanciful: it has an attitude, a frame of mind. It prefers the flowery to the plain, likes its own jokes, its own rhetoric. It can laugh at itself at home, but is immediately riled at any snicker from outside. During the years after the Civil War the region took its tone, set its style, cocked its snoot, *decided* to become set in its ways and pleasurably conscious of being so. Traditions became doubly important; the South set about glamorizing its past and transforming anecdote into legend. And among the rites and observances, none was more important than those of the table.

When I was invited to return to the United States and set foot in the South for the first time in more than two decades in order to prepare this book, I mulled over all this and wondered what I would find. In a sense I had never left home: in Rome I live as I lived in Mobile. On my terrace garden I have five kinds of mint, five kinds of onions and chives, as well as four-o'clocks and sweet olive. I take a nap after the midday meal; there is always time for gossip and for writing letters. I eat Southern dishes: fried chicken, grits and spoon bread, having learned to cook almost all of them since I left home. I enjoy guests, I stay up the nights of the full moon, my life is one long quest for a perfect cup of hot strong black coffee. And that was how it was when I was growing up in my grandmother's house on Bayou Street in Mobile, Alabama.

Ma-Ma, my grandmother, was a tiny woman with brown eyes, laugh lines, and clanking amethyst or amber or jet beads. She set a superior table and was proud of it. Her kitchen and dining room were her life. The first sound in the morning, even before the maid arrived, was Ma-Ma's carpet slippers, flap-flapping down the hall as she went to shake the ashes out of her iron stove and fire it up. She kept a four-burner gas stove alongside her older six-lidded black iron wood stove. She claimed that nobody could bake anything edible in a gas stove, or prepare a proper long-simmering gumbo or stew. The breakfast biscuits occupied her first thing; when they had been placed in the oven, she flap-flapped back to her room to dress for the morning. Rebecca, the maid, arrived to prepare the morning meal, and then she and my grandmother had a first cup of coffee and their first gossip of the day. Their conversation always included food, the dishes contemplated for that day, or raw materials to be obtained from the market.

"First crowder peas is come, Miss Annie!" Rebecca might announce with triumph. Or, angrily: "Them sparrows is back at the plums!"

If somebody was going off very early, hunting or fishing or traveling, his breakfast might be at the huge square kitchen table, but generally it was in the dining room, and a serious meal. There were flowers in the middle of the table, a small bouquet flanked by the dishes of jams or preserves and the honey pot and sorghum pitcher. The fruit juice fad was unknown, but there was usually an orange or stewed fruit to begin the meal. In summer it might be iced cantaloupe or Persian melon, with a wedge of lemon and a sprig of mint, or the much-appreciated Concord grapes. Then came grits with fried ham, or fried chicken livers or eggs in any one of a dozen ways. Calves' brains and scrambled eggs appeared once a week, and in the winter we had fried pork chops or small steaks—"breakfast steaks"—or pork sausage with fried apples. The hot biscuits, often the sort called "twin biscuits" because they were cooked in pairs, one on top of the other with butter in between, accompanied everything but came into their own as sops for sorghum. My favorite breakfast was fried fish and fried bananas. On rare occasions red plantains turned up. There was almost always a plate of bacon. Coffee with cream went along with the entire meal. Nobody drank sweet milk; it was seldom seen outside the kitchen. Buttermilk was my beverage.

By the time breakfast was over it was about 8 o'clock, and in warm weather the next hour was given over to the kitchen garden. The backyard area was enclosed by a high wooden fence. Between the kitchen and the stables was an area paved with gray flagstones, which had come to Mobile from France as ballast in ships that took cotton back. On one side of this paved area there was a wooden platform with a faucet, used when Rebecca was plucking fowl or washing greens and roots from the garden. The garden itself was small and very tidy: lettuces (several kinds), a few rows of sweet corn, a few bell peppers, carrots, radishes, okra, tomatoes

(including a small pinkish acid one I've never seen since), eggplant, parsley, dill, small-leaved basil, red peppers. There was a fig tree and a plum tree. An enormous pecan tree shaded the paved area: at its foot reposed every discarded lettuce leaf, every eggshell, every blade of grass that had been mowed on the front lawn. This compost heap was the secret of the kitchen garden's excellence.

The daily grind of weeding and tying up tomatoes or beans fell to my grandmother. Bugging was my specialty, and my grandfather had the pleasure of watering the plot in the evening. No orchid fancier in his thermostated hothouse, no breeder of rare peonies, ever showed more concern than my grandparents for that small garden, which was as pretty in its way as the flower beds in front of the house. They took their greatest pleasure in fresh things in season rushed from plant to dinner table. The corn was never picked until the water was put on the stove to boil it in. Fresh radishes were plunged into ice water an hour before the meal and served with crusty bread, fresh country butter, and a little pile of salt on each plate. To eat one of these radishes was to experience the truth of the radish, and I remember that "as sad as a store-bought radish" was one of Ma-Ma's favorite similes.

Midmorning in that house at the corner of Bayou and Conti Streets was a kind of mad levee, a morning party like those held by King Louis XIV of France, when people were received and the day's events were discussed. My grandmother would install herself in a rocking chair on the high back porch to glance at the morning Mobile *Register,* shell beans and sip a lemonade or iced tea. And hold court.

The "boboshilly" was usually the first to appear. Like the djin from the lamp, she was suddenly there. The boboshillies were the two or three old Indian women who came into town to sell gumbo filé, a few wild herbs like burnet, bay laurel leaves, sassafras root, sometimes wild persimmons in the fall after frost. This one wore a cotton print dress faded almost to white, and a kind of turban of white cloth. I don't think I ever heard her utter a sound, and she moved like a shadow, completely silent and seemingly weightless. She would never sit and never stay.

There were any number of vegetable wagons that passed in Conti Street, and according to the needs of the day, I would have to cry out, "Crowder peas?" or "What kind of squash?" or stop any wagon with promising-looking melons. I would also watch for the oyster man coming down the street with his pushcart full of ice and oysters covered by a great burlap that smelled part wet dog and part rowboat, an umbrella on a pole quaking over all. His cry carried for blocks:

"Oy-ay-ees-oy-ster man, manny-man, manny-man, manny-man!"

"There he is!" I'd cry. "He's stopping for Miss Nana!"

The oyster man would be accosted at the curb by Rebecca with a pail; he never entered the garden. But Miz Mimms, the country-butter lady, arrived by car and made a proper entry with much ado. There was a sliding section of the back fence, which was balanced on a kind of overhead trolley mechanism. Miz Mimms would heave it open with a crash and clatter most impressive. She was a pure Anglo-Saxon provincial type, every visible inch of her skin dotted with small yellow-ocher freckles. She was not

Opposite: Breakfast down South can be a sumptuous affair. It is certain to include a broad variety of foods, some of which are not usually associated with breakfast in other parts of the country. Starting below the coffee pot at top center and going clockwise are: Kentucky scramble (creamy eggs scrambled with fresh corn kernels and peppers and draped with bacon); fresh whole strawberries and peaches; squares of fried hominy grits; homemade country sausage cakes encircled by fried apple rings; molded shrimp paste (at handle end of fork); citrus marmalade; butter balls and baking-powder biscuits.

of the Southern social category known as "po' white trash," but she was "country," and her style was "tacky." She was invited to "sit and rest" a moment, have a glass of iced tea, and share those precise details gleaned in other households which she visited, always, we hoped, adhering to another of Ma-Ma's favorite pronouncements: "Gossip is no good if it doesn't start from fact."

On the back porch, outside the kitchen window, was a huge wooden chest. When one lifted the lid one found another and even thicker lid below. Boxes within boxes. The inside was heavily lined with zinc and every day a great block of ice was plonked in it, a double hunk on Saturdays. The horse-drawn ice wagon would stop at the back gate, which Miz Mimms had left ajar, and the iceman would bring the block of ice in his great tongs and open the double doors and put the ice in the wooden chest, always a drama.

> MA-MA: Mind the strawberries, mind the strawberries!
> REBECCA: *(running out from kitchen)* Oh, careful with my jelly! Not about to set yet, don't you joogle it!
> MIZ MIMMS: Let me rack my things while you have it open.
> REBECCA: No, ma'am, I needs that buttermilk inside.
> MA-MA: Lift up that watermelon for me, while you're here.

As for myself, it was a daily indecision whether to be on the back porch, or to go and climb up the back of the ice wagon to get the bits of "snow" from where the iceman had sawed our piece off the great blocks in the wagon, a clammy and dark place inside on the hottest August day, hidden by a great burlap curtain.

Miz Mimms never opened the icebox of her own accord. It would have shown unseemly curiosity. She waited for the iceman, or if his visit didn't coincide with hers, she left her fresh-churned butter, buttermilk and "yard eggs" on a wicker table in the corner of the porch. When she had drained her glass and exhausted her gossip she went back out to her battered old Chevrolet (her comestibles were in the rumble seat) and clattered off, giving the gate a slam shut that made the trolley mechanism go on trembling for a good 10 minutes. In really hot weather Miz Mimms wore a large cabbage leaf on her head, and said it was the only thing that kept off the heat of the sun.

The next arrival was Edward, the gardener, who came in to pass the time of day with Ma-Ma and Rebecca and to see if he were required "of a Saturday." Edward worked around the neighborhood, and his specialty was mowing lawns and raking leaves, but he was never entrusted even to water that jewel-box kitchen garden.

Edward was light caramel in color, with long silky black lashes, long black hair, and a great curly beard which he wore in imitation of Old Testament prophets. I have seen his face since in practically all Coptic art. He was soft-spoken and gentle, but had the strength of an ox. He collected tinfoil in all the places he worked, then brought it to a tool shed in our backyard, where he added it to a huge globe of foil larger than a bass drum. When he judged it huge enough, he would lift it—all of us gathered to see the feat—onto a coaster wagon. He would trundle it down to the Marine Junk Company and sell it, superstitiously looking for a bit of

14

tinfoil gum wrapper or any foil in the streets on his way back, to begin the next silver roc egg.

After Edward the next arrival would often be the grocery boy from over on Dauphin Street, where my grandmother kept an account and paid every Saturday, receiving a little bag of Silver Bells (chocolate kisses) as lagniappe. (The custom of giving a little something extra to a pet customer, the lagniappe, or "nappe," has all but vanished. It was the baker's-dozen idea, or the little something sweet offered when a bill was paid.) The grocer supplied flour, meal, sugar, coffee, tea, rice, black-eyed peas, red kidney beans, navy beans, Lima beans, coconut, baking powder and chocolate. The only canned goods I remember coming into the house were Heinz's peaches, tinned Magnolia Milk (an extremely sweet condensed milk that turned into a tasty candied goo under the right summer conditions) and the cans of malt my grandfather used in his beermaking.

My grandfather was in the wholesale fruit and vegetable business, down on Water Street, so weekly he sent one of his drivers with cases of grapes that vanished into the Pandora's box on the back porch, out of my reach. It was strictly forbidden to open the icebox, and sometimes one waited until two things in it were needed before the lids were lifted. Peaches and apricots were sent home with special haste, as soon as they reached grandfather's office, and there was serious discussion of their merits when the first-of-season filled the kitchen with their flowerlike smell.

Roadside vegetable stands are always a handy gauge of local taste. The stand above, on Old Shell Road in Mobile, displays an assortment of typical Southern produce. In front are the white- and red-skinned sweet potatoes called yams in the South, Spanish onions, unroasted peanuts and turnip greens. In the rear are cabbages and tomatoes.

He had friends in various shipping companies and in other produce firms, so strange and exotic things often turned up, like the occasional mango, or a bunch of plantains with a tiny Central America monkey no bigger than your hand stowed away in it, or huge avocados of the purplish-green variety. The grapes arrived in quantity, since those were Prohibition years and my grandfather made wine and beer at home and hid it under the house, which rose high off the ground with latticing between the brick supports. Under the icebox was a funnel in a hole in the floor and underneath, where the cold drip-drip-drip kept the earth cool and damp, was as close to a wine cellar as he could arrange. There was a permanent puddle of cold water about two feet wide here, and I used to like to go and put my feet in it, entering by a little door cut in the lattice under the pantry window.

In the winter the iceman came every other day, but his lapses were more than made up for by the "lide-ud man," the lightwood man who sold pine knots for the stove and fireplace and who sang out "Liiiide-ud! Get yo' liiiiide-ud!" in almost incomprehensible fashion, but who, once in the yard, spoke very clearly with the quasi-Yankee accent of certain New Orleans natives.

There were others who attended Ma-Ma's levees, like the poor widow who made wax flowers, the knife grinder and the old-fashioned tinker who soldered holes in pots and pans. Other people's servants came in a steady procession, since notes were still delivered by hand, and samples of this and that dish were constantly arriving from Ma-Ma's friends across the street. All the while there were discussions between Ma-Ma and Rebecca about what vegetables we would have for the midday meal, and Rebecca would go with her basket to pick them from the garden, if Ma-Ma had not already done so. Or if the field peas had been bought from a vegetable wagon, the shelling would begin. Usually I shelled, but sometimes I read last Sunday's funny papers out loud to Ma-Ma and Rebecca, describing the action depicted. *Little Nemo* was our favorite, with *Tarzan and the Jewels of Ophir* running a close second.

In those days everybody came home for dinner, which was lavish and at high noon. Rice was served with almost every meal and potatoes only turned up as a Saturday dish au gratin, or as potato salad or as mashed potatoes forming a ring or nest to hold peas or chopped spinach or such. There was a boiled green for dinner every day: turnip greens, collards, mustard greens, beet tops or whatever. Always there would be a good sweet course followed by fruit. Ice creams and sherbets were usually reserved for Sunday, but the luscious avocado sherbet turned up in midweek if someone was available and willing to crank the freezer (me).

Friday was fish day, and my grandfather would sometimes telephone that he had found good red snapper at the waterfront fish market, which would change all plans for the midday meal. Oyster stew was a Friday night regular, and on Sunday night we often drove down to Bayou La Batre or Coden (a corruption of *Coq d'Inde*) for an evening meal on the water, at one of the eateries on the piers where the shrimp boats tied up, or at one of the boardinghouse hotels. Public eating was very good in those years, but my family usually preferred to eat at home. Dinner at the

Opposite: In mountain areas of the South, plain country foods still survive, made from recipes that are hundreds of years old. Here before a cabin in the Black Mountains near Burnsville, North Carolina, a country woman cooks apple butter in a caldron over an open fire.

16

Battle House Hotel, or in the La Clede Hotel dining room, or at Karl's on Dauphin Street, was a birthday treat.

Ma-Ma loved to entertain Father Seydell from St. Joseph's Church. He was a jolly soul and a great trencherman, and always had appreciative words about my grandfather's wines, especially a pale-yellow Tokay-like one, made from seedless grapes. Grandmother often prepared a proper shrimp gumbo for him, which took two days.

Gumbo exists in countless forms throughout the South, with Mobile and New Orleans claiming superiority in the art. The origin of the word is not clear; it is believed to be derived from *kingombo* or *ngombo,* African words for okra, often a principal ingredient of the dish. In the South, gumbo means "all together" or "all at once," as in the phrase "gumbo ya-ya," meaning everybody talking at once. It also means a potpourri of turkey, chicken, rabbit, squirrel, fish, crab, oyster, shrimp or almost any available ingredients; or a thick kind of stew that is a close cousin to bouillabaisse, Italian fish soup, couscous or other mixed-ingredient dishes of the Mediterranean and North Africa.

In Gulf Coast versions the pleasure of the dish lies in the contrast between the high and piquant flavoring and the smooth texture, which is achieved by the addition of the glutinous okra or of the thickening agent known as gumbo filé, which is powdered dried sassafras leaves. The okra is cooked with the other ingredients but the gumbo filé, a grayish-green powder, is not added until the steaming pot is taken off the fire. Some cooks then slowly stir the filé into the gumbo. Others dip up a cupful of gumbo liquid, and gradually mix in the filé, which turns a blackish-green and begins at once to thicken and to emit a distinctive and appetizing aroma. This cupful is then stirred into the full pot. The gumbo is best if it is eaten at once, and it must never be boiled again. If it is used the day after, it must be reheated slowly, or the filé will form into stringy, unappetizing particles.

When Father Seydell dined with us the first course was a cold shrimp dish, accompanied by iced celery. Then came the gumbo, served in soup bowls, each with a little mound of rice. Pecan pie and black coffee usually completed the meal. I would have been fed and bedded long since, but some instinct brought me to the dining room at the moment the pecan pie came in. My grandfather served a cordial made of sand pears which he got from a friend at Bay Minette, and I was usually allowed a drop in a thimble-sized glass. It was white fire and tasted the way sand-pear leaves smell. After the tubby, red-cheeked priest had left, my grandmother brought out crystallized ginger—"sovereign against flatulence," she said —and we each had a piece while the family commented and laughed over all that had been done and said at supper.

Nor did the evening end there. After we had all gone to bed we could count on a bottle or two of my grandfather's wine exploding in that mysterious dining-room closet where the Christmas fruitcakes aged in port or bourbon, where the elderberry wine was locked and where the aniseed cookies were kept in stoneware jars. Sometimes we went a month without a blowup, but something about Father Seydell's presence seemed to send a bottle off. A muffled explosion and the sound of glass falling.

Thunderstorms seemed to affect the bottles under the house and I remember a spectacular cannonade one August. It always made Ma-Ma laugh uproariously.

Hurricanes were an accepted fact of life on the Gulf Coast, and they always seemed to come in years with sixes. There were hurricanes in 1896, 1906, 1916, 1926 and in 1936. (In 1946 everybody got all ready and nothing happened.) When the hurricane warnings went up, there was always a lot of scurrying about to prepare food, bake bread, polish candlesticks, fill kerosene lamps. The three sisters across the street, the Misses Nana, Evelina and Jessamina Ebeltoft, who taught shorthand and typing upstairs (a discreet side entrance in Conti Street) and piano and flower painting on cloth downstairs (the main front door) were always running over to see what Ma-Ma was planning at storm time.

Sometimes Miss Nana would appear, wild-eyed, as the storm clouds were already piling up and the air still and stifling.

"What are you going to have for the hurricane? I never know what to have," she'd say.

Ma-Ma, never stopping her work or asking Miss Nana to sit down, would mutter, "Boiled ham and pickled peaches, like always." The house would smell of bread baking. The seven yard cats would have sensed the storm and assembled on the back porch. The squirrels would have scurried along the telephone wires into the attic where pecans were stored, and where we could hear them rolling the nuts around at night.

There were not only hurricane dishes, but picnic dishes, funeral dishes and wedding dishes. One thought food, talked food; the quest for the freshest and the best never ended.

When I set out after all these years to revisit the South, I wondered whether any of this would be left, or would it all be at one with the dodo and the trumpeter swan? Well, I thought, when people ask me where I'm from . . . I'd really like to pull out a banjo or a lyre, and play and do a shuffle dance, while singing:

> *Gumbo born and gumbo bred,*
> *Tabasco follies fuzz my head.*
> *South is my blood and South my bone*
> *So haply formed on pork and pone.*
> *Incan, African move in me.*
> *You say: "South? Where can it be?"*
> *Chewing my sugar cane, I repeat:*
> *"Why, in all we like to cook and eat."*

I was to travel 5,000 miles through the South for this book, and before setting forth my findings, I should explain certain ground rules that take the form of a warning. It is to be hoped that no one on reading this book will jump in the car and expect to find all sorts of delectable dishes in the nearest Southern restaurant. What we are talking about here is not the pizza pies and hamburgers to be found in run-of-the-mill eating places, but the best of indigenous Southern cooking, something that is rarely surpassed. It exists mostly in the homes, although some restaurants are exceptions. The trick is to know what to look for and where to find it.

Overleaf: Cornbreads are legion throughout the South and run a gamut from simple mushlike mixtures to delicate spoon breads. Most Southern cooks make their cornbreads with white cornmeal —preferably the stone-ground kind —never sweeten them with sugar, and always serve them hot from the oven or skillet. The sampling shown starts at top left with hoecakes, a sort of meal-and-water pancake served with lots of butter. The skillet cornbread *(top right)* that owes its crunchy crust to a preheated frying pan, and the individual corn sticks *(bottom right)* are made from the same cornmeal, egg and buttermilk batter. At bottom left is spoon bread with corn, a soufflélike pudding laden with fresh corn kernels and the fragrance of nutmeg. For these and other cornbread recipes see the Recipe Index.

Nothing is more Southern than hot breads, especially those made of cornmeal. And no meal is as distinctly Southern as breakfast, with its omnipresent grits and such satisfying dishes as Kentucky scramble or country-style sausage with fried apple rings.

Baking-Powder Biscuits

To make about 10

2 teaspoons butter, softened plus 8 tablespoons butter, cut into ¼-inch bits
2 cups all-purpose flour
2 teaspoons double-acting baking powder
1 teaspoon salt
⅔ cup milk

ADDITIONAL INGREDIENTS FOR CHEESE-AND-HERB BISCUITS
¼ cup freshly grated imported Parmesan cheese
¼ cup finely cut fresh chives
¼ cup finely chopped fresh parsley

Preheat the oven to 400°. With a pastry brush, spread the 2 teaspoons of softened butter evenly over a baking sheet. Set aside.

Combine the flour, baking powder and salt and sift them into a deep bowl. Add the 8 tablespoons of butter bits and rub the flour and fat together with your fingertips until they resemble flakes of coarse meal. Pour in the milk all at once and mix briefly with a wooden spoon, stirring just long enough to form a smooth soft dough that can be gathered into a compact ball. Do not overbeat.

Place the dough on a lightly floured surface and roll or pat it into a rough circle about ½-inch thick. With a biscuit cutter or the rim of a glass, cut the dough into 2½-inch rounds. Gather the scraps into a ball, pat or roll it out as before and cut as many more biscuits as you can.

Arrange the biscuits side by side on the buttered baking sheet and bake in the middle of the oven for about 20 minutes, or until they are a delicate golden brown. Serve at once.

CHEESE-AND-HERB BISCUITS: Following precisely the directions for baking-powder biscuits, prepare the dough and gather it into a ball. While the dough is still in the bowl, knead into it the grated cheese, chives and parsley. Place the dough on a lightly floured surface, then roll, cut and bake the biscuits as described above.

Skillet Cornbread and Corn Sticks

To make one 9-inch bread or fourteen 5½-inch sticks

1½ cups cornmeal, preferably white water-ground
½ cup all-purpose flour
1 tablespoon double-acting baking powder
1 teaspoon salt
2 eggs
1½ cups buttermilk
1 tablespoon butter, melted

Preheat the oven to 350°. Combine the cornmeal, flour, baking powder and salt and sift them into a deep bowl. In a separate bowl, beat the eggs lightly with a wire whisk or fork, then add the buttermilk and mix well. Pour the liquid ingredients over the dry ones and, with a wooden spoon, stir them together until the batter is smooth; do not overbeat.

SKILLET CORNBREAD: Place a heavy 9-inch skillet with an ovenproof handle over high heat for about 1 minute, or until the pan is very hot. Remove the pan from the heat and, with a pastry brush, quickly coat the bottom and sides of the pan with the melted butter. Immediately pour in the batter, spreading it evenly and smoothing the top with a rubber spatula. Bake in the middle of the oven for 30 to 35 minutes, or until the cornbread begins to draw away from the edges of the skillet and the top is a rich golden brown.

To unmold and serve the bread, run a knife around the edges of the pan to loosen the sides. Place a heated platter upside down over the skillet and, grasping platter and skillet together firmly, quickly invert them.

Rap the platter sharply on a table and the bread should slide easily out of the skillet. Cut the bread into wedge-shaped pieces and serve at once.

CORN STICKS: Brush the inside surfaces of the molds in a corn-stick pan with the melted butter. Spoon the batter into the molds, dividing it evenly among them. Bake in the middle of the oven for 25 to 30 minutes, or until the corn sticks are golden brown.

Turn the corn sticks out of the pan, arrange them attractively on a heated platter and serve at once.

NOTE: An interesting variation on skillet cornbread is crackling bread. It may be made in the following fashion: Place ¼ pound of finely chopped salt pork or fat back in an ungreased 9-inch skillet with an oven-proof handle. Fry the pork over moderate heat, stirring frequently until the bits are crisp and brown and have rendered all their fat.

With a slotted spoon, transfer the browned pork bits (called cracklings) to paper towels to drain; then stir them into the cornbread batter. Discard all but a thin film of fat from the skillet and heat the pan until it is very hot but not smoking. Pour in the batter, spread and smooth it with a rubber spatula and bake the bread in a preheated 350° oven for 30 to 35 minutes, or until the top is golden brown. Unmold and serve the crackling bread as described in the recipe for skillet cornbread.

Spoon Bread with Corn

To serve 6 to 8

Preheat the oven to 350°. With a pastry brush, spread 1 tablespoon of the softened butter evenly over the bottom and sides of a 2-quart casserole. Set aside.

Using the teardrop-shaped holes of a hand grater, shred the corn into a bowl. Then, with a rubber spatula, scrape the corn and the liquid that has accumulated around it into a heavy 2- to 3-quart saucepan. Add 2 cups of the milk and the salt and bring to a boil over high heat.

Pour in the cornmeal slowly enough so that the boiling continues at a rapid rate and stir constantly with a wooden spoon to keep the mixture smooth. Reduce the heat to low and, stirring from time to time, simmer uncovered until the mixture is so thick that the spoon will stand up unsupported in the middle of the pan.

Remove the pan from the heat and immediately beat in the remaining 8 tablespoons of softened butter, a few spoonfuls at a time. Add the remaining cup of milk and, when it is completely incorporated, beat in the egg yolks, one at a time, and the sugar, nutmeg and red pepper.

In a deep mixing bowl, preferably of unlined copper, beat the egg whites with a wire whisk or a rotary or electric beater until they are stiff enough to form unwavering peaks on the beater when it is lifted out of the bowl. Scoop the egg whites over the corn mixture and, with a rubber spatula, fold them together gently but thoroughly.

Pour the mixture into the buttered casserole, spreading it evenly and smoothing the top with the spatula. Bake uncovered in the center of the oven for 35 to 40 minutes, or until the top of the spoon bread is golden brown and the center barely quivers when the casserole is gently moved back and forth.

Serve the spoon bread at once, directly from the casserole.

9 tablespoons unsalted butter, softened
3 medium-sized fresh ears of corn, husked
3 cups milk
2 teaspoons salt
1 cup white cornmeal, preferably water-ground
3 egg yolks
1 tablespoon sugar
¼ teaspoon ground nutmeg, preferably freshly grated
⅛ teaspoon ground hot red pepper (cayenne)
3 egg whites

To serve 4 to 6

5 cups water
1 teaspoon salt
1 cup regular white hominy grits,
    not the quick-cooking variety
1 tablespoon butter, softened

To serve 4 to 6

2 tablespoons butter, softened, plus
    4 to 8 tablespoons butter
5 cups plus 2 tablespoons cold water
2 teaspoons salt
1 cup regular white hominy grits,
    not the quick-cooking variety
1 egg
½ cup flour

To serve 6 to 8

2 pounds lean boneless pork,
    coarsely ground
¼ pound fresh pork fat, finely
    chopped
1 tablespoon crumbled dried sage
    leaves
1 teaspoon ground nutmeg,
    preferably freshly grated
¼ teaspoon ground hot red pepper
    (cayenne)
1 tablespoon salt
1 teaspoon freshly ground black
    pepper
3 large firm tart cooking apples,
    cored but not peeled, cut
    crosswise into ½-inch-thick
    rings
Cinnamon sugar made from ¼ cup
    sugar combined with 2 teaspoons
    ground cinnamon

Boiled Grits

In a heavy 1½- to 2-quart saucepan, bring the water and salt to a boil over high heat. Pour in the hominy grits slowly enough so that the boiling continues at a rapid rate. Stir constantly with a wooden spoon to keep the mixture smooth.

Reduce the heat to low and, stirring occasionally, simmer the grits tightly covered for 30 minutes. Stir in the butter and mound the grits in a heated bowl. Serve at once with more butter, salt and black pepper to taste.

Fried Grits

With a pastry brush, spread 1 tablespoon of the softened butter over the bottom and sides of a shallow 9-by-13-inch baking dish and set aside.

In a heavy 1½- to 2-quart saucepan, bring 5 cups of water and the salt to a boil over high heat. Pour in the hominy grits slowly enough so that the boiling continues at a rapid rate. Stir constantly with a wooden spoon to keep the mixture smooth.

Reduce the heat to low and, stirring occasionally, simmer the grits tightly covered for 30 minutes. Stir in the remaining tablespoon of softened butter. When it is absorbed, spoon the hot grits into the buttered dish and smooth the top with a metal spatula. Cool to room temperature, cover with plastic wrap or foil, and refrigerate for at least 4 hours, or until the grits are firm to the touch.

Preheat the oven to its lowest setting. Line a large shallow baking dish with paper towels and place it in the middle of the oven.

With a sharp knife, cut the chilled grits into cakes approximately 2 inches square. Beat the egg lightly with the remaining 2 tablespoons of cold water and, one at a time, immerse the cakes in the mixture. Then roll each cake in the flour to coat both sides lightly and evenly.

In a heavy 10- to 12-inch skillet, melt 4 tablespoons of butter over moderate heat. When the foam begins to subside, add 7 or 8 of the hominy-grit cakes and fry them for about 3 minutes on each side, turning them over with a spatula. When the cakes are a golden brown, transfer them to the lined dish to drain and keep them warm in the oven while you fry the rest, 7 or 8 at a time. Add more butter to the skillet as necessary.

Arrange the fried grits attractively on a heated platter and serve them at once, with sorghum or corn or maple syrup.

Country-Style Sausage with Fried Apple Rings

Combine the ground pork, pork fat, sage, nutmeg, red pepper, salt and black pepper in a deep bowl and knead vigorously with both hands until the sausage mixture is smooth. On a firm, flat surface, pat and roll the mixture into a thick cylinder about 8 inches long and 3 inches in diameter. Wrap tightly in wax paper or foil and refrigerate for at least 2 hours, or until the sausage is firm. (Covered and refrigerated, the sausage can safely be kept for 3 or 4 days.)

Preheat the oven to its lowest setting. Then line a large shallow baking dish with paper towels and place it in the center of the oven.

Slice the sausage cylinder crosswise into ½-inch-thick round cakes.

24

Place 5 or 6 cakes in an ungreased heavy 10- to 12-inch skillet and set it over moderate heat. Turning the cakes frequently with a slotted spatula, fry them for about 10 minutes, or until they are richly browned on both sides and no trace of pink shows when a cake is pierced with the point of a small sharp knife. As the fat accumulates, draw it off with a bulb baster and reserve in a heatproof bowl.

Transfer the fried cakes to the lined baking dish and keep them warm in the oven. Place 5 or 6 more cakes in the skillet and repeat the entire procedure until all the sausage is fried.

Return enough of the reserved fat to the skillet to come about ½ inch up the sides. Drop half of the apple rings into the hot fat, cover the pan tightly and cook over moderate heat for 2 minutes. Turn the apple rings over with the slotted spatula and sprinkle them evenly with 1 tablespoon of the cinnamon sugar. Then cover the skillet again and cook for 2 minutes longer, or until the apples are tender. Turn the rings over, sprinkle them with 1 tablespoon of cinnamon sugar and drain them on paper towels. Place the rest of the apple rings in the skillet and fry them as before.

Mound the sausage cakes attractively in the center of a large heated platter and arrange the apple rings around them. Serve at once.

Kentucky Scramble

In a heavy 10- to 12-inch ungreased skillet, fry the bacon over moderate heat. Turn the slices with tongs until they are crisp and brown, then transfer them to paper towels to drain.

Pour off all but 3 tablespoons of the fat remaining in the skillet and in its place add the butter. Drop in the corn and stir over moderate heat for 1 or 2 minutes until the kernels glisten. Then add the green pepper, pimiento, salt and black pepper and cook uncovered, stirring frequently, for 5 minutes, or until the vegetables are soft but not brown.

Break the eggs into a bowl, beat them lightly with a table fork, and pour them into the skillet. Stirring with the flat of the fork or a rubber spatula, cook over low heat until the eggs begin to form soft, creamy curds. Mound the eggs on a heated platter, arrange the bacon slices attractively on top and serve at once.

To serve 4

6 slices lean bacon
1 tablespoon butter
1 cup fresh corn kernels, cut from 3 medium-sized ears of corn, or substitute 1 cup canned or defrosted frozen corn kernels, thoroughly drained
½ cup finely chopped green pepper
¼ cup finely chopped pimiento
1½ teaspoons salt
⅛ teaspoon freshly ground black pepper
6 eggs

Hoecakes

Combine the cornmeal and salt in a bowl. Stirring the mixture constantly with a spoon, pour in the boiling water in a slow, thin stream and beat until the batter is smooth. For each hoecake, scoop up 2 tablespoons of batter and pat it into a flat round about 4 inches in diameter.

In a heavy griddle or 10- to 12-inch skillet, melt 1 tablespoon of the bacon fat or butter over high heat. When the fat is very hot but not smoking, reduce the heat to low. Add 4 of the hoecakes and fry for about 2 minutes on each side until they are golden brown, turning them with a wide metal spatula. Transfer the crisp, browned cakes to a heated platter, add more fat to the pan if needed, and fry the remaining 4 cakes.

Serve the hoecakes at once, accompanied by sweet butter or cane syrup.

To make eight 4-inch round cakes

1 cup white cornmeal, preferably water-ground
½ teaspoon salt
¾ cup boiling water
1 to 2 tablespoons bacon fat or butter

II

Where Grab and Chicken Are King

Conveniently close to Chesapeake Bay's famous crabs, Baltimore proudly calls itself the crab capital of the world. When Dave Gordon *(head of table),* owner of Gordon's, one of the city's leading restaurants, plays host to family and friends, hotly spiced steamed crabs are the order of the day. Guests attack the crabs with paring knives and mallets, and offset their spiciness with steins of beer or Coke.

Somewhere near Wilmington I sniffed something in the air that said "South" to me. Setting out from New York early that morning, I had driven down the New Jersey Turnpike, then crossed the Delaware Memorial Bridge and come onto the broad concrete expanse of Interstate Highway 95. The pale sky was up there somewhere above the haze of industrial smoke. The new superhighways, constructed since I left the United States to work and study in Europe, seemed with their sweeping curves and wide spaces to be the essence of America in the 1970s. Space—and speed. On these roads where one travels for miles without seeing a sign of life other than whizzing vehicles there was a sameness, a kind of insistent anonymity. Clearly, if I wanted to find Delaware, I would have to leave the superhighway and dawdle a while. I turned off and suddenly, along a rambling country road, caught a whiff of mud and leaves, a fecund ditch smell that, to me, meant the South.

Actually, my detour was more than casual. I was in search of a superior boardinghouse I had known many years ago at the pleasant village of Arden, site of one of the colonies founded on the single-tax philosophy of the high-minded Henry George. I remembered a kitchen presided over by two plump artists, one white, one black, whom I thought I would query concerning the Great Controversy over the preparation of the most Southern of all foods, fried chicken. It was, as I had feared, a futile quest. The old boardinghouse had disappeared, and a modern picture-window residence had taken its place.

But disappointment was soon tempered by an encounter with a dish almost as beloved by true Southerners as fried chicken. I stopped at a filling station with a single gas pump and there, in a window under a metal awning, was a hand-lettered sign that read "Crab cakes." I have always been a believer in hand-lettered signs. They seem to say, "There's something here that we don't always have," and I have found them to be a reliable guide to good eating.

I could smell the crab cakes the moment I opened the door. And when my order came, the cakes proved as big as jumbo hamburgers and golden brown, with lots of crabmeat, held together by mashed potatoes and seasoned with plenty of good black pepper. I ate three, and washed them down with cold pale-blond beer, a drink that always goes well with salty things. I liked the crab cakes immensely, and it wasn't until I chatted with a Maryland friend later that I learned that there was an even better way of preparing them *(Recipe Index)*. When I mentioned the mashed potatoes to her, she exclaimed, "You must have been eating in a restaurant. We never fix crab cakes that way. We use beaten egg, crabmeat, salt and pepper." After I had eaten some of *her* crab cakes, I realized the lady had a point.

The filling-station stop proved to be merely the overture to a greater feast that same night at a seafood restaurant in east Baltimore with pine-paneled rooms and walls decorated with fishnets. Steamed crabs *(Recipe Index)* were the specialty of the house, and after I placed my order, a ritual that was long familiar to me ensued. The waitress brought some brown wrapping paper and covered the table. She tied a bib around my neck, handed me a wooden mallet and a paring knife and set a wooden chopping block before me. Then she brought half a dozen good-sized crabs on a tray and deposited them on the table. The crabs were a dull reddish-brown, from the spices with which they had been cooked. They had been arranged in layers in a pot of shallow steaming water and vinegar, and each layer had been covered with a mixture of ground rock salt, black pepper, ginger, mustard seeds, celery seeds and paprika.

I went to work on the first crab by twisting off the large front claws. Then I removed the six side legs, pried open the crab shell with the paring knife, discarded the spongy gray matter known as "dead man's fingers" and broke the crab in half. (See pages 30-31 for illustrations of proper way to attack a crab.) Next I gave a twist to one of the back legs, exposing a beautiful snowy-white chunk of crabmeat. I ate every bit of it, picking the strands from the shell with the paring knife and using the mallet to smash the claws on the chopping block and extract the tender meat from them. The crabmeat was sweet but hot and spicy from the seasonings, and as I ate it, I found myself quaffing cold beer after almost every mouthful to soothe the slightly burning though pleasant taste.

Eating crabs this way was by no means a new experience for me. They are available in great quantities all the way down the Atlantic Coast and along the Gulf as well, and I had enjoyed them many times in Mobile. Only there we ate them boiled instead of steamed. The crab boil is a cherished pastime in the Deep South, on a summer evening at the beach, in the backyard or even in the kitchen. A great vat, washtub or lard tin is filled with water (formerly, seawater was dipped up for this, but many people nowadays, thinking of pollution, get nervous at the idea) and put to boil on a driftwood fire or charcoal burner, with bay leaves, a bit of lemon or vinegar, bird's-eye pepper, cloves and whatever you fancy. The crabs are first put into plenty of cool water, to clean them and keep them fresh. When the cooking water is ready they are dropped alive into the boiling vat, completely immersed instead of being steamed in shallow water as they were at the restaurant in Baltimore. After about 10 minutes they are stirred up so the top and bottom ones change places, and then they are cooked another 10 or 15 minutes, depending on their size.

Tradition also rules the serving of the crabs. You must spread old newspapers on the table. You give everybody a big napkin or dish towel to tie about the neck, and you must be sure to have plenty of paper napkins on hand. You put out nutcrackers or heavy-handled knives for each guest; if you have a set of old-fashioned nutpicks with single tines, they are just right for this occasion. Beer, of course, is icing in a tub, and in the middle of the table are lined up all or some of these: melted butter, lemon juice, tartar sauce *(Recipe Index),* chilled celery, large green olives, tomato relish, a plate of oyster crackers or cold biscuits, a bottle of Tabasco (if you're on the Gulf Coast), pepper sherry (if you're in Charleston, South Carolina), dill pickles (if you're anyplace). Five or six crabs per person are about right, but some dainty pickers are satisfied with three or four. Quite often at a crab boil in the family kitchen, half the crabs are eaten there and then, and half are saved for the next day, perhaps to be used as creamed crab in pastry shells or crab in avocado that will be eaten at a garden-club do.

By the time the full moon has risen out of the crape myrtle and the last crab claw has relinquished the last shred of sweet white meat, the newspaper tablecloth is folded and piled on the general wreckage and mess, and a new layer of newspaper is put down for the chilled watermelon that ideally follows. If you're eating outdoors, it's customary to see how far you can spit the seeds. I learned how to do this in Mobile long ago, and once put it into practice in a fancy New York seafood restaurant where I lunched with the poet Jean Garrigue, who was born in Indiana but had lived in seafood and melon country in the south of France. We had finished our dinner with melon, and the idea of spitting the seeds came to us at the same instant, without any words exchanged. We waited for our rather severe waitress to leave, then erupted simultaneously. We tied, both of us spitting all the way to the end of the room. She hit the mirror, I conked the coatrack. Once a seed spitter, always a seed spitter.

So far as my Maryland friends were concerned, the steamed crabs I ate in Baltimore were but a paltry hint of the joys the state had to offer my palate. Marylanders' pride in their cuisine, its quality and variety, goes back a long way—almost to the time when King Charles I of England carved off a slice of Virginia and granted it to his friend Sir George Calvert, the first Lord Baltimore. The original Maryland settlers, some 200 strong, who came up Chesapeake Bay in 1634 in two little ships—the *Ark* and the *Dove*—and settled on a promontory between the Bay and the Potomac River, were goggled-eyed at the bounty they found: rich soil, timber, game, wildfowl, seafood.

Continued on page 32

HOW TO EAT A STEAMED CRAB

Steamed red and flecked with dabs of spices, the hard-shell blue crabs at left are fit for a feast. (For the recipe, see the Recipe Index.) All the diner needs is a wooden mallet and a small sharp knife to crack and clean them. The step-by-step photographs at right show how to go about eating a steamed crab. No need to stand on ceremony; simply enjoy the meat as you pick it out.

1. The first step is to twist and break off the two large claws that come together below the crab in this picture. Then twist off the three small legs on each side, which are partially hidden here. Set the claws aside and suck any meat from the legs before you discard them.

2. Turn the crab on its back and, with the point of the knife, carefully pry off the pointed flap or "apron." In a she crab, the orange roe will be visible now. Do not pass it up; the crab roe is edible and excellent.

3. Turn the crab again and, holding it tightly in one hand, break off the entire top shell with the knife, pick out the morsels of yellow liver and "fat" from inside the shell, then discard the shell. Pull off the spongy gray lungs or "dead man's fingers" at each side, scrape the intestines from the center and discard these.

4. Holding the crab in both hands, snap it in half. Scrape off any cartilage from the exposed meat.

5. Gently twist the back fin off one half the body, leaving the meat intact. Eat this piece of back-fin crabmeat, twist the back fin from the other half of the body and enjoy the crabmeat there. Then with the aid of the knife, remove the large lumps of crabmeat still remaining inside the shell and eat them.

6. Set the blade of the knife upright on one claw close to the pincers. With the mallet, drive the blade through the top shell to get at the claw meat in one piece. Or, if you are feeling impatient, simply smash the claw with your mallet.

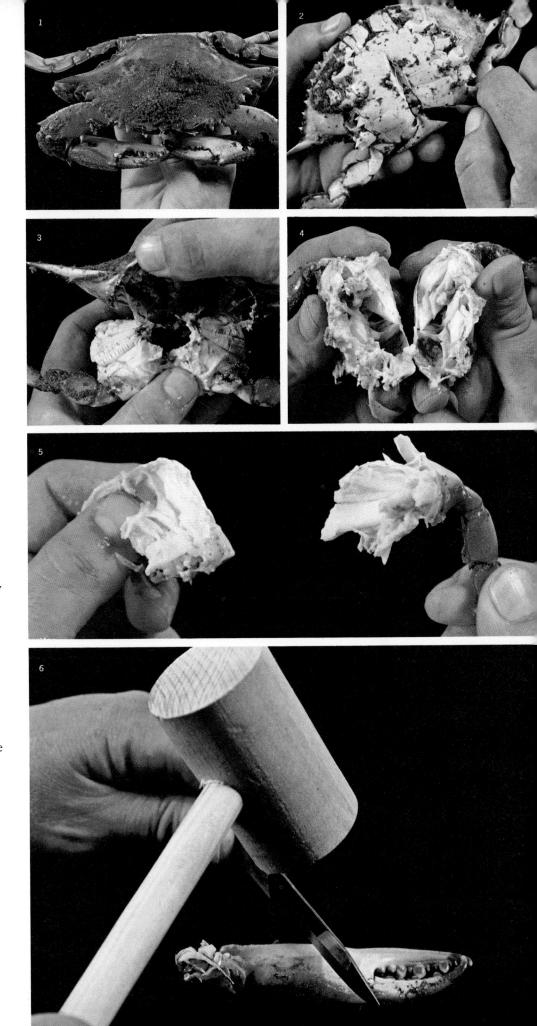

They soon prospered, of course, and the tables they spread reflected their prosperity. Legends arose of the existence of a corner of the New World where baked chickens and roast pigs went about with knives and forks stuck into them, begging to be eaten. These fables of plenty were well mixed with fact.

The tradition of good eating founded by the colonists survives to this day, along with some rather special preferences. Marylanders stuff their hams with greens *(Recipe Index),* serve roast turkey with sauerkraut, and breakfast on fried green tomatoes cooked with salt, pepper, flour and butter. A Maryland specialty that is well worth a trip for itself is shad roe, available in the spring when the fish are spawning. It is broiled or browned in a skillet, and served with raw cucumbers and sour cream. Another famous delicacy is diamondback terrapin *(Recipe Index),* boiled and flavored with butter and sherry—although the cost of this exotic item ($13 to $17 for enough terrapin to feed four) has largely confined it to exclusive clubs and expensive restaurants.

The preparation of terrapin, a member of the turtle family, is such an elaborate, time-consuming ritual that some restaurants require three days' notice before serving it. For a party of four people, six terrapins are prepared. They are about five to seven inches in length, measured from front to back along the bottom. The terrapins are washed first, then plunged into boiling water and cooked for 10 minutes. The toenails and skin of the heads, necks and legs are removed, then the terrapins are again placed in a pot of fresh boiling water, covered and cooked until tender, which usually takes from one to two hours. After this, they are taken out of the water, the shells are removed and all of the innards except the livers discarded. If the terrapins are females, the eggs are carefully saved. The yellow skin under the shell is removed; the meat is deboned and chopped fine. The terrapin livers are sliced and the eggs are washed (there are usually a dozen or fewer eggs in the female terrapin). The broth in which the terrapins have been cooked is then boiled down until nothing but a strong, thick gravy is left. After that, the chopped meat, sliced livers and eggs are reheated in butter and the reduced broth. They are seasoned with salt and cayenne pepper, and a final zesty touch of sherry is added.

When ready for serving, terrapin is a rich, heady dish tasting of the salt marshes where this strange creature dwells. Like snails or octopus it is one of those either-you-like-it-or-you-don't dishes that some people rave about, and others compare with rubber tires.

In my search for more of Maryland's marine splendors, I pushed on from Baltimore toward Annapolis, the state capital, a pretty town, quiet and clean with a look that is more early American than Southern, but on the streets I heard the "g" quite definitely being dropped in the Southern way, and I caught a few "you-alls." I was also cheered by a brisk salt breeze blowing up the Severn River, and I caught a glimpse of oyster boats putting out of the little harbor.

Just beyond Annapolis, I crossed the nicely curved bridge over the Chesapeake into the Delmarva peninsula, the tristate area of Delaware, Maryland and Virginia lying between the Chesapeake Bay and the Atlantic Ocean. On the map this region (which is called the Eastern Shore by the people who live here) is shaped like a raccoon, one paw tickling Wilmington and the tail pointing down toward Norfolk, Virginia. Delmarva is a self-contained place; like the American South itself, it is a country within a country. With its countless bays and coves and meandering inlets and streams, like the delightful Choptank River, it has long been a busy summer place for the messing-about-in-boats set. The quiet communities are made up of neat white wooden houses, old churches and graveyards. The small farms, laid out with a kind of four-square dignity and old sense of tidiness, are all definitely Anglo-Saxon, and one senses even now a little of the early settlers' nostalgia for England, if only in the names of the towns: Dover, Milford, Salisbury.

All the sea creatures that prefer less salty waters or mingled salt and fresh water throng about Delmarva: hard-shell or littleneck clams; blue crabs that spawn in the inner waters of the Chesapeake, and their growing offspring that cast off their shells and become briefly the delicious soft-shell crabs that are fried and eaten with tartar sauce; the rightly famed Chincoteague and Tangier oysters (deplorably, the latter are being eliminated by a blight that has been creeping northward in the Bay since 1959). There are scallops and lobsters and delicious herring with its marvelous roe (eaten fresh or salted, a breakfast favorite with hot biscuits).

Off the coast the fat and delicately flavored butterfish is found; the bluefish, abundant in spring, flits off to New England in summer and returns in fall; cod come on unpredictable visits. There are seven or eight species of flounder in the Chesapeake and Atlantic here, and some are eaten as "fillet of sole" because the flavor and texture reminded the early colonists of England's Dover sole. There is the king whiting or kingfish (no relation to that game fish called the kingfish), which is prized for its delicate flavor. The sheepshead is a favorite breakfast dish, fried golden-brown. Another favorite for pan-frying is the little spot, which is sometimes served in pairs. The striped bass, or rockfish, is the pet of sportsmen everywhere in the Chesapeake; one sees them surf casting and trolling for it. The spotted seatrout is another sportsmen's favorite. But of all the fish found in the waters off Delmarva the most beautiful is the Spanish mackerel, deep blue with a play of mauve or cerulean when it is first caught, and a flash of gold in its scales. Much esteemed, it is broiled or baked and eaten with drawn butter and a little lemon juice.

This region, as might be expected, is the hub of the crab universe. Crab-cake stands are almost as common as hamburger joints, and crab is enjoyed here in all sorts of ways: stuffed, deviled, imperial, creamed, au gratin, croquettes; crab burgers, crab loaf, and crab casserole; crabmeat omelets, soups, salads; crabs used in variants of deviled eggs or to stuff avocados or merely "tossed on toast." This is crabmeat cooked in a little butter, laced with a splash of cream and a splash of sherry, lightly sprinkled with cayenne pepper and poured over hot toast. As in the case of the crab cakes, the garnish for "tossed on toast" varies; one excellent version consists of a bit of finely chopped sweet onion, sliced tomatoes or crumbled crisp bacon. All these variations of crab dishes, of course, are also available all down through the coastal South.

Along with its wealth of fish and seafood, the Delmarva peninsula is fa-

Diamondback terrapins, like the one above, were at the peak of their popularity around the turn of the century and sold for as much as $10 apiece. The supply dwindled in the 1920s, but thanks to strict protective laws enacted during that period turtles are becoming plentiful again in the Chesapeake Bay area. Above right, Benny Daisey of Crisfield, Maryland, hauls a catch into his boat. He will keep the terrapins in pens until he has an order, then sell them alive.

mous for another reason. It is one of the most highly concentrated poultry-raising areas on earth, producing 330 million broiler-fryer chickens per year. (The poultry industry defines a broiler-fryer simply as "a young tender-meat chicken.") These birds are mechanically hatched and kept in thermostat-controlled houses until they are about eight weeks old and weigh from two to three and a half pounds, which means that they are just right for frying or broiling.

In Maryland—as throughout the South—the great classic dish is, of course, fried chicken. Southern fried chicken is such a byword that it produces a conditioned reflex: mention it and the mouth waters and Pavlov's ghost smiles. It probably comes as close to being the ideal all-purpose, all-occasion dish as anything in this country. (Recipes for Maryland fried chicken, Kentucky fried chicken, oven-fried chicken and Southern fried chicken appear in the Recipe Index.) It is equally good hot or cold; it can be enjoyed by young and old and appreciated in all circumstances, from the most formal of seated dinners to the most casual of lap lunches, or snacks in a car, on a train or in your own backyard. Properly prepared, with its crisp, savory crust and its tender meat inside, it is a superb dish that goes especially well with chicken biscuits (fried in the leftover fat, *Recipe Index*) and fresh vegetables, such as corn on the cob, butter beans and home-grown tomatoes. And what better picnic fare could anyone ask for than cold fried chicken with potato salad, followed by a generous slice of ice-cold watermelon?

34

Any attempt to prescribe the best way to prepare fried chicken is likely to start the Civil War all over again, or it may, at best, lead into a storm of prolonged arguments, widely diverse local and even neighborhood differences, not to say family bickerings.

Southern cooks disagree on just about every step in the frying process. Some of them salt and pepper the chicken pieces and then dredge them with flour, while others put the flour, salt and pepper—and sometimes paprika—in a brown paper bag and shake the chicken pieces in it. A Middle South variant soaks the pieces in buttermilk, then does the bag trick, and after that dips the chicken in cream and returns it to the flour mix before frying; all this, it is claimed, makes an especially crunchy crust.

Then there is the matter of cooking time. One faction says you simply cook the chicken until it is golden brown. Another insists you must brown the pieces thoroughly, then drain off the excess fat, add a little water, cover the pan and cook the chicken slowly for another 10 to 20 minutes. A Virginia version calls for browning the chicken in a skillet and then baking it in a slow oven for the last 30 minutes.

To lid or not to lid is also a question. Friends of mine in Gaithersburg, Maryland, take a dim view of recipes that call for covering the chicken during part of the cooking. One of them smiled a superior smile and said: "When you fry chicken you have to expect a lot of grease popping all over the place. It's only people who don't want to scrub the stove afterward who use a lid for cooking fried chicken."

Terrapin stew is a culinary tradition nurtured by generations of Marylanders. After the terrapins are boiled and shelled, the meat is chopped fine and cooked with the livers and terrapin eggs (*Recipe Index*). Devotees of the stew, gathered here at the Baltimore home of Bruce P. Wilson (at head of table), make a ritual of eating it. The delicacy is presented in a silver bowl, ladled into soup plates, and accompanied by beaten biscuits and glasses of dry sherry.

These same friends scoff at cooks who insist that the gravy must be poured over the chicken; they say it should be served separately in a sauceboat. They also serve boiled rice with the chicken. This is rank heresy to other Marylanders, who say the proper accompaniment is hot cornbread.

My own home town of Mobile also has its strong views on how to fry chicken. I used to know two sisters, music teachers, who had a lifelong battle about the question. One of them, named Georgia, used a recipe from her father's family. She would cut up two or three fryers and put them in a bowl with a little milk to soak for about half an hour, turning the pieces often while they were in the milk. Then she would shake the chicken pieces and dip them in a mixture of flour, salt and pepper. She would fry the pieces in bacon drippings and lard—not too hot—watching them carefully and turning them frequently, and finally sprinkling a little paprika over them before they were done.

Her sister, whose name was Kittiebelle, utterly disdained this method. She used her mother's fried chicken recipe. On this side of the family, the chicken pieces were washed and dried carefully, then rubbed lightly with garlic. The recipe, which Kittiebelle wrote down, included a word of reassurance about the garlic: "Don't worry; you can't really taste it. It only adds an indefinable flavor vibration." The garlic rubbing was followed by a liberal sprinkling of salt and pepper. Then Kittiebelle would make a batter of eggs, milk, flour and lemon juice. She would dip the pieces in the batter, then dip them in flour, and fry them golden brown in an iron skillet in hot lard and butter. Every step was different from the way her sister Georgia did it.

Chicken plays such an important role in the Delmarva peninsula's economy that in 1949 the poultry industry created a festival, in the spirit of an old-time country fair, with beauty queens, vintage motorcar displays and a national chicken-cooking contest. At the most recent festival held on the campus of Maryland State College in Princess Anne, there were junior and senior contestants, and they cooked chicken in just about every combination imaginable: with crabmeat, maple syrup, orange marmalade, grape jelly, sake, peanut butter, lime juice, chopped oysters, soy sauce, cornmeal, pineapple juice, applesauce, green beans, frozen orange juice and even instant oatmeal.

Of the 98 recipes that reached the finals of the competition the winning entry, which brought a prize of $5,000, was prepared by a dimpled lady named Arletta Lovejoy from—of all places—Indiana. Jefferson Davis must have whirled in his grave at this Yankee triumph. There was some consolation for Southern cooks, however, for Mrs. Lovejoy coated her chicken with pecans, an ingredient that is as Southern as mockingbirds or a mess of grits. Mrs. Lovejoy's prize-winning prescription called for dipping the chicken in buttermilk and egg, then dredging it in a mixture of flour, ground pecans, paprika, salt, pepper and sesame seeds. She covered the chicken with pecan halves, and baked it "until tender and golden brown." Then, when it was done, she garnished it with parsley and cherry tomatoes.

At first glance Mrs. Lovejoy's recipe may seem exotic, but it has credentials going back to ancient times. The Romans were fond of ground pine nuts and various seeds, and cooked their meats with them in the same way that Mrs. Lovejoy used pecans and sesame seeds. Closer to home, the American Indians used ground pecans and ground hickory nuts as a thickening in many dishes.

Although fried chicken leads all the rest, there is an almost endless variety of ways in which Southern cooks prepare this ubiquitous, inexpensive bird: broiled, roasted, fricasseed, stuffed, baked, smothered, barbecued or made into chicken pie.

The pie ranks as a classic. The chicken is cooked; then a sauce is prepared with hard-boiled egg yolks, black pepper, boiled-down chicken broth and light cream. The chicken meat is cut up, placed in a pastry-lined pan, and the sauce is added. All of this is topped by a light flaky crust with an air vent, and a special sign of some sort is pricked in the pastry to indicate to the server where he will find the dark meat and where the light. In Virginia carrots go in the pie, and in north Georgia fresh green peas. The farther south you go the more celery and bell pepper are used. One old Mississippi recipe calls for asparagus tips and a knob of butter along with the chicken and the cream gravy. A South Carolina recipe —known as Beaufort chicken pie—specifies that the bottom of the baking dish be lined with an inch of cooked, buttered rice. Over this goes the chopped chicken that has been cooked with onion, celery, red pepper, mace and black pepper. Sweet corn is added, along with the juice that is saved when the corn is pared from the cob. Then the cook pours a cup of broth over this mixture, adds some butter and covers the whole mixture with another inch of rice. She covers the pie with an egg glaze, bakes it until it is a pale golden brown and serves a sweet relish with it.

There is, in short, no end to the things that Southern cooks can do with chicken. But my own favorite way of preparing it is to fry the chicken in bacon drippings, butter and light olive oil. I grow fresh herbs in the garden on the balcony of my apartment in Rome, and in a spirit of adventure I like to add a different herb whenever I prepare fried chicken. A little fresh marjoram, chopped very fine, lends a delightful, surprising flavor. So does dill, thyme, or summer savory. I use each herb separately and always in very small quantities.

Many Southern cooks add some light wine to the pan scrapings when they are making chicken gravy. They prefer it to milk or cream. In Rome, where I serve fried chicken the year round, I like milk gravy in winter and wine gravy in summer. Either way there is nothing better.

NATIONAL CHICKEN COOKING CONTEST
OUTDOOR DIVISION

Uniformed in a "Delmarvalous Chicken" apron, a contestant pauses beneath one of the outdoor signs.

Chicken Rules the Roost at Delmarva's Annual Festival

Every year since 1949, poultry growers of the Delaware-Maryland-Virginia peninsula have played host at a national chicken festival. The scene shifts year to year from one Delmarva town to the next, and there is always a parade, a pageant and a Poultry Princess, but most of the excitement centers around the National Chicken Cooking Contest held during the final two days. At a recent contest, shown here, 10,000 entrants submitted chicken recipes. Judges winnowed the finalists from the hopefuls, who came to Delmarva to demonstrate the dishes they had invented. On an outdoor grill *(below)* one finalist, Mrs. Charles Kuether of Milwaukee, wearing heavy gloves, bastes her "Lemony Barbecued Chicken."

The seven and a half tons of chicken eaten by festival visitors were fried in this steel skillet, 10 feet across and eight inches deep.

Contest judges, like those shown blindfolded at right, were chosen from among the nation's newspaper, magazine, radio and television food editors. The judges scored each recipe on originality, clarity and practicality —the finished product on taste and appearance. To give cooks of all ages a chance, there were both junior (8 to 18) and adult divisions. Two adult and junior finalists were chosen from each state and the District of Columbia. Cash prizes were awarded. The contest has grown so rapidly that while the prizes totaled only $7,200 in 1969, by 1971 a total of $26,000—hardly chicken feed—was distributed.

A pair of prize winners—Mrs. Jack
Wiseman of Searcy, Arkansas
(above), and Miss Travis Holcomb
of Farmington, New Mexico, savor
their triumphs. Mrs. Wiseman took
honors for "Chick Kabobs":
chicken breasts, mushrooms, small
onions and green pepper squares
marinated in a pineapple, catsup
and curry sauce, then grilled over
charcoal. A high school sophomore,
Travis owed her triumph to a
creation called "Cock-A-Noodle-
Do": chicken dipped in butter
flavored with soy sauce and rolled
in crushed chow mein noodles.

The Delmarva Chicken Festival attracts around 30,000 people every summer. The main events are the chicken-cooking contest and the beauty pageant at which a Poultry Princess is plucked from the young chicks in the surrounding towns. The visitors may also enjoy a carnival, an art show, an antique car display and a flea market, along with the parade of costumed marchers. But mostly the guests just stand around *(above and right),* doing what comes naturally at a chicken festival —munching on fried chicken.

Fried chicken is as Southern as a mint julep—and stirs as many debates. Almost every cook uses a different recipe; there is no King James version. In Maryland, traditionally the bird is seasoned and floured before frying, and it is served with gravy made from the pan drippings. Even so, Marylanders themselves do not agree on whether to pour the gravy over the chicken or present it in a sauceboat. Below and on the following pages are recipes for three of the best ways of preparing fried chicken.

Maryland Fried Chicken with Cream Gravy

To serve 4

1½ to 2 pounds lard, or substitute
 3 to 4 cups vegetable oil
A 2½- to 3-pound chicken, cut
 into 8 serving pieces
2½ teaspoons salt
Freshly ground black pepper
½ cup plus 2 tablespoons flour
1 cup milk
1 cup heavy cream

Preheat the oven to its lowest setting. Then line a large shallow baking dish with a double thickness of paper towels and place the dish on the middle shelf of the oven.

Melt 1½ pounds of the lard over high heat in a heavy 10-inch skillet at least 2 inches deep or in a large heavy saucepan. When melted the fat should be about 1 inch deep; if necessary, add more lard. Or pour the vegetable oil into a comparable skillet or saucepan to a depth of 1 inch. Heat the fat until it reaches a temperature of 375° on a deep-frying thermometer, or until it is very hot but not smoking.

Pat the pieces of chicken completely dry with paper towels and season them on all sides with 2 teaspoons of the salt and a few grindings of pepper. Dip each piece of chicken in ½ cup of the flour, turn to coat it evenly, and vigorously shake off the excess flour.

Fry the chicken thighs and drumsticks, starting the pieces skin side down and turning them frequently with tongs, for about 12 minutes, or until they color richly and evenly. To be sure that the bird is cooked to the proper degree of doneness, lift a piece from the pan and pierce it deeply with the point of a small skewer or sharp knife. The juice that trickles out should be clear yellow; if it is still tinged with pink, fry the pieces for 2 or 3 minutes more. As they brown, drain the pieces of chicken in the paper-lined dish and keep them warm in the oven.

Then fry the wings and breasts, in two batches if necessary to avoid crowding the pan. The white meat pieces should be fully cooked in 7 or 8 minutes. When they are brown, add them to the dish in the oven.

Pour off all but a thin film of fat from the pan and in its place add the remaining 2 tablespoons of flour. Mix well. Then, stirring the mixture constantly with a wire whisk, pour in the milk and cream in a thin stream and cook over high heat until the gravy comes to a boil, thickens lightly and is smooth. Reduce the heat to low and simmer for 2 or 3 minutes to remove the taste of flour. Add the remaining ½ teaspoon of salt and a few grindings of pepper and taste for seasoning.

Arrange the chicken on a platter and pour the cream gravy over it, or ladle the gravy into a bowl or sauceboat, arrange the chicken on a heated platter and serve at once. Maryland fried chicken is traditionally accompanied by fried biscuits *(Recipe Index)*. If you wish to serve the biscuits, fry them in the hot fat after the chicken and keep them warm in the oven in the same lined baking dish while you prepare the gravy.

Maryland's famous fried chicken comes with cream gravy that may be poured over the bird or served separately.

To serve 4

2 to 4 pounds lard
A 2½- to 3-pound chicken, cut
 into 8 serving pieces
2 teaspoons salt
Freshly ground black pepper
1 egg, lightly beaten and combined
 with ½ cup milk
1 cup flour

Kentucky Fried Chicken

Preheat the oven to its lowest setting. Then line a large shallow baking dish with paper towels and place it in the center of the oven.

Melt 2 pounds of the lard over high heat in a deep fryer or large heavy saucepan. When melted, the fat should be 1½ to 2 inches deep; add more lard if necessary. Heat the lard to a temperature of 375° on a deep-frying thermometer, or until it is very hot but not smoking.

Pat the pieces of chicken completely dry with paper towels and season them on all sides with the salt and a few grindings of pepper. Immerse the chicken pieces one at a time in the egg-and-milk mixture, then dip them in the flour and turn to coat them lightly but evenly.

Fry the chicken thighs and drumsticks, starting them skin side down and turning them frequently with tongs, for about 12 minutes, or until they color richly and evenly. As they brown, transfer them to the paper-lined dish and keep them warm in the oven. Then fry the wings and breast, separately if necessary to avoid overcrowding the pan. The white meat will be fully cooked in 7 or 8 minutes.

When all the pieces are fried, mound the chicken attractively on a heated platter and serve at once.

To serve 4

A 2½- to 3-pound chicken, cut
 into 8 serving pieces
2½ teaspoons salt
Freshly ground black pepper
1 cup plus 2 tablespoons flour
1½ to 2 pounds lard
2 medium-sized onions, peeled and
 cut crosswise into ⅛-inch-thick
 slices (2 cups)
2 cups water
1 tablespoon distilled white vinegar

Southern Fried Chicken with Onion Gravy

Preheat the oven to its lowest setting. Then line a large shallow baking dish with paper towels and place it in the center of the oven.

Pat the pieces of chicken completely dry with paper towels and season them on all sides with 2 teaspoons of the salt and a few grindings of pepper. One at a time dip the pieces in 1 cup of the flour and turn to coat them evenly. Shake each piece vigorously to remove the excess flour.

Melt 1½ pounds of the lard over high heat in a heavy 12-inch skillet at least 2 inches deep and equipped with a tightly fitting lid. When melted, the fat should be about ½ inch deep; add more lard if necessary. When the lard is very hot but not smoking, place the pieces of chicken skin side down in the skillet and set the lid on top. Fry over high heat for 5 minutes, turn the pieces of chicken with tongs and continue to fry, still tightly covered, for 4 to 5 minutes longer, or until the chicken is richly and evenly browned on both sides.

Transfer the chicken to the paper-lined dish and keep it warm in the oven while you prepare the onion gravy. Pour off all but about 1 tablespoon of the fat remaining in the skillet and in its place add the onions. Sprinkle them with the remaining 2 tablespoons of flour and, stirring frequently, cook over high heat for 3 or 4 minutes, or until the onions are soft and golden brown. Stirring them constantly with a spoon, pour in the water in a slow stream and cook until the gravy comes to a boil, thickens and is smooth. Stir in the vinegar, the remaining ½ teaspoon of salt and a few grindings of pepper. Remove the skillet from the heat and taste the gravy for seasoning.

To serve, arrange the chicken attractively on a heated platter and pour the onion gravy over it. Or, more traditionally, mound Southern dry rice *(Recipe Index)* in a serving bowl, pour the onion gravy over the rice, and serve the gravy-smothered rice with the chicken.

Fried Biscuits

In Maryland, these are called chicken biscuits and are fried in the fat remaining in the pan after the chicken is finished.

Combine the flour, baking powder and salt and sift them into a deep bowl. Add the butter bits and, with your fingers, rub the flour and fat together until they resemble flakes of coarse meal. Pour in the milk and toss lightly together with your fingers or a table fork.

Gather the dough into a ball and place it on a lightly floured surface. Then roll the dough about ¼ inch thick. With a biscuit cutter or the rim of a glass, cut the dough into 1½-inch rounds. Collect the scraps in a ball, roll them out again and cut as many more rounds as you can.

Melt 1½ pounds of lard in a heavy 12-inch skillet set over high heat. Or pour vegetable oil into a 12-inch skillet to a depth of about 1 inch. Heat the fat until it reaches a temperature of 375° on a deep-frying thermometer, or until it is very hot but not smoking. Fry the biscuits for about 4 or 5 minutes, turning them with a slotted spatula until they are evenly browned on both sides. Transfer them to paper towels to drain.

Serve at once. Traditionally, the biscuits are placed on the dinner plates with Maryland fried chicken and masked with gravy.

Crab Cakes

In a deep bowl, beat the egg lightly with a wire whisk. Add the mayonnaise, mustard, red pepper, Tabasco, salt and white pepper and whisk until the mixture is smooth. Then add the crabmeat, parsley and cracker crumbs and toss together all the ingredients with a fork. Divide the mixture into 8 equal portions, and shape each of these into a ball about 2 inches in diameter. Wrap in wax paper and chill the cakes for 30 minutes.

Pour oil into a deep fryer or large heavy saucepan to a depth of 3 inches and heat the oil to a temperature of 375° on a deep-frying thermometer.

Deep-fry the crab cakes 4 at a time, turning them with a slotted spoon for 2 or 3 minutes until they are golden on all sides. As they brown, transfer them to paper towels to drain. Arrange the crab cakes with the lemon wedges on a heated platter. Serve at once, accompanied by the tartar sauce in a separate bowl.

Imperial Crab

Preheat the oven to 375°. With a pastry brush, spread the softened butter over 4 medium-sized natural or ceramic crab or scallop shells.

In a deep bowl, beat the egg lightly with a wire whisk. Add the mayonnaise, Worcestershire, salt and white pepper and whisk until the mixture is smooth. Then add the crabmeat and the green and red pepper and toss together gently but thoroughly with a rubber spatula.

Spoon the crab mixture into the buttered shells, dividing it evenly among them and mounding the centers slightly. Dot the tops with the butter bits. Bake in the upper third of the oven for 15 to 20 minutes, then slide them under a hot broiler for 30 seconds to brown the tops, if desired. Serve the imperial crab at once, directly from the shells.

To make about a dozen 1½-inch biscuits

1 cup flour
2 teaspoons double-acting baking powder
¼ teaspoon salt
2 tablespoons butter, cut into bits
6 tablespoons milk
Lard or vegetable oil for frying

To serve 4

1 egg
2 tablespoons freshly made mayonnaise *(Recipe Index)*, or substitute bottled mayonnaise
½ teaspoon dry mustard
⅛ teaspoon ground hot red pepper (cayenne)
⅛ teaspoon Tabasco
½ teaspoon salt
½ teaspoon ground white pepper
1 pound fresh, frozen or canned crabmeat, drained and picked over to remove all cartilage
3 tablespoons finely chopped fresh parsley
1½ tablespoons fresh crumbs made from unsalted soda crackers, pulverized in a blender or with a rolling pin
Vegetable oil for deep frying
1 lemon, cut into 8 wedges
Tartar sauce *(Recipe Index)*

To serve 4

2 teaspoons butter, softened, plus 2 tablespoons butter, cut into bits
1 egg
2 tablespoons freshly made mayonnaise *(Recipe Index)*, or substitute bottled mayonnaise
2 teaspoons Worcestershire sauce
½ teaspoon salt
¼ teaspoon ground white pepper
1 pound fresh, frozen or canned crabmeat, drained and picked over to remove all cartilage
¼ cup finely chopped green pepper
¼ cup finely chopped red pepper

In Maryland crab cooking is a high art. The masterpieces assembled here, from the bottom left clockwise, are: deep-fried soft-shell crabs with tartar sauce; butter-fried soft-shells; imperial crab baked in its own shell; deep-fried crab cakes; and Maryland deviled crab in a scallop shell. All are in the Recipe Index.

To serve 4

12 soft-shell crabs, cleaned
   (below)
1 tablespoon salt
1 cup flour
11 tablespoons butter
3 to 6 tablespoons vegetable oil
6 tablespoons finely chopped fresh
   parsley
3 tablespoons strained fresh lemon
   juice

Fried Soft-Shell Crabs

Preheat the oven to its lowest setting. Then line a large shallow baking dish with a double thickness of paper towels and place it on the middle shelf of the oven.

Wash the crabs under cold running water, pat them completely dry with paper towels and season them evenly with the salt. One at a time, dip the crabs in the flour to coat both sides and shake vigorously to remove the excess flour.

In a heavy 10- to 12-inch skillet, melt 3 tablespoons of the butter with 3 tablespoons of the oil over moderate heat until the foam begins to subside. Fry the crabs, 2 or 3 at a time, for about 5 minutes, turning them frequently with tongs and regulating the heat so that they color richly and evenly without burning. As they brown, transfer the crabs to the lined dish to drain and keep them warm in the oven while you fry the rest. Add the remaining 3 tablespoons of oil to the skillet, a spoonful at a time, if necessary.

Just before serving, melt the remaining 8 tablespoons of butter over moderate heat in a 6- to 8-inch skillet, regulating the heat and stirring to prevent the butter from browning. Remove the pan from the heat and stir in the chopped parsley and lemon juice.

Arrange the crabs attractively on a heated platter and dribble a few tablespoonfuls of the butter sauce over them. Present the rest of the butter separately in a small bowl or sauceboat.

To serve 4

12 soft-shell crabs, cleaned
   (below)
1 tablespoon salt
Freshly ground black pepper
1 cup flour
3 cups soft fresh crumbs made from
   homemade-type white bread,
   pulverized in a blender or finely
   shredded with a fork
4 eggs
½ cup milk
Vegetable oil for deep frying
Tartar sauce (Recipe Index)

Deep-fried Soft-Shell Crabs

Wash the crabs under cold running water, pat them completely dry with paper towels and season them on both sides with the salt and a few gridings of pepper.

Spread the flour and bread crumbs on separate plates or pieces of wax paper. In a wide bowl, beat the eggs lightly with a wire whisk or rotary beater, then beat in the milk.

One at a time, dip a crab into the flour to coat both sides. Shake off the excess flour, immerse the crab in the egg-milk mixture, then coat it with the crumbs, covering the crab completely.

When all of the crabs have been floured, dipped in the egg mixture, and breaded, arrange them side by side on 1 or 2 large baking sheets and refrigerate them for at least 20 minutes to firm the coating.

Preheat the oven to its lowest setting. Then line a large shallow baking

To clean a live soft-shell crab, first freeze the crab briefly to numb it, then peel back the triangular apron.

With a small sharp knife, scrape out the stomach and intestines, which lie beneath the apron.

Turn over the crab, lift the shell at the tapering points on each end and insert knife into the grayish lungs.

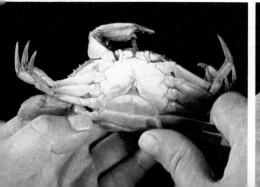

dish with a double thickness of paper towels and place it on the middle shelf of the oven.

Pour vegetable oil into a deep fryer or large heavy saucepan to a depth of 3 inches and heat until the oil reaches a temperature of 360° on a deep-frying thermometer.

Deep-fry the crabs, 2 or 3 at a time. Turn them occasionally with tongs or a slotted spoon and fry them about 5 minutes, or until they are golden brown. As they brown, transfer them to the lined dish and keep them warm in the oven while you deep-fry the rest.

Arrange the crabs attractively on a heated platter and serve them at once, accompanied by a bowl of tartar sauce *(Recipe Index)*.

Maryland Deviled Crab

To serve 4

Preheat the oven to 375°. With a pastry brush, spread the 2 teaspoons of softened butter over the bottoms of 4 medium-sized natural or ceramic crab or scallop shells.

In a heavy 8- to 10-inch skillet, melt 2 tablespoons of butter over moderate heat. Drop in the bread crumbs and stir until they are crisp and golden. With a rubber spatula, scrape the entire contents of the pan into a small bowl and set aside.

In the same skillet, melt the remaining 2 tablespoons of butter over moderate heat. When the foam begins to subside, add the flour and mix well. Stirring the mixture constantly with a wire whisk, pour in the milk in a slow stream and cook over high heat until the sauce comes to a boil, thickens and is smooth. Then reduce the heat to low and simmer the sauce for 2 or 3 minutes.

Remove the skillet from the heat and stir the sieved egg yolks into the sauce. When they are well incorporated, beat in the lemon juice, Worcestershire sauce, Tabasco, dry mustard, red pepper, salt and a few grindings of black pepper. Now add the crabmeat, chopped green pepper and chopped egg whites and toss the mixture together gently but thoroughly with a table fork. Taste for seasoning.

Spoon the crab mixture into the buttered shells, dividing it evenly among them and slightly mounding the centers. Sprinkle the reserved crumbs over the tops.

Bake the deviled crab in the upper third of the oven for 15 to 20 minutes, then slide them under the broiler for 30 seconds to brown the tops, if desired. Serve at once, directly from the shells.

2 teaspoons butter, softened, plus 4 tablespoons butter
6 tablespoons soft fresh crumbs made from homemade-type white bread, pulverized in a blender or finely shredded with a fork
2 tablespoons flour
¾ cup milk
2 hard-cooked eggs, the yolks rubbed through a fine sieve with the back of a spoon, and the whites finely chopped
2 teaspoons strained fresh lemon juice
1 teaspoon Worcestershire sauce
¼ teaspoon Tabasco
½ teaspoon dry mustard
¼ teaspoon ground hot red pepper (cayenne)
1 teaspoon salt
Freshly ground black pepper
1 pound fresh, frozen or canned lump crabmeat, thoroughly drained and picked over to remove all bits of cartilage
3 tablespoons finely chopped green pepper

Clean out the spongy lungs, or "dead man's fingers," until the cartilage is completely exposed.

With a pair of sharp scissors, cut off and discard the head of the crab, just behind the eyes.

Squeeze the body and the sand sac will pop out of the head opening. Wash the crab in cold water.

A Tradition That Has Been Pounded into the Southern Way of Life

For close to 200 years, Maryland and Virginia cooks have prided themselves on their beaten biscuits. By pounding the dough, they beat air into it and made it light, in days before baking powder was available. Freshly baked, these crisp morsels are still considered an essential accompaniment to the famous Smithfield ham—and the time and energy spent beating the dough is neither grudged nor stinted. Mrs. J. Millard Tawes *(left)*, the wife of a former Maryland governor, who lives on the Eastern Shore is a talented cook and an authority on traditional biscuit-making techniques. Her recipe, which produces about 6 dozen biscuits, calls for 2 pounds of flour, ½ teaspoon of sugar, a scant teaspoon of salt, 6 ounces of lard, 1 cup of cold water and a dab of baking soda no larger than a pea. After she works all the ingredients together thoroughly, Mrs. Tawes places the dough on a chopping block. She then pounds it with a hammer, flailing away for 20 minutes (although other cooks use a mallet or even the flat of an ax). Whatever the implement, it takes anywhere from 20 to 30 minutes of steady beating to make the dough "blister" and appear smooth and glossy. Although the pounding need not be unduly vigorous, it should be regular, and this procedure is best accomplished while sitting down.

When the dough has achieved a satiny texture, Mrs. Tawes begins to shape it into biscuits. Unlike Virginia cooks who roll the dough flat and stamp out the biscuits with a cutter, Maryland-born Mrs. Tawes forms each biscuit with her hand *(left)*. She scoops a piece of dough into her fist and squeezes it up between her thumb and forefinger to form a ball. Then she pinches the ball off, pats it flat and pricks the top with the tines of a fork. She recommends that the biscuits bake for 25 minutes in a 400° oven, so they will emerge golden brown like the panful shown below.

III

The Secrets of
Virginia's Hams

Virginia's proudest gift to
gastronomy is the Smithfield ham.
It is cured with salt, smoked
and aged according to a centuries-old
method. Then it is boiled, glazed
with brown sugar and bread crumbs
and baked. Served with beaten
biscuits, the ham is carved paper
thin. It may be sliced vertically or,
for even thinner slivers, sliced
horizontally as shown on page 75.

To the serious traveler and eater, Virginia means two things above
all: history and ham. The best way to approach both subjects is to drive
down the Delmarva peninsula and cross the spectacular 18-mile-long
Chesapeake Bay Bridge-Tunnel to Norfolk. From here it is only an hour's
drive to Jamestown, where the first permanent English settlement in
America was established in 1607. And once you reach Jamestown, you
are little more than a stone's throw from Smithfield, a shrine hallowed by
food lovers everywhere—home of Virginia's world-famous hams.

Smithfield is, appropriately, just a few miles from Hog Island, where
the original Jamestown settlers kept their hogs. It is a placid little town,
with only one hostelry, Sykes Inn, which was built in 1752. The inn has a
high, wide front porch and spotless rooms furnished with old wooden
beds and wardrobes. My experience of its dining room reassured me that
there are, indeed, places in the South where public eating is a pleasure.

The young man who presently runs Sykes Inn is Russell Thompson, a
conscientious and ingratiating host. I questioned him point-blank:

"What *is* a Smithfield ham?"

He smiled, took a breath and began, "Well. . . ." I realized it was a question as vast as "What is a rose?" so I waited until he ruminated a bit. He
then put down his coffee cup and said: "It has to have been cured in Smithfield or hereabouts; it has to have that special flavor our way of curing produces. The hog has to be the lean type, part razorback, and usually it has
been at least partly peanut-fed. And you have to know how to cook it!"

"And how *do* you cook it?"

"We use Mrs. D. W. Sykes's method which she passed on to us. You begin by scrubbing the cured ham in hot water with a stiff brush until you get off all the mess—all the mold and salt. Then you put it in the boiler with enough water for it to float, and soak it overnight. The next day you bring the water to a boil, then turn the fire down, down, down until the water doesn't even bubble, just seems to tremble. This keeps the ham from flaking or coming to pieces. You cook it like that until the hock —the bone on the small end—pokes through the skin so that it sticks out about one inch. Then you take the ham out; we don't leave it to cool in the water. When it's cooled enough to handle, we skin it and trim off some of the fat. Then we cover it with brown sugar and bake it in a hot oven for about 10 minutes. You don't ever cut the hock off the ham. That keeps the juices in while the ham is cooking and makes a natural handle for you when you're carving."

Technically, as Russell Thompson indicated, a ham must be produced within the corporate limits of the town of Smithfield in order to be called a Smithfield ham (the Virginia state legislature having passed a law to that effect in 1968). But in actual practice it is not the specific area where the ham is produced, but the way it is cured, smoked and aged that makes the difference. The E. M. Todd Co. in Richmond, for example, produces marvelous Smithfield-type hams, as good as you will find anywhere. These are called "Old Virginia Hams," but they are Smithfield hams in everything but name.

The first requirement for Smithfield or Smithfield-type hams is that they must come from hogs that are peanut-fed for part of their lives. The animals themselves may be from Virginia, Georgia or North Carolina. For the first eight or 10 months they feed on acorns, grass or hickory nuts. Then, when peanuts are harvested, they are allowed to forage through the fields. The peanut diet gives the hams their amber color, their translucent fat and their distinctiveness of texture. The curing begins when the hams are rubbed with dry salt, a preservative process that goes back 2,000 years. From here on the steps vary. At the Todd Company the hams are stacked in mountainous piles in a cool room allowing the salt to seep through the meat. After some weeks they are taken down from the huge piles and salt is rubbed into them again. Then they are washed in scalding water and scrubbed with brushes. Next they are covered with ground black pepper, hung on metal trees or steel railway tracks, and smoked 24 hours a day with hickory smoke. At first hickory logs are burned, but then hickory sawdust is substituted, because it is cooler, providing lots of smoke and very little heat. The hams are smoked for about six weeks, then taken down and set in boxes in a cool place to age for three months or more. The total time for curing, smoking and aging usually ranges from nine to 21 months.

The curing, smoking and aging give the Smithfield ham the distinctive salty-smoky-spicy flavor that sets it apart from all other hams. A Smithfield ham usually weighs anywhere from 12 to 16 pounds, and it will keep indefinitely. Some people have tales of heirloom hams stashed away at the birth of a child and enjoyed—miracles of delicacy—at his or her wedding years later.

54

In Virginia and throughout the South, you also hear much talk about the "country ham." This is a ham from the rural South—especially Virginia, North Carolina, Georgia, Kentucky and Tennessee—and it differs substantially from the Smithfield ham. In the first place, the hog is not necessarily peanut-fed; it may feed on corn or other grains. Moreover, the cut of meat is different from the Smithfield ham; the full butt and the shank bone are not left on the ham, as is the case with the Smithfield, but are removed before packing.

The processing of a country ham varies from one place to the next. At the Todd Company it is hand rubbed with salt, sugar and nitrate or saltpeter, which makes it take the cure more quickly. Then the ham is stored in a stainless-steel or fiberglass vat. Here the juices run out of the ham, and over a period of three months it is cured by these juices. The country ham is smoked with hickory smoke, just as the Smithfield ham is. After that, the procedure differs, but at the Todd Company a country ham is not aged. The ham is ready for eating after three months, and the meat is noticeably different from that of the Smithfield ham. It is leaner, because the hogs are not fed on peanuts; it has a mahogany color; it is not so salty and not so rich as the Smithfield. Many people will argue long and loud that it is better than a Smithfield ham, although this is a subjective judgment that is just about as easy to decide as whether Bordeaux wines are really better than Burgundies.

The preparation of ham for the table stirs other heated debates. Whether the ham is a Smithfield or a country ham, it is usually scrubbed and soaked, then boiled very slowly in water. But every Southern household seems to have a different opinion as to what, if anything, to add to the water. The list is long—tart apples, bay leaves, brown sugar-and-vinegar, peppercorns, molasses, wine, dried apricots, blackberry jam. Caprice rules, except in one regard: however many transformations the cooking water goes through, it is never thrown out. It is used to cook beans, cabbage, greens of all sorts; and one of the great soups of the South is made of ham stock, white beans and milk, with shredded ham scraps thrown in.

What happens to the ham when it comes out of the water also differs from one household to the next. If it is to be browned or glazed in the oven it is not boiled very long. The skin is removed, and the ham is roasted until the fat is golden. For fancy occasions the skin is coated with a mixture of bread crumbs and brown sugar *(Recipe Index)*, or peanut butter and brown sugar, or fruit juice and ham broth. The ham is accompanied by a sweet dish or relish. Two classic accompaniments are brandied peaches and watermelon rind preserves *(both Recipe Index)*.

Good ham goes well with almost anything. One of the marriages made in heaven is a beaten biscuit *(Recipe Index)* with a slice of ham inside. A breakfast classic all through the South is ham with red-eye gravy (a gravy made from the ham juice), hot grits and sometimes fried apples. In Maryland's Charles County the Easter ham *(Recipe Index)* is stuffed with fresh greens and served in cold slices with hot biscuits. Roast ham is a popular dish at Christmas or Carnival time in the Deep South. The traditional recipe calls for baking the ham in a blanket of stiff flour-and-water paste. After you bake it for six hours in a moderate oven, you remove the paste,

Smithfield hams are salt-cured, then smoked for about two weeks. At the Smithfield Ham and Products Co., in Smithfield, Virginia, the hams are coated with black pepper before being hung on racks in a smokehouse, where they are exposed to smoke from burning hickory, apple wood and oak. Finally the hams are taken to a smoke-free house to age for six to 18 months.

sprinkle the ham with a few fine crumbs and return it to the oven for half an hour, dusting it lightly with cayenne and basting it every five minutes with a mixture of one cup of light dry red wine and two tablespoons of sherry. This ham is good either hot or cold.

No matter how they prepare it, Southern cooks pride themselves on using every bit of the ham. The hambone goes with black-eyed peas or beans of any kind for slow simmering; the fat is carefully saved for cooking uses; the scraps and last remnants of the ham become potted ham or delightful ham puffs, or they end up in a ham, celery and crisp apple salad. The Southern boast that "we use everything in the pig but the squeal" applies as much to ham as it does to the pork dishes that belong in the soul food category.

Yet all this palaver about ham proves pointless until you have tasted one, preferably a Smithfield ham at its best, and the purpose of my visit to Sykes Inn was to do just that. When the great moment arrived and I was properly seated in the dining room my cheerful waitress, Margaret Reese, brought in a plate of cold sliced ham and hot crisp biscuits, along with sweet relishes, and placed this feast before me. I thought, here goes. I have drunk from the centaurs' mint-verged spring in Thessaly, eaten apples and goat cheese in Arcadia, goose-liver pâté in Strasbourg, oysters at Colchester, *couscous* in North Africa, and perhaps only in the light of those experiences could I now come back to my native land and properly partake of Smithfield ham . . . in Smithfield.

I looked at it respectfully for a moment before I lifted knife and fork. For an instant I remembered a pig I had known personally, on the east

Throughout the aging process, Smithfield hams are checked regularly. At left, Alton H. Gwaltney, who is foreman of Smithfield Ham and Products Co., demonstrates the test by plunging a "try pick," which resembles an ice pick, into the ham until it touches the bone. If the pick gives off a winey, salty aroma, he knows the ham is good. But if the pick smells like rotten onions, the ham has spoiled and is discarded.

coast of Italy, who danced every morning at 6 o'clock when his pen was cleaned (pigs are very clean by nature, even though they like to cool their precious layer of fat in nice mud). I remembered that the poet Robert Herrick had a pet pig that he taught to sit at table and drink from a tankard. I remembered also that in the Scandinavian world the pig is regarded as a kind of minion of the sun, since his fat serves to heat people up in the winter. I thought how grateful our first settlers must have been, in the long damp winters of the South, for the true "central heating" qualities of pork fat and flesh.

Margaret Reese and Russell Thompson were hovering in the middle distance, she at the big old dark sideboard, he at the front desk, both awaiting my reaction. I put down my knife and fork and picked up a nugget of ham in my fingers. The dark red meat was framed by delicate old-ivory fat, and there was something almost flowery in its perfume. I tasted it. It was superb. The succulent consistency of the meat contrasted with the delicate firmness of the fat. The basically salt flesh; the basically sweet fat. Some overtone of flavor in which there was a hint of autumn woods or wine barrels, or early spring and broom grass. Margaret Reese and Russell Thompson were now a little in suspense. But my mouth was full: all I could manage was, "Yes, oh yes, oh yes!"

In Virginia past and present are closely interwoven. You drive along a modern four-lane highway with cars roaring all around you, and you pass a sign noting that near this spot the Indian maid Pocahontas married John Rolfe, the man who introduced a new strain of tobacco into the Jamestown Colony and helped save it from extinction. Farther along, you come to another marker telling how Lord Cornwallis blundered into a trap at Yorktown and, with his back to the sea, surrendered to George Washington. And everywhere you see signs explaining troop movements and great battles of the Civil War: Seven Pines, Five Forks, Petersburg, Fredericksburg, Chancellorsville and The Wilderness.

I stopped off in Williamsburg, a living museum itself, where costumed ladies bustle about showing legions of tourists through the Governor's Palace, and other renovated colonial landmarks. I decided to dine at a restaurant there, and must confess I was a little uneasy about it. I felt that if so much attention had been lavished on "atmosphere" (which I don't like in dining rooms unless it is natural), and on waiters' ruffles, buckles and knee breeches, the food must surely be a mess. Yet there was one thing that reassured me: the big square napkins. I hate dainty tea doilies and paper napkins, and when the yard-square heavy cloth napkins appeared at the table, I decided that this restaurant must be a serious eating place after all.

I ordered a sweet-potato soufflé, beefsteak pie and greengage-plum ice cream. The soufflé is what I remember most. It was the first time I had eaten one, although this is surely a dish that must have originated in the South. The soufflé was a nice golden brown. It didn't seem a bit nervous, but held its shape so well that I did not have the uneasy feeling that it might collapse at any moment. The sweet potatoes had been as finely puréed as if for a sweet-potato pie. They had a winey sort of taste, and were a little spicy, but not enough to crowd out their own flavor.

Between Williamsburg and Richmond, the banks of the James River are dotted with new chemical and synthetic fiber plants. Yet history asserts itself again here, for scattered through the area are some of the loveliest old plantations in all the South: Brandon with its fluted Corinthian columns and formal boxwood gardens; Westover, the magnificent home of William Byrd II; Carter's Grove, a stately mansion on a terraced rise overlooking the river; and Berkley, with its tall chimneys and gabled roof, birthplace of one President of the United States, William Henry Harrison, and home of another, William Henry's grandson Benjamin.

Having accomplished one mission at Smithfield, I was now bent on another. I wanted to try to capture some sense of what life had been like on a plantation, to see for myself where some of the finest traditions of Southern eating had evolved. I meandered through this part of Tidewater Virginia, the lowland area of the state extending as far inland as the tides reach. Then I turned northward to Westmoreland County and Stratford Hall, home of Virginia's most distinguished family, the Lees.

Stratford Hall was built around 1725 by Virginia's first native-born colonial governor, Thomas Lee. Two brothers who signed the Declaration of Independence, Richard Henry Lee and Francis Lightfoot Lee, were born here. So was the South's great hero, General Robert E. Lee.

The red brick house itself is plain but imposing, with a Jacobean English air. The two clusters of four chimneys rise to a dignified height, and the broad stairway leading up to the front door lends a sweep to the facade. The outlying buildings are set at equal distances from the four corners of the main house, accentuating the grand-square design. Both house and grounds have been thoughtfully restored and tended; the 1,200 acres are run today much as they were when the Lees lived here.

I wandered about for a while, then strolled over to the kitchen outbuilding, with its huge fireplace and its collection of utensils and kitchen paraphernalia, including a magnificent copper alembic for distilling brandy. An old black woman in a turban was polishing this vessel while chatting with a younger woman. As the two women talked, I sat on a low stone wall and watched an orange cat play with a mouse it had caught. Sitting there enjoying these old Virginia surroundings, I found myself harking back to history, conjuring up a picture of daily life on a Tidewater plantation.

The first sound in the morning, coming from just such a kitchen outbuilding near where I now sat, would be the *thonk! thonk!* of beaten biscuit dough being prepared. This procedure made the biscuits light and airy in the days before baking powder was invented. The dough was beaten with a hammer, the flat of an ax or a hatchet on a chopping block—usually a tree stump that had been hewn clean—and when it became soft and malleable it was cut and baked. This produced crisp, compact, powdery biscuits that are still made this way and are still a Southern favorite.

At daybreak the guinea fowls would start up their *pot-rack, pot-rack* call. The roosters would join in and wake up the ducks to add to the chorus. From the springhouse came the hollow wooden sound of the churn making fresh butter for the biscuits. From the slave cabins—a tobacco plantation in Virginia maintained around 100 slaves—came the pungent aroma of sowbelly frying.

The people at the big house usually got up at sunrise, and if it were winter they often took something hot upon awakening. Breakfast itself was an ample affair, with ham, venison pasty or whatever meat was left over from the night before. These would be taken with beaten biscuits, hominy grits and hoecakes, crisp round cakes of cornmeal so called because they were sometimes baked on the blade of a hoe. The beverage to go with this usually was coffee, tea, chocolate or cider.

After this serious meal, the master of the house might go off to visit the stables, issue orders to the overseer, exercise his favorite mount or watch the trees being felled on a remote part of his property. Or upon receiving a report that turkey gobblers were roosting in a particular tree, he might set out to hunt them. Even then Virginians were building a reputation for their hospitality, and he might amuse himself by "capturing" wayfarers on the nearest highroad and taking them home with him, perhaps to stay overnight, perhaps only to dine.

The plantation house was a ceaseless hive of activity. There were a thousand and one tasks to be done in the food department alone. If the peaches were ripe, they had to be put into crocks to make brandy; or they were sliced, arranged in shallow trays and covered with net, then placed in the sun to cook and be turned daily, finally to emerge as delectable "peach chips" or "peach leather." Leftover ham bits had to be deviled; tougher bits of beef had to be cooked and chopped for mincemeat; the fermenting vats of beer, wine and spirits had to be stirred or the scum ladled off. Butter had to be covered with leaves and placed in the springhouse. In a

Continued on page 68

The classic beauty of Monticello is reflected in a pond where the mansion's gourmet-owner often kept shad and carp.

America's First Great Gourmet

Anyone who was invited by Thomas Jefferson to dine at Monticello, his mountaintop home near Charlottesville, Virginia, could expect some scintillating conversation and an exceptional meal. For the third President was not only a witty and urbane talker, able to draw on his expertise as architect, philosopher, musician, lawyer, astronomer, inventor, mathematician, botanist and farmer, he was also America's first gourmet of note. Like most epicures, Jefferson placed great value on fresh foods taken at the peak of their season. In the spring, when the shad were running in Virginia's James River, he had the fish transported by the barrelful to Monticello, then kept them alive in a pond *(above)* until he was ready to eat them. In the summer, when dinner was being prepared in the kitchen at Monticello (as re-created on the opposite page), there were deviled crabs from the Chesapeake Bay and a wealth of fresh fruits and vegetables—green peas, cucumbers, cymlings, salad greens, apples and peaches—grown on the premises of Monticello. But Jefferson's tastes in food were eclectic. Often a favorite French soup—*consommé julienne* —would be simmering over the kitchen's open fire. When dinner was served, the local foods were supplemented by fine French dishes and imported wines.

60

Fellow-Virginian Patrick Henry once accused Jefferson of being "so Frenchified that he abjured his native victuals." Jefferson had served as America's envoy to France and was indeed so impressed by the French cuisine that at Monticello he often served such dishes as *boeuf à la daube,* cold jellied beef *(at top in the picture above).* But Jefferson also relished such native delicacies as Jerusalem artichokes, grown and pickled at Monticello, and that Southern specialty, beaten biscuits, particularly when taken with a freshly made cream cheese. Garden peas *(left)* appealed to him so much that he grew 30 different varieties at Monticello. With this un-Frenchified food and with another of his favorites, rice, Jefferson often enjoyed turkey giblet gravy, a dish that was every bit as American as Patrick Henry.

Jefferson was so fond of corn that when he was living in Paris, he grew the vegetable in his garden and served corn on the cob to startled French guests. At Monticello he served corn in many different ways, one of which was a delicate, golden corn pudding *(far left)*. With it he was likely to offer *(top to bottom at immediate left)* celery with almonds, scalloped tomatoes baked with brown sugar, and puréed cymlings with bacon.

Overleaf: In the dining room at Monticello, the table is set for a dinner for 10, just as it might have been in Jefferson's day. Displayed from left to right on the table are many of Jefferson's favorite foods: a Virginia ham, corn pudding, celery with almonds, scalloped tomatoes, puréed cymlings, *boeuf à la daube,* a pair of dishes of damson plum preserves, Jerusalem artichoke pickles and a wild turkey. Decanters of red and white wines stand at either end of the dining table. On a small table in the corner at far right is a silver coffee urn that was designed by Jefferson.

63

Monticello's Gastronomic Gadgets

Jefferson was fascinated by gadgets of all sorts. In the dining room a handy gadget *(above)* was installed by Jefferson because he did not want a lot of servants in the dining room (he thought that they picked up conversations inaccurately and were the source of many false rumors). The set of semi-circular shelves could be loaded with dishes in the pantry and, at the press of a button, revolved into the dining room. Empty dishes could be returned to the pantry the same way. As seen above, the shelves are loaded top to bottom with cream and sugar holders, macaroons, ladyfingerlike Savoy biscuits, tinted meringue kisses and fresh peach ice cream. When dinner was over, guests could serve themselves *(right)* from a glass epergne, laden with clustered raisins, candied violets, crystallized ginger, almonds and pecans.

A lover of fine wines, Jefferson kept his cellar full of casks of imported vintages. The wine was drawn off into bottles, and conveyed to the dining room by this dumbwaiter. The bottles were so expensive that when used, they were reloaded onto the dumbwaiter and returned to the cellar for further use.

Mr. Jefferson's Garden Book

Although Thomas Jefferson served as President of the United States, Governor of Virginia and Minister to France, farming was the career that he preferred above all others. "No occupation is so delightful to me as the culture of the earth," he said. At Monticello, Jefferson kept a diary of his garden, recording everything that happened there in meticulous detail. Known as his *Garden Book,* the diary was begun in 1766 and concluded in 1824, two years before Jefferson died. There is no entry for the fateful year of the Declaration of Independence, 1776. The book's editor notes simply that "Jefferson seems to have been too busy to make any recordings" that year. Below and opposite are some observations that Jefferson recorded, with the dates of the entries.

MAR. 30, 1766.
Purple hyacinth begins to bloom.

MAY 4, 1766.
Wild honeysuckle in our woods open—also the Dwarf flag & Violets.

FEB. 20, 1767.
Sowed a bed of forwardest and a bed of midling peas.

MAR. 9, 1767.
Both beds of peas up.

APRIL 7, 1767.
Planted strawberry roots.

APRIL 25, 1767.
Asparagus 3 inches high, and branched.

(Continued on opposite page)

world without refrigeration, the icehouse was opened only once a day, to get ice for the melons or iced tea or juleps. Fish were never stored there; they were cleaned and put to cook the moment they arrived, or salted and set aside for future use. Fat had to be clarified for lard or soap; candles had to be made. For all these chores, of course, there was a small army of servants, but tradition required that the mistress of the house watch over everything that was done.

Always in these great houses, the tables were bountifully laid. When Philip Fithian came down from New Jersey in the 1770s to tutor the children of the Robert Carters at Nomini Hall with its 2,500 acres (part of Carter's holdings of 70,000), he was surprised to find Southern life pleasanter than he had expected. In a letter home he reported Carter's own estimate that the family and guests consumed annually "27,000 pounds of pork, 20 beeves, 550 bushels of wheat, besides corn, four hogshead of rum and 150 gallons of brandy." He also noted that one dinner included: "Beef and Greens; roast-Pig; fine boil'd Rock-Fish, Pudding, Cheese, etc. Drink: good Porter-Beer, Cyder, Rum and Brandy Toddy."

Another visitor subsequently described the splendors of the table at Shirley Plantation, built by Edward Hill who married into the illustrious Carter family. "His service is all of silver and you drink your porter out of silver goblets. . . . The finest Virginia hams, and saddle of mutton, Turkey, then canvas back duck, beef, oysters. . . . Then comes the sparkling champagne—after that the dessert, plum pudding, tarts, ice cream, peaches preserved in Brandy . . . then the table is cleared and on comes the figs, almonds and raisins, and the richest Madeira, the best Port and the softest Malmsey wine I ever tasted. . . ."

This heady vision of plenty is further expanded in a book entitled *The Old Virginia Gentleman,* by one of the state's most noted 19th Century chroniclers, George Bagby. One premise Bagby sets forth is the superiority of Virginia bacon and greens to the bacon and greens of other places, pointing out that the Virginia pig, like its Westphalian counterpart, is free-ranging, never penned up. Then Bagby goes on: "I am tolerably certain that a few other things beside bacon and greens are required to make a true Virginian. He must, of course, begin on pot-liquor. He must have fried chicken, stewed chicken, broiled chicken, and chicken pie; old hare, butter-beans, new potatoes, squirrel, cymlings, snaps, barbecued shoat, roas'n ears, buttermilk, hoe-cake, pancake, fritters, pot-pie, tomatoes, sweet-potatoes, June apples, waffles, sweet milk, parsnips, artichokes, carrots, cracklin' bread, hominy, bonny-clabber, scrambled eggs, gooba-peas, fried apples, popcorn, persimmon beer, apple-bread, milk and peaches, mutton stew, dewberries, batter-cakes, mushmelons, hickory nuts, partridges, honey in the honey-comb, snappin'-turtle eggs, damson tarts, catfish, cider, hot light-bread, and cornfield peas all the time; but he must not intermit his bacon and greens."

Stratford Hall and the other great plantations of Tidewater Virginia were built by Englishmen or their descendants. Some of these men were Cavaliers, aristocratic supporters of Charles I who fled England when the king was executed in 1649. But mostly they were middle-class Englishmen who came to Virginia and made their fortunes in tobacco. Even so, they still looked to England as their model in nearly all things. They copied the Georgian architecture of English country homes, stocked their mansions with English china and crystal and Chippendale furniture, and sent their sons across the ocean to study in English schools, their daughters to learn proper English manners. And the Virginians' taste in food was English too. The first cookbook to be printed in America, *The Compleat Housewife, or Accomplish'd Gentlewoman's Companion* (printed in Williamsburg in 1742), was of English authorship, and in July 1746 a traveler to Virginia reported in the *London Magazine:* "All over the colony . . . full Tables . . . speak somewhat like the old Roast-beef Ages of our Forefathers . . . Their Breakfast Tables have . . . Coffee, Tea, Chocolate, Venison-pasty, Punch, and Beer, or Cyder . . . their Dinner, good Beef, Veal, Mutton, Venison, Turkies and Geese, wild and tame, Fowls . . . Pies, Puddings. . . ."

The English influence is still much in evidence at the more elegant tables of Tidewater Virginia. People eat rich dark fruitcakes and plum puddings with brandy sauce. They drink eggnog at Christmas, and top festive meals the year round with wine jelly in rich yellow custard flecked with nutmeg. They favor roast beef and roast lamb. They bake delicate buns called Sally Lunn, made with yeast, from an English recipe.

Along with their English culinary heritage, Virginians make much of authentic Southern specialties. This is not to say that they spend all of their time sitting around strumming on banjos and munching on hush puppies. The South is a part of the United States, both from a political and a gastronomic point of view. Virginians eat steak and other standdard American dishes, but their menus also have strong English and authentic Southern overtones. They like spoon bread *(Recipe Index)*, golden puddinglike cornbread known as "batter bread" in Virginia, that is served swimming in butter and so hot you have to roll it around on the tongue. Few true Virginians will pass up cornpone—cornbread shaped into oval mounds baked or fried on a griddle—or sweet-potato pie *(Recipe Index)* or turnip salad. And a particular favorite in the state is Brunswick stew *(Recipe Index)*. Virginians claim to have originated it and say it was named after Caroline of Brunswick, wife of King George IV. (Georgians dispute this point, claiming that it originated in their state and was named after the town of Brunswick, Georgia.) It is a robust, soul-satisfying brew of chicken, hambone, beef or veal, rabbit, onions, tomatoes, celery, butter beans, corn and potatoes—all highly seasoned with red pepper, basil, bay leaf, parsley and lots of black pepper.

There was one place in Virginia I wanted above all others to see, both for historic and culinary reasons: Monticello, the home of Thomas Jefferson. Just about everybody knows that Jefferson was the author of our Declaration of Independence and our third President, but relatively few realize that he was also America's first great gourmet.

En route to Monticello I stayed overnight in Richmond. This was something of a sentimental stopover; I had not visited the old capital of the Confederacy for many years, and wanted to do a bit of sightseeing. Along tree-lined Monument Avenue, a kind of Champs Élysées of the South, statues of the old Confederate heroes stand: Jefferson Davis, Robert E.

MAY 28, 1767.
Snap-dragon blooming.

JULY 5, 1767.
Cucumbers come to table.

NOV. 22, 1767.
8 or 10 bundles of fodder are as much as a horse will generally eat thro' the night.
9 bundles × 130 days = 1170 for winter.

JULY 27, 1769.
A bed of mortar which makes 2000 bricks takes 6.hhds. [hogsheads] of water.

MAY 8, 1771.
The greatest flood ever known in Virginia.

SEPT. 11, 1771.
Stephen Willis sais it takes 15 bushels of lime to lay 1000 bricks.

MARCH 15, 1774.
Sowed the following seeds . . .
Succory, or Wild Endive . . .
The Spanish onion . . .
Salsafia.
Cabbage.
Lettuce.

FEB. 28, 1782.
A flock of wild geese flying to N.W.

JUNE 10, 1782.
Raspberries come & last a month.

FEB. 1, 1823.
Lettuce. radish. spinach. carrots. from this time to Sept. 30. sow lettuce every Monday morning . . .
[NOTE: At this point Mr. Jefferson was 80 years old. He died July 4, 1826.]

Lee, Stonewall Jackson and "Jeb" Stuart, the flamboyant cavalryman astride a spirited horse. The Virginia Museum of Fine Arts, a model of how miscellaneous collections should be arranged, displays a stunning array of precious objects by the great jeweler Fabergé, created for the last Czars of Russia. I also prowled through the Edgar Allan Poe Museum, to see its relics of the poet's life and a delightful scale model of Richmond as it looked when Poe lived in the city. Miss Edith Ragland, the lady who created the model many years ago, comes every spring to freshen its miniature trees and gardens and dust off the roofs and cupolas.

I stayed at the old Jefferson Hotel, its lobby a glory of marble, gilt and red plush, its atmosphere still redolent of the 1880s and 1890s, of a South recovering from hard times. There once was a pond with alligators in the lobby. The alligators have long since disappeared, but the freshly stenciled gilt-patterned walls and gleaming columns quickly chased this disappointment from mind. The red-carpeted stairway, the hotel people proudly point out, served as the prototype of the one used in the movie *Gone With the Wind*. I walked up the stairs to the restaurant in the gallery overlooking the lobby, and enjoyed dinner in circumstances that summoned up the real old take-your-time South. The waiters, mostly elderly, showed a finesse that was tantamount to high art. They never interrupted a conversation, they observed one's personal rhythm of dining, so that no plate arrived too soon or was whisked away too quickly. The biscuits were hot and kept coming; the parade of sauces, relishes and preserves was lavish. Corn relish, pepper sauces, watermelon-rind pickles, piccalilli, chutney—all made on the premises, or at least locally. The only sound while I dined was the gentle tinkle of glass and cutlery. I am told that the infamous canned music occasionally does violence to the quiet in these marble halls. I am glad I did not hear it, because I am constitutionally unable to eat steak to a polka or to munch my way through a salad to Latin-American beats.

The next day I drove to Monticello, passing through Charlottesville and going by the University of Virginia with its splendid white columns, its sweeping lawn and serpentine walls. As I approached Monticello, I thought of Jefferson's special interest in food and wines, farming and gardening, his range of interests of all sorts, so typical of the enlightened 18th Century man. His house, begun in 1768 and never really completed during his lifetime, what with all the changes and alterations he was constantly making, is lovely and full of repose. Its domed center portion was inspired by the Hôtel de Salm in Paris, now the palace of the Legion of Honor. Jefferson, in adapting the scale and proportions to the rolling hills of Virginia, created something less grandiose but every bit as noble.

Actually Monticello is more revolutionary in design than it appears. All the other plantation houses had a cluster of buildings surrounding them. Jefferson gathered all these outbuildings into the two wings of the main house, devising a half-submerged arrangement concealed under a promenade. Kitchens and smoke-rooms were built under the south terrace going off at a right angle from the south promenade, while a similar arrangement on the north provided space for carriage house, stables and the brick-walled ice house. There were different cellars for cider, beer and wine. Off at a distance stood a weaver's workroom, a shoemaker's shop and a carpenter's workshop—all the services required for a household that never counted fewer than 180 persons, excluding guests.

The epitaph that Jefferson selected for his tomb in the burying ground at Monticello tells us that he took his greatest pride in having written the Declaration of Independence and the Virginia Statute of Religious Freedom, and in having founded and designed the University of Virginia. On occasion, he was poet and inventor and mathematician and statesman. But the field of interest that absorbed him all his life was food and wine, in all their ramifications from garden to table.

Jefferson built a round dining room at Monticello and kept a gracious, convivial table there. Even when he dined alone places were always laid for six or seven. He believed that "Man was destined for society," and since he also felt that "good talk and good wine" bring out the best in man, he considered wine "a necessity of life." He kept agitating for a reduction of wine duties levied by the federal government, remarking that "no nation is drunken where wine is cheap." He established vineyards not far from Monticello, but after many attempts achieved only a modestly successful table wine; in concert with neighboring plantation owners, he imported six vineyard workers from Italy, but differences in climate and soil defeated their best efforts. He was the first citizen of the United States to import the finest wines from France, Germany, Italy, Spain, Portugal and Hungary. Never before or since his presidency has the White House served such excellent potables.

While serving in Paris as American Minister to the Court of Louis XVI, Jefferson became enamored of the subtlety of French cooking. He collected recipes for his favorite French dishes and sauces, and often went to market with his servants in search of superior products and the best ingredients. He systematically studied the markets and kitchens of Paris; then went on to the provinces. He collected almond samplings in Lyon, and hundreds of plants and seeds for the gardens and greenhouses at Monticello. Extending his travels to Italy, he risked the death penalty by smuggling pocketfuls of a jealously guarded, special strain of rice out of the province of Lombardy. Yet in spite of his absorption with culinary matters, when he was at Monticello, his old slave Isaac reported that he never went into the kitchen except to wind the clock. The dinner table was his preferred place: he played host to as many as 50 guests at a time, with "plenty of wine, best old Antigua rum and cider."

Jefferson is still very much a force and a presence at Monticello. I found him everywhere, and I learned that every year his gourmet spirit comes alive there. To celebrate his birthday on April 13, Mrs. Helen Duprey Bullock of the National Trust for Historic Preservation, who is an authority on Jefferson's eating habits, serves a special dinner featuring shad roe, fresh garden peas, elegant French wines and other delicacies that he especially enjoyed. When Mrs. Bullock learned that we were doing this book, she planned a special Jefferson dinner for us (details of which appear on pages 60-67); not the least part of this memorable occasion was that the dinner was served in the same dining room and at the same table which Jefferson himself graced.

Overleaf: Preserves of all descriptions are staples of the Southern larder. There are marmalades and jellies for breakfast, relishes and chutneys at dinner and supper, fruit conserves to spoon over ice cream. Spicy vegetable pickles and relishes, canned after the summer harvest, grace the table year round. But the Southern sweet tooth, and the region's lavish fruit crops, ensure a regular array of sweet preserves as well. Used as toppings and condiments, these are prepared with everything from mangoes, oranges, lemons, grapefruit, peaches, apricots, pears and cherries to watermelons and pineapples. For recipes for all the preserves shown, as well as for other Deep South favorites, see the Recipe Index.

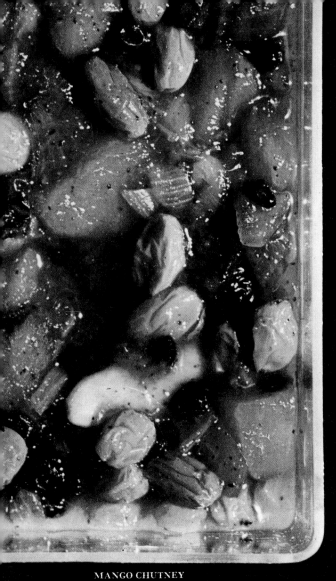

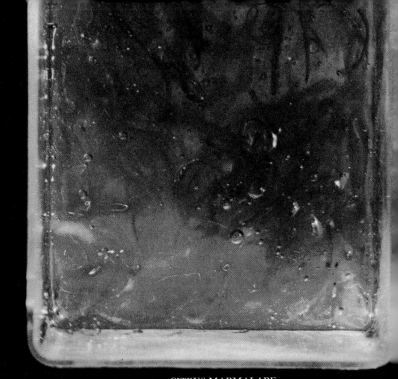

CITRUS MARMALADE

MIXED VEGETABLE PICKLES

MANGO CHUTNEY

PALM BEACH PINEAPPLE RELISH

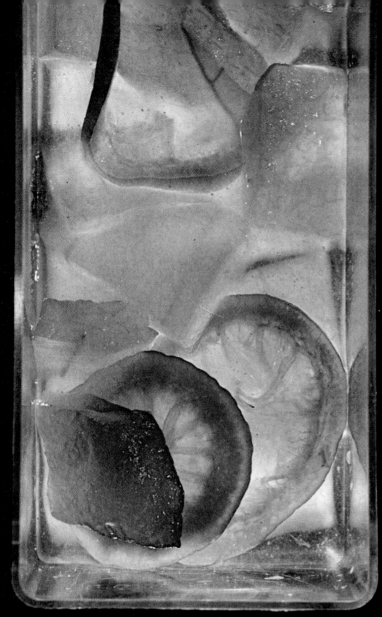

PEAR CHUTNEY

SUMMER FRUIT CONSERVE

PICKLED WATERMELON RIND

PEPPER RELISH

In the South, Smithfield and other types of country ham are never served as a main meat course; instead, paper-thin slivers of the smoked, salty hams are presented as a first course or as an accompaniment to chicken or other fowl. They are also a traditional part of buffet tables. All of these hams are available baked and ready to serve—but at a higher price than the uncooked ones command. If you would like to prepare your own ham, the following recipe describes the basic procedures.

Baked Ham with Brown-Sugar Glaze

A 12- to 16-pound Smithfield ham or a 12- to 16-pound Virginia, Kentucky, Tennessee or Georgia country ham
½ to ¾ cup fine dry bread crumbs
1 cup dark-brown sugar
¼ cup whole cloves (optional)

Starting a day ahead, place the ham in a pot large enough to hold it comfortably and pour in enough water to cover the ham by at least 1 inch. Let the ham soak for at least 12 hours (for 24 hours if possible), changing the water 2 or 3 times. Remove the ham from the pot and discard the soaking water. Then, under lukewarm running water, scrub the ham vigorously with a stiff brush to remove any traces of pepper or mold.

With a dampened kitchen towel wipe the ham and return it to the pot. Pour in enough water to cover the ham by at least 1 inch and bring to a simmer over high heat. Reduce the heat to low and simmer partially covered for 3 to 4 hours, allowing 15 to 20 minutes to the pound. When the ham is fully cooked, you should be able to move and easily pull out the small bone near the shank.

Transfer the ham to a platter and, if you wish, set the cooking water aside to be used for cooking greens. When the ham is cool enough to handle remove the rind with a small sharp knife, leaving only a ⅛-inch-thick layer of fat. If you intend to stud the ham with cloves, make crisscrossing cuts about 1 inch apart on the fatty side, slicing down through the fat to the meat.

Preheat the oven to 400°. With your fingers, press enough of the bread crumbs into the fatty side of the ham to coat it thoroughly. Then sift the brown sugar evenly over the crumbs. If you are using cloves, insert them where the scoring lines intersect. Place the ham on a rack set in a shallow roasting pan and bake it uncovered in the middle of the oven for about 20 minutes, or until the glaze is richly browned.

Set the ham on a large platter and let it cool to room temperature before serving. Smithfield or country ham is carved into paper-thin slices as shown opposite. Tightly covered with foil or plastic wrap, the ham can safely be kept in the refrigerator for at least 1 month.

Monticello Salad Dressing

To make about 1 cup

1 medium-sized garlic clove, finely chopped
1 teaspoon salt
½ teaspoon ground white pepper, preferably freshly ground
⅓ cup tarragon or wine vinegar
⅓ cup domestic sesame-seed oil, combined with ⅓ cup olive oil

Combine the garlic, salt and white pepper in a small bowl and, with the back of a spoon, crush to a smooth paste. Beat in the vinegar by the tablespoonful. Stirring constantly with a wire whisk, pour in the sesame-and-olive-oil mixture in a slow, thin stream and continue to beat until the salad dressing is smooth.

Taste for seasoning and serve at once.

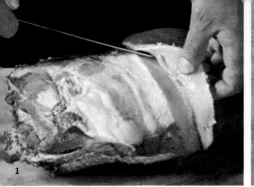

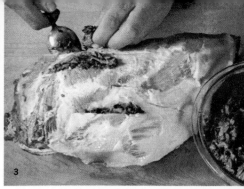

How To Stuff a Country Ham with Greens

One way to vary the preparation of a country ham is to stuff it with spicy greens. (1) Begin by cutting off and discarding the rind and most of the fat. (2) With a large knife, make 6 to 8 deep incisions in the ham, each about 2 inches long and spaced about 2 inches apart. (3) Holding the incisions apart with a spoon, fill them evenly with the greens. (4, 5 and 6) Wrap the stuffed ham in a double thickness of cheesecloth. (7) Then sew up the ends of the cheesecloth with kitchen cord. Following the recipe instructions on the next page, cook, cool and chill the wrapped ham. As shown below, carve the ham horizontally into paper-thin slices, each slice including a sliver of the stuffing.

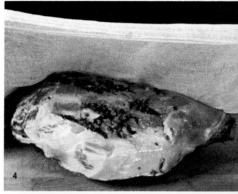

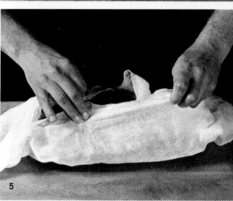

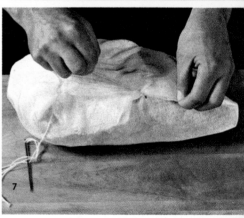

Country Ham Stuffed with Greens

A 12- to 16-pound country ham
3 tablespoons butter
¼ cup finely chopped scallions, including 2 inches of the green tops
½ cup finely chopped celery
½ pound fresh mustard greens, trimmed, washed and coarsely chopped (about 4 cups)
½ pound fresh spinach, trimmed, washed and coarsely chopped (about 4 cups)
1 teaspoon crushed dried hot red pepper
½ teaspoon salt
Freshly ground black pepper

Starting a day ahead, place the ham in a pot large enough to hold it comfortably and pour in enough cold water to cover the ham by at least 1 inch. Let the ham soak at room temperature for at least 12 hours.

When you are ready to cook the ham drain off the soaking water and replace it with fresh cold water to cover the ham by 1 inch. Bring to a boil over high heat, then reduce the heat to low and simmer the ham partially covered for 1 hour. Transfer the ham to cool on a large platter or cutting board. Discard the cooking liquid, wash the pot and set it aside.

With a large sharp knife, cut the rind off the ham and discard it. Then remove the excess fat from the entire outside surface of the ham, leaving a layer no more than ⅛ inch thick all around. Set the ham aside.

In a heavy 4- to 5-quart saucepan, melt the butter over moderate heat. When the foam begins to subside, add the scallions and celery and, stirring frequently, cook for about 5 minutes until they are soft and transparent but not brown. Stir in the mustard greens, spinach, red pepper, salt and a few grindings of black pepper. Reduce the heat to the lowest possible setting, cover the pan tightly, and cook for 15 minutes, or until all the vegetables are tender.

Following the directions on page 75, cut 6 to 8 incisions in the ham and stuff them with the mustard-green-and-spinach mixture. Wrap the ham, as shown, in cheesecloth.

Return the ham to the original pot and add enough water to cover by at least 1 inch. Bring to a boil over high heat, reduce the heat to low and partially cover the pot. Simmer for 3 to 4 hours, allowing about 15 minutes to the pound, or until the ham is tender and shows no resistance when pierced deeply with the point of a small skewer or sharp knife. (The ham should be kept constantly immersed in water. Check the pot from time to time and add more boiling water if necessary.) The cooking liquid can be saved, if you like, for cooking greens.

Transfer the ham to a large platter and, without removing the cheesecloth, cool to room temperature and refrigerate for at least 12 hours. Just before serving, unwrap the ham and with a large sharp knife, carve it into paper-thin slices as shown on page 75.

Pickled Peaches

To make about 2 quarts

12 medium-sized firm ripe peaches (about 3 pounds)
12 whole cloves
4½ cups sugar
3 cups cider vinegar
4 one-inch-long pieces of stick cinnamon, broken into bits with a mallet or the side of a heavy cleaver

Drop the peaches, 3 or 4 at a time, into a pot of boiling water and let them boil briskly for about 2 or 3 minutes. With a slotted spoon, transfer the peaches to a colander and run cold water over them. Then peel them with a small sharp knife. Pierce each peach with a whole clove and drop the peaches into wide-mouthed canning jars.

In a 2- to 3-quart enameled or stainless-steel pan, bring the sugar, vinegar and cinnamon to a boil over high heat, stirring until the sugar dissolves. Immediately ladle the hot liquid over the peaches, a few tablespoonfuls at a time, allowing the liquid and bits of cinnamon to flow through to the bottom of the jars before adding more.

Cover tightly, cool to room temperature and refrigerate for at least 3 days to let the peaches pickle before serving them. Pickled peaches are a traditional Southern accompaniment to baked ham.

Baked Ham in Pastry

In a large chilled mixing bowl, combine the flour, butter and lard. With your fingertips rub the flour and fat together until they look like coarse meal. Mix the egg yolks thoroughly into the dough. Pour ½ cup of the ice water over the mixture all at once, knead vigorously and gather the dough into a ball. If the dough crumbles, add up to ½ cup more ice water, a tablespoonful at a time, until the particles adhere. Dust the dough with a little flour, wrap it in wax paper and refrigerate one hour.

Preheat the oven to 350°. Cut off about ¼ of the dough and return it to the refrigerator. Place the remaining dough on a lightly floured surface and pat it into a rough square about 1 inch thick. Then roll the dough into approximately an 18-inch square.

Pat the ham completely dry with paper towels and, following the directions on page 78, enclose it securely in the square of dough. Place the covered ham on a large ungreased baking sheet and set aside.

On the lightly floured surface, roll the reserved ¼ of the dough into a rough circle ⅛ inch thick. With pastry cutters or a sharp knife, cut out leaves, crescents and other decorations like those in the photograph on page 78. With a pastry brush, moisten the bottom of each decoration lightly with the egg-yolk-and-cream mixture and set each decoration in place on the ham as illustrated on page 78. Finally, brush the entire surface of the ham with the remaining egg-yolk-and-cream mixture. Bake in the middle of the oven for 1 hour, or until the crust is golden brown.

To serve, transfer the ham to a heated platter. Let the ham cool to room temperature before carving it into ½-inch-thick slices.

6 cups flour
12 tablespoons butter, chilled and cut into ¼-inch bits
12 tablespoons lard, chilled and cut into ¼-inch bits
6 egg yolks
½ to 1 cup ice water
A 12- to 14-pound precooked ham with the rind removed
1 egg yolk, lightly beaten and combined with 3 tablespoons heavy cream

Summer Fruit Conserve

Drop the peaches and apricots into enough boiling water to cover them completely and boil briskly for 2 to 3 minutes. Drain in a sieve or colander, then remove the skins with a small sharp knife. Cut the peaches and apricots in half, discard the pits, chop the fruits coarsely and combine them in a 6- to 8-quart enameled or stainless-steel pot.

Wash, stem and pit the cherries and add them to the pot. Slice the unpeeled grapefruit, orange and lemons into ¼-inch-thick rounds and pick out the seeds with the point of a small knife. Put the slices through the coarsest blade of a food grinder and add all the pulp and juices to the peach-and-cherry mixture. Stir in the sugar, cover the pot with foil or plastic wrap and set aside at room temperature for at least 12 hours.

Stirring constantly with a wooden spoon, bring the fruit mixture to a boil over high heat. Reduce the heat to low and simmer uncovered for 1 to 1½ hours, or until the mixture is thick enough to hold its shape almost solidly in a spoon. As the conserve begins to thicken, stir deeply from time to time to prevent it from sticking to the bottom of the pot.

Add the raisins and, stirring frequently, continue to simmer for 15 minutes. Stir in the pecans and the bourbon and mix well. Immediately ladle the conserve into hot sterilized jars. Fill the jars to within ⅛ inch of the top and follow the directions for canning and sealing in Recipe Booklet.

Summer fruit conserve is used as a topping for ice cream and is also served as an accompaniment to game and roast meats.

To make about 3½ quarts

16 medium-sized firm ripe peaches (about 4 pounds)
¾ pound medium-sized firm ripe apricots
1 pound firm ripe cherries
1 large grapefruit
1 large orange
3 lemons
6 cups sugar
2 cups (½ pound) seedless raisins
2 cups (½ pound) shelled pecan halves
1 cup bourbon

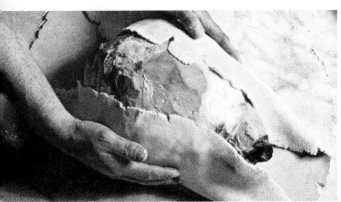
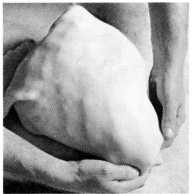
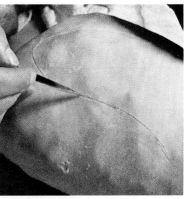

To enclose a precooked ham in pastry, set it on an 18-inch square of thin pastry dough and fold two ends of the dough over the sides of the ham. Holding the dough firmly in place, turn the ham over.

Gently fold the dough under and around the ham, following its shape *(above center)*. To decorate the ham as on the opposite page, sketch the outline of the stems *(above right)* in the dough with a knife point.

Roll out the remaining pastry dough and, with a cookie cutter or small knife, cut out pastry leaves. Gently lift up the leaves with the knife. Reroll the pastry scraps to make as many more leaves as you need.

With the knife, firmly delineate the veins of a leaf *(above center)*. Brush the leaves' bottoms with an egg-and-cream mixture. Set them along the stem outlines on the ham, overlapping them slightly *(above right)*.

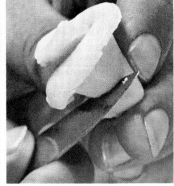

To make roses, cut out 3-by-1-inch strips. Roll up each strip *(above left)*, then pull the outer flap down slightly while pushing up the center. Trim off ½ inch from the bottom of the rose *(above center)*.

Brush the pastry flowers with the egg-and-cream mixture and set in place on the ham. Now brush the entire surface of the pastry-enclosed ham *(right)* and bake one hour, until golden brown.

The baked, cooled ham *(above)*, with its traditional complement of pickled peaches, is ready to be carved crosswise into ½-inch-thick slices, each with its own border of pastry. Recipes for the ham and peaches are on pages 77 and 76.

IV

Pokeweed to "Purloo" in the Carolinas

Shrimp pilau, sometimes called purloo, pelos, or pilaw in the Charleston patois, combines two Carolina specialties: shrimp and rice. First the rice is baked with onions, tomatoes and chicken stock that are flavored with bacon fat, Worcestershire, mace and red pepper. Then, when the grains plump up, shrimp are mixed in and cooked until pink and tender.

There is an old saying that North Carolina is "a vale of humility between two mountains of conceit." This may be a bit hard on Virginia and South Carolina, but it *is* true that North Carolina is noticeably different from its neighbors to the north and south. The state itself is more progressive and more heavily industrialized and its people tend to be more egalitarian, more down to earth and less prone to ancestor worship than Virginians or South Carolinians.

Yet, North Carolina has not altogether shaken off the past. That is particularly evident when you drive down the western part of the state through the Blue Ridge Mountains, with their receding subtleties of blue-green and gray-green. Suddenly, in the foothills here, you come upon a surprising modern factory or plant in the middle of nowhere. But more often the landscape is dotted with fine old barns and wooden farmhouses that are empty to the winds, with roofs sagging and doors standing ajar. Here and there you see farmers with horses plodding around in circles to provide the power to grind sorghum stalks into syrup.

The inhabitant of this region has a jaunty character, a kind of spit-in-your-eye independence; there is still some of the old frontier in his make-up. In the more remote communities, the English language of Raleigh, Bacon and Shakespeare persists. The original Elizabethans came to this part of the world seeking a new way of life, but modern Elizabethan scholars come in search of lost stanzas of ancient ballads and echoes of Tudor speech. The first light of day is the "morn gloam," while the mottled clouds announcing a shower are "rain seed." The cucumber is still "cowcumber"; a dish of turnip greens is a "mess of turnip sallet." If you want a small piece of pie you say, "I'll settle for a tee-toncey bit." Homemade "corn likker" is "giggle soup" here.

As elsewhere in the South, the divisions between mountain people and coastal people are striking, and nowhere more than in their eating habits. In the back country people have always preferred heartier dishes and ampler portions, with fewer courses and less subtle flavorings. Looking back at the old days, an observer recalled: "You may expect, in a healthy country like that, there would be big eaters. Their food was plain and simple . . . bacon and cabbage, chicken soup and pot pies, Irish potatoes and hominy . . . buckwheat pancakes, tarts, and puddings by way of dessert." Every sort of occasion—reapings, quiltings, corn shuckings, ground clearings, barn raisings—has served as an excuse for enormous quantities of food and drink to be consumed. Lusty appetites have made rich, nourishing stews, based on beef and even venison, a favorite in this part of the world, and have encouraged the local production of distinctive hams, sausages and hog's headcheese. Foods are mixed together with notable nonchalance. At a four-table café behind a filling station on a side road I ate a dish of dark-bronze mixed greens, which had been prepared with rather large spiced sausages, and biscuit dumplings cooked on top of the lot. It was all very hot and very good. When I asked the little honey-haired waitress what greens were in the dish she said only, "Eh law', what I could find of a morning."

There's good eating in many parts of North Carolina, even though the dishes one encounters are more likely to be variations on tested Southern themes than original specialties. One such variation is North Carolina's superb way with barbecued pork, prepared on a much grander scale than the ordinary backyard barbecuing. Whole pigs are cooked all night over smoldering coals, and when the meat has taken on an amber color it is hauled off to a chopping house where it is cut into pieces or sliced. Seasoned with chopped red peppers and salt, and usually further accompanied by hot-pepper sauces, the pork has a rich, smoky, piquant flavor.

Hush puppies *(Recipe Index)* are another favorite, especially along the coast, where they are eaten with fish and other seafood. In former times these crisp, crunchy balls of cornbread, fried in deep fat, were thrown to howling puppies to make them hush, but nowadays hush puppies are a staple at roadside stands and everybody eats them. A country cousin of the hush puppy is the dodger, an oven-baked cornmeal biscuit that gets its name from its cannonball quality—it is so heavy that you had better dodge when you see one coming at you.

In the mountainous part of the state, where I began my survey, one runs into pokeweed or poke salad, so called because it is often gathered in a poke, the local term for a brown paper bag. Pokeweed grows wild, and is picked in the spring when the young leaf is reddish green. The berries and roots are poisonous, but the shoots are perfectly safe and the leaves are good eating once they have been properly cooked. They must first be parboiled for about 10 minutes, then boiled again in a pot of fresh water. Pokeweed is seasoned with a slab of fat or lean pork; it tastes like spinach and actually is richer in vitamins.

Two places I particularly wanted to see before turning east toward the Carolina coast were Asheville and Chapel Hill, the first the home of one of the South's literary titans, Thomas Wolfe, and the second the home of one of the South's finest educational institutions. Like any book lover who grew up in the South in the years before World War II, I had been enchanted by Tom Wolfe's *Look Homeward, Angel.* Now, prowling Asheville's streets, I could almost see Eliza Gant standing on the steps of her boardinghouse, pursing her lips and exclaiming, "That's going to be a good piece of property some day." I remember Brother Ben, dying long before his time, and the inimitable old Gant himself, swaggering through life in a drunken rage, spouting rhetoric like an Old Testament prophet. I remembered, too, what prodigious eaters the Gants were, and how vividly Wolfe described their meals: "In the morning they rose in a house pungent with breakfast cookery, and they sat at a smoking table loaded with brains and eggs, ham, hot biscuit, fried apples seething in their gummed syrups, honey, golden butter, fried steak, scalding coffee. Or there were stacked batter-cakes, rum-colored molasses, fragrant brown sausages, a bowl of wet cherries, plums, fat juicy bacon, jam. At the midday meal they ate heavily: a huge hot roast of beef, fat buttered lima-beans, tender corn smoking on the cob, thick red slabs of sliced tomatoes, rough savory spinach, hot yellow corn-bread, flaky biscuits, a deep-dish peach and apple cobbler spiced with cinnamon, tender cabbage, deep glass dishes piled with preserved fruits—cherries, pears, peaches. At night they might eat fried steak, hot squares of grits fried in egg and butter, pork-chops, fish, young fried chicken."

The university town of Chapel Hill proved to have an un-Southern bustle about it. Definitely a small town in the best sense, it is filled with lively young people doing their thing, as they say, in civilized fashion. The town stays up late, and one can eat and drink into the small hours, something that delighted me, for I am used to Rome's nocturnal habits, and was alarmed by the early closing hours of many American cities.

I questioned a number of the university students, those from Southern homes, about their food likes and dislikes. When I asked what kind of dinner they would choose after a heavy day of classes or exams, "good steak" was the predominant reply, with spaghetti or macaroni and cheese as runners-up. But when it came to the matter of breakfast, the vote was solid South: grits, ham, biscuits and molasses. There were only two dissenters, and they were obviously rugged individualists. One young lady wanted "trout fried alongside the water where they were caught," and one young man preferred to start his day with whiskey sours.

Going from North to South Carolina you cross two borders: one man-made, the other a natural frontier that marks the start of the real Deep South. I became aware of this not long after I crossed into South Carolina, when the road passed through a thick forest festooned with Spanish moss. Studying it, I could see how this wispy grayish-green growth that looks like so many thousands of yards of torn used cheesecloth dustrags had given rise to so many ghost stories and ballads throughout the South. Hanging from a tree limb or a fallen branch, it takes on—even in daylight —whatever shape of human, beast or fiend one may conjure, and in the

Scripture Cake
THE RECIPE

The Baptist ladies of the Deep South look to the Scripture for guidance in all things, even cooking, as may be seen by one of their favorite recipes, Scripture cake. The ingredient list below gives the amounts to be used, followed by a reference to a passage in the Bible in which the ingredients appear. On the opposite page are the Scriptural passages referred to.

3½ cups I Kings 4:22
1 cup Judges 5:25 (last clause)
2 cups Jeremiah 6:20
2 cups I Samuel 30:12
2 cups Nahum 3:12
2 cups Numbers 17:8 (last clause)
6 Jeremiah 17:11
1 cup Judges 4:19 (last clause)
6 tablespoons I Samuel 14:25 (last clause)
2 teaspoons Amos 4:5
A pinch of Leviticus 2:13 (last clause)
Season to taste with II Chronicles 9:9

trees, inevitably, a single tatter eerily moves while all the rest is still. Yes, I was in the Deep South now.

The area through which I was traveling was originally the province of Carolina, a land grant from the British Crown, which included what is now North Carolina, South Carolina and the northern part of Georgia. English explorers first came here in 1663, returning home with accounts of a mild climate and rich soil. The first settlement was established on the banks of the Ashley River in 1670 and was named Charles Town, after England's Charles II. (The town moved 10 miles southeast to its present location a decade later, and after the Revolutionary War its name was changed to Charleston by patriots who thought Charles Town too British.) The first settlers, 148 strong, brought indigo seed, ginger roots, sugar cane and olives, fruits and vegetables. In 1680 the first group of French Huguenots arrived, and others later followed, driven out of their homeland by the revocation of the Edict of Nantes, which deprived Protestants of religious freedom. That same year Captain John Thurber sailed into the Charleston harbor, bringing with him a bag of Madagascar rice. The rice was given to Dr. Henry Woodward who planted it and found that it flourished in the Carolina climate. Soon afterward, slaves were introduced into the colony and cleared the swampy riverbanks for rice plantations. By the 18th Century rice was important enough so that South Carolinians used it for currency and called it "Carolina gold."

Indigo proved even more profitable than rice, although the preparation of this valuable dye required huge vats of water where mosquitoes and flies bred, and everything about the dye works took on a blue tone. In time indigo production declined and the rice-growing areas proved too swampy to support heavy modern machinery. Today Texas, Louisiana, Arkansas and California are the leading rice-producing states, and "Carolina rice," the long-grain product on supermarket shelves, is a brand name. Rice is still very popular in the Charleston area, the most celebrated way of preparing it being the pilau—pronounced pilaw, pelos or even purloo.

Yet the great prosperity rice and indigo once brought to Charleston helped make it one of the loveliest cities on earth. During the late 18th and early 19th Centuries some of America's most beautiful houses were built here. Many of them echo the Georgian style. The details of these English-type houses—their hand-carved mantels and cornices, their finely rounded balustrades—are delightful. The Huguenot influence on the architecture here is also apparent. Throughout the Battery, the city's harbor area, you see overhanging balconies, stuccoed walls, hipped roofs, convex roofing tiles—all common features of the Huguenot centers in France. And many of Charleston's houses are a startling variety of pastels and bright hues: lavender, salmon pink, deep yellow, deep rose, blue and green. An added touch of color is supplied by the traditional street vendors, among them shrimp sellers and the strawberry women, whose cries Gershwin set to music in *Porgy and Bess*.

In the past two decades more than 2,000 old Charleston houses have been restored, without a tinge of the artificiality that has attended the restoration of some colonial towns. Credit for this achievement belongs to the Historic Charleston Foundation, which was founded in 1947 with the purpose of preserving and sprucing up the city's historic buildings. I was so impressed with the restoration work that I called on Mrs. Frances R. Edmunds, the animated lady who directs the foundation. When Mrs. Edmunds received me in her office in the Battery area, I was puzzled to see her barefoot, although smartly dressed. She quickly explained that she had had to remove her shoes after bogging down in a mud puddle while inspecting an old garden wall that was being scraped.

Mrs. Edmunds told me that most of the restoration is done by individual owners with private dollars. "We help them," she said. "We pick out another house that was built at the same time and go in and study it. We have the finest architects. We try to see that the houses are as authentic as possible. We leave the backyards alone, so you can raise hell out there, because people have to live in these houses."

Charleston's highly distinctive flavor extends beyond its architecture to its speech and its food as well. The Charleston accent is famous throughout the South: people say "bo-it," for boat, "kyar" for car, "gyarden" for garden and "swimp" for shrimp. Many African words or words of African origin crop up in Charleston speech. These derive mostly from Gullah, a dialect spoken by Negroes living along the Carolina and Georgia coast. This strange patois is a mishmash of English and African that is difficult for outsiders to fathom. One Gullah saying goes, "Better belly bus' dan good bittle spile," (it is better for your belly to burst than for you to let good food spoil). And many foods in Charleston bear Gullah names. Cornmeal dough is called "cush." The yellow-bellied turtle that comes from the rice fields is called a "cooter," the white man is called a "buckra," and Irish, or white, potatoes are "buckra yams."

The African influence on Charleston's food is much in evidence. The slaves who arrived in the late 1600s brought benne (sesame) seeds with them, and today these spicy seeds are an essential in every Charleston larder. They are used in stews, cookies and other pastries and to make a crunchy benne brittle. Hot biscuits made with toasted benne seeds (Recipe Index) are enjoyed with a drink called Sherry Bolo, a mixture of sherry, lime juice and sugar.

More important than the benne seeds, however, is the fact that the African cooks who held forth in the Charleston kitchens were formidable women, artists who were thoroughly conscious of their artistry and ruled their domains with a high hand. They were used to the spicing of a hotter climate, and they gave the old recipes lively new twists and flavors.

Still, it is the seafood dishes that are the glory of this region. Shrimp paste—made of finely ground shrimp, butter, onions and spices—is a favorite breakfast dish (Recipe Index). Fish abound along the coast: shad, mullet, pompano and porgy, sometimes called the scuppy or scup, which is usually eaten broiled.

Oysters are a particular seafood delight in the Charleston area, and the tradition of the oyster roast is well entrenched. One massive and memorable feast, described by Richard Barry, took place in the 18th Century when a young blood named John Rutledge came back from his law studies in England and decided to go into politics in Christ Church Parish near Charleston. To charm the voters of his parish he planned a great oys-

Scripture Cake
THE SOURCES

I Kings 4:22 And Solomon's provision for one day was 30 measures of fine FLOUR
Judges 5:25 She brought forth BUTTER *in a lordly dish*
Jeremiah 6:20 To what purpose cometh there to me incense from Sheba, and the sweet cane [SUGAR] *from a far country?*
I Samuel 30:12 And they gave him . . . two clusters of RAISINS
Nahum 3:12 All thy strong holds shall be like fig trees with the first-ripe FIGS
Numbers 17:8 And behold, the rod of Aaron . . . yielded ALMONDS
Jeremiah 17:11 As the partridge sitteth on EGGS, *and hatcheth them not*
Judges 4:19 And she opened a bottle of MILK, *and gave him drink*
I Samuel 14:25 And there was HONEY *upon the ground*
Amos 4:5 And offer a sacrifice of thanksgiving with leaven [BAKING POWDER]
Leviticus 2:13 With all thine offerings thou shalt offer SALT
II Chronicles 9:9 And she gave the king . . . SPICES *in great abundance*

ter roast, organizing it in a way that would have put many a latter-day politician to shame.

At dawn on the appointed day, the wagons came hauling materials and supplies from all over the Rutledge plantation to the front lawn where the oyster roast was held. Pits were dug and parallel lines of ovens set up, and long tables were laid with the best table linen, china and silverware, some of it brought from England with the original grant holder. Before noon the guests began to arrive; everyone was aware that the oysters would be ready shortly after 1 o'clock and had to be eaten while they were piping hot. Rutledge led his mother along the tables to inspect the elaborate settings; whereupon, her approval being given, everything was packed away again in wicker baskets and quite another kind of setting was laid out on the bare cypress boards of the tables: individual linen mats, wooden platters and special oyster knives, large tumblers and a kind of protectional armrest clamped to the table at each place.

Rutledge had expected perhaps 100 families; but more people flocked to the oyster roast and carpenters quickly set up more tables, which finally stretched out for a quarter of a mile. At 1 o'clock sharp a hunter's horn sounded and the oysters were heaped on the coals. The guests hurried to their seats, and servants filled the tumblers with hot drinks—whiskey punch for the men and eggnog for the ladies. Then a battalion of black children ran from the coals to the tables, bringing the hot roast oysters. This relay race from pits to plates went on for more than an hour. Afterward the guests all wandered off while the wreckage was removed and the fine napery, china and silver were once more laid in place. At 3 o'clock, the guests resumed their places to deal seriously with crayfish in aspic, shrimp and watercress salad, red snapper in wine sauce, terrapin stew and venison patty, beaten biscuits, choice wines. The feasting went on until it was almost sundown. At last John Rutledge struggled to his feet and asked his guests for their vote. But by that time so much food and drink had been consumed that, as the author puts it, "there may have been confusion in grasping what he meant."

Oyster roasts are still a popular pastime in this part of the world, but they are much simpler affairs, and are held as close to the supply as one can get. The oysters are roasted on a metal grill or sometimes on chicken wire stretched over the coals, and turned occasionally with a shovel. Each guest is given a little bowl of melted butter or one of the special piquant sauces that differ with each household. A dish of hot Hopping John (black-eyed peas and rice, *Recipe Index*) with biscuits usually follows, although sandwiches may be served or, a little farther down the coast from Charleston, a crab omelet *(Recipe Index)* sandwiched between lightly toasted slices of bread.

One seafood delicacy that kept popping up everywhere I went in Charleston was she-crab soup *(Recipe Index)*. I heard so much about it that I finally persuaded a young lawyer who is highly interested in kitchen mysteries and traditions to show me just how it is prepared. He made me promise not to mention his name because he said his mother and sister were great cooks and would be furious not to have been included in our kitchen fest.

He began by explaining this exotic morsel. "She crabs are more delicate than the male crabs and cost more," he said. "But the roe, you know, the eggs, gives a smooth texture and an extra flavor to the soup."

Amid the glittering array of polished pots and pans in his kitchen, he went to work. In the top of a big double boiler he mixed some butter and flour to make a white roux; then he slowly added a quart of milk, constantly stirring the mixture with a big wooden spoon. Into this he put two cups of white she-crabmeat, the crab roe, a few drops of onion juice, a bit of powdered mace, a nice bit of freshly ground black pepper, some Worcestershire sauce, salt and a hint of cayenne. Then he stirred all this thoughtfully and kept it cooking slowly in the top of the double boiler for about 20 minutes.

"Part of the secret of the flavor is in the sherry," he said mysteriously.

"What sherry?" I asked; I hadn't seen any.

"Look," he said. He poured some sherry into a heat-proof glass measuring pitcher and set it in a bowl of hot water to heat. Then he whipped half a cup of cream. He put about a tablespoon of warmed sherry in each soup bowl, filled the bowl with she-crab soup and put a dollop of whipped cream on top. After that he sprinkled chopped parsley on the cream, and the she-crab soup was ready for serving.

"If you can't get she crabs," he said, "you just substitute crumbled-up hard-boiled egg yolks in each dish with the sherry."

The flavor of the soup was delightful. The texture, so smooth and creamy, seemed like a bass accompaniment to the melody: the taste of the sea played up by the small and knowing amounts of spices.

We next had a fine green salad, and my host prepared another dish that is a classic along the Carolina coast—okra pilau, known locally as Limping Susan. Okra was not in season, and so he had availed himself of frozen okra to show me how to make the dish.

"There's no secret ingredient or special flavoring," he said. "But my, it's good. And so easy I'm kind of embarrassed to show you!"

He chopped four slices of bacon into pieces about the size of thumbnails, put them in a deep skillet and started them frying. Next he put in about a package of okra, sliced in rings. When the okra was tender, he added a cup of washed rice, some salt, freshly ground black pepper, a pinch of cayenne and a cup of water. He mixed all of these well, put the mixture into the top of a rice steamer and cooked it about an hour and a half until the rice was fluffy and the mixture had cooked dry. The result was a dish fit for Charles II or any other king.

Charleston, of course, is unique, but many of its characteristics are shared by Savannah, 105 miles down the coast and across the border in Georgia. Both are fine old cities, proud, charming and eminently Southern. Whereas Charleston is a busy seaport, a bustling city with all sorts of military installations around it, Savannah is larger but its pace is more leisurely.

Many distinguished visitors have been taken by its attractions. In 1855 Thackeray wrote of "a tranquil old city . . . no tearing Northern hustle, no ceaseless hotel racket, no crowds." In the same decade, the Swedish writer Fredrika Bremer spoke of Savannah as an "assemblage of villas, come together for company." During the Civil War the Confederate General Jeremy Francis Gilmer wrote, "The place is too beautiful to be occupied by Yankees," but two years later General Sherman captured the city and gave it to President Lincoln as a Christmas present along with 150 heavy guns and about 25,000 bales of cotton.

Savannah got its start quite differently from Charleston, in a way that was to have a crucial effect on its development. An idealistic Englishman named James Oglethorpe, concerned with the plight of debtors languishing in British prisons, conceived the idea of transporting large numbers of them to America and developing a new colony with them. Later, Oglethorpe expanded his concept to provide a refuge in America for Protestants who were persecuted in Europe. In 1732, Olgethorpe and his fellow trustees were granted proprietary rights for 21 years for the area between the Savannah and Altamaha Rivers, and the colony was named Georgia after Britain's reigning monarch, George II.

Some time later, writing home to his fellow trustees, Oglethorpe reported: "The river here forms a half moon, along the south side of which the banks are about 40 foot high. . . . Upon the river-side in the center of the plain, I have laid out the town." This modest phrase gave little idea of Oglethorpe's achievement. It was his design for Savannah that enabled the city to develop along orderly and beautiful lines, although actually the plan was not entirely his. It was based on a sketch in a book called *Villas of the Ancients* by Robert Castell, who died in one of the English debtor prisons that Georgia was established to relieve. As worked out by Oglethorpe and an engineer named Colonel William Bull, the plan was a model of simplicity and good sense. It called for a clearly organized ward or square design for the town, with a green square at the center of every four squares of buildings. Through the years, Savannah has grown according to that design, even though the city has twice been all but destroyed by fire (in 1796 and 1820).

Oglethorpe and his cohorts hoped to produce wine and silk in Georgia, but failed in their efforts. The real beginning of Savannah's wealth and style dates from 1793, with a revolution as quiet as Charleston's when Dr. Woodward planted his sackful of rice. Only here the revolution was made of cotton and its prime mover was a Yankee named Eli Whitney.

The son of a New England farmer, Whitney graduated from Yale, then took a job tutoring in Georgia to earn money for further studies. En route to his new job, he met Mrs. Catharine Greene, widow of the Revolutionary War hero, Nathanael Greene. Whitney's job fell through, and he accepted an invitation to visit Mrs. Greene at Mulberry Grove Plantation, near Savannah. Like all Southern planters, she was complaining that although there was a wide new market for cotton across the Atlantic, the only kind of cotton the South could grow was the upland, short-fiber type with its adamantly clinging green seeds. The seeds had to be removed by hand and it took a whole day for a slave to clean a pound of cotton. A young man of unusual mechanical ability, Whitney decided to tackle the problem, and in 10 days produced a model of a simple machine. One roller, full of metal spikes, pulled the fiber through a metal grid and separated it from the seeds. A revolving brush removed the cotton from the spikes. This simple product of genius made it possible for a

 Continued on page 94

Tar Heels Still Have a Tooth for Old-Time Sorghum Syrup

Saccharine-sweet sorghum syrup is an old Southern favorite that has largely disappeared in the past 50 years. In the mountains of western North Carolina, however, the Tar Heels, as the people of this state call themselves, still grow sweet sorghum and prize the syrup they make from it. The syrup is called sorghum molasses, although strictly speaking molasses must be made from sugar cane. Except for sales to health-food stores where the syrup is valued for its high mineral content, most sorghum molasses is now consumed in the areas where the stalks are processed into syrup, as shown here and on the following pages.

Sorghum grows in tall, cornlike stalks. The stalks are first cut, then trimmed to remove their seeds and leaves. The sweet, juicy sorghum variety shown here is ground up for syrup, while the more common grain sorghum is used as a feed for livestock or in making alcohol.

Overleaf: The trimmed stalks of sorghum are fed by the bundle into a horse-powered grinder or cane mill. There, heavy rollers—not unlike those on clothes wringers —squeeze the stalks dry. The foamy greenish juice flows down a trough into a big tub, ready to be boiled down into sorghum syrup.

Sorghum juice is boiled down to syrup—60 to 80 gallons at a time—in open boilers, like the one at left. Boiling reduces the juice to six to eight gallons of syrup, and may take as long as five or six hours. When boiling begins, scum rises to the surface and is skimmed off with a long-handled scoop like the homemade one at top right. As the syrup thickens, it is stirred continuously until it reaches the consistency and the color of molasses. Then it is funneled into jars, ready to be poured over hoecakes and cornbread or spooned into coffee as a substitute for sugar.

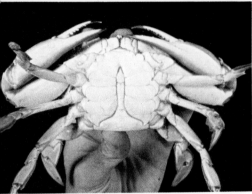

In Charleston she-crab soup *(page 102)* is a highly touted summer dish. Crabbers identify the female *(top)* by the broad apron, or flap, on the bottom shell; the male crab *(bottom)* has a narrow pointed apron. The spawning season extends from April through October, but the orange-roe-laden she-crabs are most sought after from late April through June, when spawning is at its peak.

slave to clean 50 pounds of cotton a day. The South was changed overnight, Savannah with it, and the effects are still with us today. Young Eli Whitney never was able to capitalize on his invention, but he went on to pioneer other machine tools and modern production methods. Meanwhile, his invention made cotton king and Savannah a bustling river port.

Physically, Savannah has been saved by a restoration as imaginative as Charleston's. By the 1950s, many of Savannah's oldest and loveliest buildings had been destroyed in the unholy name of Progress. Then Mrs. Anna Hunter organized a group of interested citizens into the Historic Savannah Foundation. The demolitionists and their bulldozers were foiled. Crumbling houses that had been marked for slum clearance and tall new office buildings and residences were rescued in the nick of time.

The Historic Savannah Foundation's passion for reclaiming the old buildings caught on. Oglethorpe's plan provided an unexpected boon; for the green squares which he insisted on including in Savannah's lovely design now seem effective antidotes for such basic urban ills as air pollution, overcrowding, tension and alienation.

I thought it a good idea to have a word with Mrs. Hunter, who launched Savannah's rescue. Contrary to what one might expect, she lives not in a restored mansion but in a former cotton-grading office turned studio, on the street level above Factors' Walk on the waterfront.

Mrs. Hunter is a grandmother, but her eyes have kept that glance-around-the-ballroom animation we associate with the Southern belle. And her views on her city are equally lively. "We're not against modern structures, mind you," she told me, explaining the foundation's purpose. "But we want to preserve what we have, and add to it in a modern way that is tasteful. We work through the city planning board and try to protect certain areas and control the kind of buildings that are going up."

I asked Mrs. Hunter how it happened that she was living in a cotton-grading office instead of a restored Savannah home.

"Everybody raised eyebrows right up to their hairlines when I moved in here," she said. "Even more so when I started raising herbs in the patch of earth between the sidewalk and the street, and most of all at my furnishings." She flashed a smile and nodded vaguely about. Mrs. Hunter is a painter and her furnishings are a wonderful higgledy-piggledy attic and storeroom assortment, put together with humor and fantasy. "I gave everything to the children," she said, "and decided to live like a gypsy." There were dried bouquets and living plants, a fern flourishing in a bidet, no two pieces related to each other. There was also a fine view of the river, and altogether I found her studio delightful.

Mrs. Hunter proved to be as knowledgeable about culinary matters as about Savannah's restoration. "Life has changed so rapidly in the South in the past 20 or 30 years," she remarked. "Nobody has many servants any more and now that the lady of the house has to go into the kitchen and actually make the dinner as well as decide what to have and go shopping for it, a great many things just aren't seen on the dinner table. Besides, so many men have died before their wives, and when you are not catering to hearty appetites, you tend to make lighter and easier things. For the old dishes and elaborate menus you have to look to a few people who make a hobby of it, or actually, to some of the young men who have gourmet societies and take turns preparing fine dinners."

Mrs. Hunter allowed that a dish she particularly likes is the tiny river shrimp of Savannah. "There are three sizes of shrimp," she said. "But I still love the little ones—especially with hominy. Others call it grits, but we call it hominy. I think a good shrimp pilau is awfully good—made with sweet onions, a little bell pepper and fresh mace, and, of course, rice. Sometimes I like to eat the big shrimp just cooked with a little butter." The local oysters, she explained, are "fat and sweet—come mostly from around Hilton Head Island and are smaller and tastier than those from the Chesapeake Bay."

Next I went to see the poet Conrad Aiken and his charming wife, Mary, in their old house. Mr. Aiken, a gentle Buddha, is a kind of unofficial Prince of Savannah in the fashion that William Faulkner was unofficial Prince of Oxford, Mississippi. Mr. Aiken, who had recently celebrated his 80th birthday, was recovering from a hospital stay and a reaction to antibiotics, and so he was forced to forgo a reading of his work at the Poetry Society that night. His wife had promised to make her recipe of oysters on toast and she led the way to the kitchen.

"Nothing to it," she said, "but everybody likes them so much. It's child's play to make. Look, you have to use a saucepan of a size that allows the oysters to be about two inches deep. You put them in, with their juice, and add a little salt and pepper and a dash of Tabasco. In Savannah we like hot seasonings. You put the pan on low heat, and stir with your forefinger until the edges of the oysters curl and the heat begins to be uncomfortable for your finger. You spoon the oysters and juice over hot buttered toast and garnish with lemon wedges and a bit of cress or parsley."

In a few minutes she offered this delicious dish along with chilled white wine. All the salt-sea flavor of the oysters was intact, heightened —but not disguised—by the seasonings.

Mary Aiken also told me the secret of another fine dish, her crumb-fried oysters. Again, they were simplicity itself. "You drain the oysters, salt and pepper them," she said. "You roll them in plain cracker crumbs and sauté them in a heavy skillet in corn oil, about one minute each side. Be sure to eat them while they are hot."

Later, while visiting Savannah, I had my first chance in more than two decades to enjoy a full-fledged Deep Southern meal when I was invited to dinner by Mrs. Henrietta Waring, widow of Dr. Antonio Waring, a well-known pediatrician. Mrs. Waring is president of the Savannah Poetry Society, a devotee of painting and the theater, an omnivorous reader and an adept at the lost art of conversation. Still she finds time to organize a thoughtful, quietly paced meal, finely balanced in flavors.

We dallied in Mrs. Waring's library before dinner and drank a Maharajah's Burra Peg—a champagne cocktail with a nice sliver of lime peel —made after a recipe of her father's. Then we went into the dining room and began our meal with okra soup, a standard Savannah as well as Charleston item, except that Mrs. Waring had invented her own version. The slightly acid flavor of the okra was balanced with the sweet-acid of tomato and the clean flavors of celery and parsley.

When the blueberries are ripe in rural North Carolina, farmers open their fields to the public. In the White Lake area local families, such as Mrs. Eva Mae Cartwright and her youngsters Billy and Joyce, can come and fill their baskets for only 25 cents a quart.

"Gosh, it's good!" I exclaimed, as I savored the soup.

"Well, not bad, if I do say so. It's my own variation. I think one should be flexible with recipes. Naturally I have a secret with this soup, but I'll tell you, it's a classic Savannah okra soup but I use V-8 juice instead of water and tomato paste. One has to be adventurous."

She pushed a twinkling cut-glass cruet toward me. The cruet contained a golden liquid; in the bottom were some small red fruits, which I made out to be bird's-eye pepper. I had seen these peppers growing in pots on almost every Savannah porch, and on occasional windowsills.

"We're mad about red pepper in Savannah. Sometimes we crush a bird's-eye pepper in each soup bowl, then toss it away before pouring the soup. It makes such an aroma. We always have pepper sherry—that's what you have there—to hot up your soup as much as you like. You just scald the peppers and put them in the cruet and pour good dry sherry over them. You let it stand 24 hours and it's ready. In the old days, gentlemen in Savannah carried little silver boxes full of bird's-eye peppers to add to whatever they were eating."

I sniffed it. Ah, I thought, that would clear a clogged sinus. It was really a kind of essence of pepper. Cautiously I added a drop or two to the soup. It gave a flowerlike aroma, and a slight heat on the tongue, and it lent an added special zest to the soup.

The main course now appeared: Dr. Waring's invention—stuffed corn. On a platter were packages of pale-green corn leaves, tied tightly with lengths of corn silks. A delicate perfume wafted up from each steaming

96

little package, and Mrs. Waring showed me how to open them, bending back the top leaves to reveal the pudding within.

She explained that in preparing this dish the corn had first been carefully removed without disturbing the leaves, and then the kernels were cut off the cobs. "You catch all the juice," she said, "then you add cream or milk to the corn and its juice. You salt and pepper it and add two beaten eggs. You put in some little whole boiled shrimp, then you spoon this mixture into the shucks, and tie them together with the silk. You put this package in the skillet with about half an inch of water, lowering it into the skillet very carefully. Then you cover it tightly, and cook it over low heat for about half an hour. It must not be runny, but firm." Chicken and bacon may be substituted for the shrimp *(Recipe Index)*.

When I opened one of these little gift packages the pudding was a light gold color that contrasted beautifully with the pale pink of the shrimp. The corn flavor was almost as pure as in corn on the cob. Everything about it was extremely delicate and extremely fresh, so much so that our conversation stopped—more or less—while we savored this excellent and satisfying dish.

By now I was so intrigued that I wanted to stay a year in Savannah and explore every dish. But I still had a long way to go in my travels, and so I reluctantly set out through the rolling pine woods. As I turned away from the Atlantic, the sudden sight of a man and a mule walking in that lackadaisical, every-day's-a-century way caught me up short. The man had a rifle and a string of quail. And I hadn't seen a mule for years.

Berrying pays off in lush cream-dolloped pies like the one above at left, which won first prize at the annual Blueberry Festival in Elizabethtown. Above right, Mrs. Cartwright and her children polish off generous wedges of the prizewinner *(Recipe Index)*.

Bushels of oysters are carted to the roast in a barrow.

After hosing them clean, Harold Chisholm heaps oysters on a metal sheet set over a hot fire. To ensure plenty of steam for opening the shells, he drapes the oysters with burlap sacks that have been dunked in salt water. Thus covered, the oysters roast for about 20 minutes.

Oyster Roasts R Classic along the Carolina Shore

Like the New England clambake, the Southern oyster roast is a time-honored excuse for gourmandizing. While especially popular in the Carolinas, oyster roasts are enjoyed from Maryland to Georgia in the months with an "R" in them (American oysters spawn during the summer and some states prohibit harvesting them from May through August). Generations of Southerners have doted on fresh oysters cooked over an open fire—often eating them by the barrowload. When Mr. and Mrs. Joseph Harrison of Savannah entertained relatives and friends at their Bluffton, South Carolina, weekend retreat, shown here and on the following pages, five bushels of oysters were consumed. Freshly harvested from the nearby Atlantic, the tangy oysters were dunked in catsup or sprinkled with lemon juice, and washed down with ice-cold beer. Hardy eaters then went on through a full-course picnic dinner.

Prying an oyster open is a challenge for the inexperienced. But to the old, properly gloved hand, it is no trick at all. Steaming opens the bivalves slightly; then the expert inserts the tip of an oyster knife at the broad end, gives it a quick twist, and the two halves fall apart.

The oyster roast on the May River included a buffet-style spread of baked Georgia ham, red rice, avocado-and-grapefruit salad,

and caramel cake decorated with pecans. The oysters were then piled on an old cable reel, and everybody came back for more.

CHAPTER **IV** RECIPES

To serve 4 to 6

6 medium-sized firm ripe tomatoes,
  or substitute 2 cups chopped
  drained canned tomatoes
2 cups uncooked long-grain white
  rice, not the converted variety
2 pounds medium-sized raw shrimp
  (about 21 to 25 to the pound)
8 slices bacon, cut into ¼-inch dice
2 cups finely chopped onions
3 cups chicken stock, fresh or
  canned
2 teaspoons Worcestershire sauce
1 teaspoon ground mace
½ teaspoon ground hot red pepper
  (cayenne)
2 teaspoons salt
2 tablespoons finely chopped fresh
  parsley

To serve 4

4 quarts water
2 tablespoons plus 1½ teaspoons
  salt
12 live blue she crabs, each about 4
  inches wide and weighing about
  ½ pound
4 tablespoons butter
1 tablespoon flour
2 cups milk
2 cups heavy cream
1½ teaspoons finely grated onions
1 teaspoon finely grated fresh lemon
  peel
½ teaspoon ground mace
½ teaspoon ground white pepper
3 tablespoons pale dry sherry
1 tablespoon finely chopped fresh
  parsley

Shrimp Pilau

If you are using fresh tomatoes, prepare them in the following fashion: Drop 2 or 3 at a time into a pan of boiling water for 15 seconds. Run them under cold water and peel them with a small sharp knife. Cut out the stems, then slice each tomato in half crosswise. Squeeze the halves gently to remove the seeds and juice, then finely chop the tomatoes.

Place the rice in a sieve and wash it under cold running water, stirring the grains with a fork until the draining water runs clear. Set aside.

Peel the shrimp. Devein them by making a shallow incision down their backs with a small sharp knife and lifting out the black or white intestinal vein with the point of the knife. Wash the shrimp, then refrigerate until ready to use.

Preheat the oven to 350°. In a heavy 3- to 4-quart casserole, fry the bacon dice over moderate heat, stirring until they are crisp and brown and have rendered all their fat. With a slotted spoon, transfer the bacon to paper towels to drain.

Pour off all but about 3 tablespoons of the fat remaining in the casserole and drop in the onions. Stirring frequently, cook the onions over moderate heat for about 5 minutes, or until they are soft and translucent but not brown. Add the rice and stir until the grains glisten with the fat, then mix in the chicken stock or water, the tomatoes, Worcestershire, mace, red pepper and salt.

Bring to a boil over high heat, cover the casserole tightly and place it in the middle of the oven. Bake for 30 minutes, then add the shrimp and bacon and toss together gently but thoroughly. Cover tightly and continue to bake 10 minutes longer, or until the liquid in the pan has been absorbed and the shrimp are pink and tender.

Remove the casserole from the oven and set it aside without removing the cover for 10 minutes. Fluff the shrimp pilau with a fork, strew the parsley over the top and serve at once, directly from the casserole.

She-Crab Soup

Bring 4 quarts of water and 2 tablespoons of salt to a boil in an 8- to 10-quart pot. Drop in the crabs and return the water to a boil. Reduce the heat to low, cover tightly and simmer for 15 minutes. Drain the crabs, then clean *(pages 48 and 49)* and shell them. Set the meat and roe aside.

In a heavy 3- to 4-quart saucepan, melt the butter over moderate heat. When the foam begins to subside, add the flour and mix well. Stirring the mixture constantly with a wire whisk, pour in the milk and cream in a slow thin stream and cook over high heat until the sauce comes to a boil, thickens slightly and is smooth.

Stir in the crabmeat and the crab roe, the onions, lemon peel, mace, the remaining 1½ teaspoons of salt and the white pepper. Reduce the heat to low and simmer partially covered for 20 minutes. Stir in the sherry, taste for seasoning, and pour the soup into a heated tureen or individual soup plates. Sprinkle the top with the parsley and serve the soup at once.

Roast Wild Duck

To serve 6 to 8

Preheat the oven to 450°. In a small pan, melt the bacon fat and butter over low heat. Remove the pan from the heat and set aside.

Wash the ducks under cold running water and pat them dry inside and out with paper towels. Season the cavities and the skin with salt and a few grindings of pepper. Combine the oranges, apples, celery and sherry in a bowl and toss together. Then fill the cavity of each bird with the fruit-and-celery mixture and close the openings by lacing them with skewers and kitchen cord or sewing them with heavy thread. Truss the birds and fasten the neck skin to the back with small skewers.

Place the ducks on their side on a rack in a shallow roasting pan. With a pastry brush, spread about 2 tablespoons of the bacon-fat-and-butter mixture evenly over each bird. Roast in the middle of the oven for 15 minutes, then turn the duck over onto the other side and brush them again with the melted fat. Roast for another 15 minutes. Reduce the oven temperature to 350°. Turn the ducks breast side up and brush them with fat again. Roast for about 1 hour longer, turning the birds every 15 minutes and brushing them each time with the remaining fat. To test for doneness, pierce the thigh of a duck with the point of a small sharp knife. The juice that trickles out should be pale yellow; if it is still tinged with pink, roast the birds for 5 to 10 minutes longer.

Transfer the ducks to a cutting board and, with poultry scissors, remove the trussing strings and cut each bird in half lengthwise. Discard the stuffing. Arrange the duck halves on a large heated platter and serve at once, accompanied, if you like, by pepper relish *(Recipe Index)*.

½ cup bacon fat, or substitute ½ cup vegetable oil
4 tablespoons butter
Four 1½- to 2-pound oven-ready wild ducks (such as mallard or teal)
Salt
Freshly ground black pepper
2 navel oranges, cut crosswise into ¼-inch-thick slices
2 large firm ripe apples, unpeeled but cored and cut into ½-inch-thick wedges
4 medium-sized celery stalks, trimmed of all leaves, cut lengthwise in half and crosswise into 1½-inch-long strips
¼ cup pale dry sherry

Shrimp Paste

To make about 3 cups

Drop the shrimp into enough boiling water to immerse them completely and boil briskly, uncovered, for 3 minutes, or until they are firm and pink. Drain the shrimp, spread them on paper towels and pat them completely dry with fresh towels. Then put the shrimp through the finest blade of a food grinder. If you lack a food grinder, chop the shrimp as fine as possible and pound them to a smooth paste with a mortar and pestle or in a bowl with the back of a spoon.

In a deep bowl, cream the butter by beating and mashing it against the sides of the bowl with the back of a wooden spoon until it is light and fluffy. Beat in the sherry, lemon juice, onion, mace, mustard, red pepper, salt and white pepper. When thoroughly incorporated, add the shrimp and continue to beat until the mixture is smooth. Taste for seasoning.

Transfer the shrimp paste to a 3-cup serving bowl or mold, spreading it and smoothing the top with a spatula. Cover with foil or plastic wrap and refrigerate for at least 4 hours, or until the paste is firm to the touch.

Serve the paste directly from the bowl, or unmold it in the following fashion: Run a thin-bladed knife around the edges of the mold to loosen it and dip the bottom in hot water. Place an inverted serving plate over the bowl and, grasping plate and bowl together firmly, turn them over. Rap the plate on a table and the shrimp paste should slide out easily.

In Charleston, shrimp paste is traditionally served for breakfast, or with wafers or crackers as an accompaniment for drinks.

1½ pounds raw shrimp, shelled and deveined *(see shrimp pilau, opposite)*
8 tablespoons unsalted butter, softened
2 tablespoons pale dry sherry
4 teaspoons strained fresh lemon juice
4 teaspoons finely grated onion
½ teaspoon ground mace
½ teaspoon dry mustard
½ teaspoon ground hot red pepper (cayenne)
2 teaspoons salt
½ teaspoon ground white pepper

To prepare stuffed corn, cut cob from husk, then slice off kernels; stuff husk with corn-chicken mixture, then tie with a strip of husk.

To serve 4

2 pounds chicken breasts
4 teaspoons salt
Freshly ground black pepper
4 cups water
6 slices lean bacon
8 medium-sized unhusked ears of
  fresh corn
4 eggs, lightly beaten
½ cup heavy cream
¼ cup finely chopped ripe black
  olives

Chicken-stuffed Corn

Place the chicken breasts in a heavy 2- to 3-quart saucepan, add 2 teaspoons of the salt and a few grindings of pepper, and pour in 4 cups of water. Bring to a boil over high heat, reduce the heat to low, cover the pan partially and simmer for about 20 minutes, or until the chicken feels firm when pressed with your finger. Drain the chicken; strain the cooking stock and reserve it for another use. With a small knife, remove the skin and bones from the breasts and discard them. Cut the chicken into ½-inch pieces and set aside.

Meanwhile, in a heavy 10- to 12-inch skillet, fry the bacon slices over moderate heat, turning them frequently with tongs until they are crisp and brown. Transfer the bacon to paper towels to drain, then crumble it into small pieces.

Shuck one ear of corn at a time, turning the husks back carefully so that they remain intact. Break off each cob at its base, pull out the corn silk, and set the husks aside.

With a sharp knife, slice the kernels from the corn into a deep bowl, taking care not to cut too deeply into the cob. Add the eggs, cream, the remaining 2 teaspoons of salt and a liberal grinding of pepper to the corn kernels and mix well. Stir in the chicken, bacon and the black olives. Taste for seasoning.

To stuff each cornhusk, stand it on its base in a tall, straight-sided tumbler 3 or 4 inches in diameter as shown above. Separate the tops of the leaves and spread them apart so that the lower half of the cornhusk forms a boatlike shell. Spoon about ½ cup of the chicken mixture into the cornhusk shell, then draw the tops of the leaves together again to enclose the stuffing completely. Secure the stuffing by tying a few strips of husk or kitchen string snugly around the end of the cornhusk.

Place the stuffed cornhusks one on top of the other in a large colander set inside a deep pot. Pour enough water into the pot to come to within

Opened at the table, the stuffed corn makes a neat package of chicken-and-corn custard, steamed and served in its own cornhusk packet.

an inch of the bottom of the colander, and bring to a boil over high heat. Cover the pot tightly, reduce the heat to low, and steam the chicken-stuffed corn for 20 minutes. With tongs, arrange the corn on a heated platter, and serve it at once.

Benne-Seed Cocktail Biscuits

Preheat the oven to 350°. Spread the benne seeds evenly in a shallow baking dish and, stirring occasionally, toast them in the middle of the oven until golden brown. Remove from the oven and set the seeds aside.

Combine the flour, baking powder and salt and sift them into a large chilled bowl. Add the butter bits and, with your fingertips, rub the fat and flour together until they resemble flakes of coarse meal. Pour in the milk and mix with your hands or a spoon until the dough is smooth. Then blend in the benne seeds, wrap the dough in wax paper and refrigerate for at least 1 hour before using.

Preheat the oven to 350°. Cut the chilled dough in half and shape each half into a rectangle. Place one half at a time between two sheets of lightly floured wax paper and roll out the dough paper thin. Gently peel off the top sheet of wax paper and, with a biscuit cutter or the rim of a glass, cut the dough into 1½-inch rounds. Using a metal spatula, carefully transfer the rounds to ungreased baking sheets. Gather the scraps into a ball, shape it into a rectangle and roll it out between sheets of wax paper as before; then cut as many more biscuits as you can.

Bake the biscuits in the middle of the oven for 10 to 12 minutes, or until they are a pale golden color. Slide them onto wire racks and at once sprinkle the tops lightly with the coarse salt. Serve the biscuits at room temperature. The benne-seed cocktail biscuits can safely be kept in a tightly covered jar or tin for 2 or 3 weeks. Before serving, warm and crisp them for a few minutes in a low oven (250°).

To make about 8 dozen 1½-inch biscuits

½ cup benne seeds (sesame seeds)
2 cups flour
1 teaspoon double-acting baking powder
½ teaspoon salt
8 tablespoons butter, chilled and cut into ¼-inch bits
4 tablespoons milk
Coarse (kosher) salt

105

Pickled shrimp get their distinctive tang from a blend of lemons, onions and spices such as ginger, mustard and mace.

106

Pickled Shrimp

To make about 2 quarts

Shell the shrimp. Devein them by making a shallow incision down their backs with a small sharp knife and lifting out the black or white intestinal vein with the point of the knife. Drop the shrimp into enough lightly salted boiling water to immerse them completely and boil briskly, uncovered for about 3 minutes, or until they are firm and pink. Drain the shrimp, spread them on paper towels and pat them completely dry with fresh paper towels.

Place the shrimp in a deep bowl, add the onion rings, lemon slices, ginger root and parsley, and toss them together gently but thoroughly. Transfer the mixture to two wide-mouthed quart jars, dividing it evenly between them. Tuck 2 bay leaves down the sides of each jar.

Combine the vinegar, pickling spice, mustard, mace and salt in a 1- to 1½-quart enameled or stainless-steel saucepan and bring to a boil over high heat, stirring until the mustard and salt dissolve completely. At once pour the hot spiced liquid over the shrimp mixture by the tablespoonful. Allow each spoonful of liquid to flow completely through to the bottom of the jars before adding more.

To make the jars of pickled shrimp airtight, place a tablespoon upside down in the top of each jar and very slowly pour the olive-and-vegetable-oil mixture over the back of the spoon, letting it trickle off onto the top of the shrimp. Cover the jars with their lids and chill the shrimp for at least 24 hours before serving. (Tightly covered and refrigerated, the shrimp can safely be kept for about 1 month.)

2 pounds medium-sized raw shrimp (about 21 to 25 to the pound)
1 large onion, peeled, cut crosswise into ¼-inch-thick slices and separated into rings
2 lemons, cut crosswise into ⅛-inch-thick slices
A 1-inch piece of fresh ginger root, scraped and cut into paper-thin slices
¼ cup finely chopped fresh parsley
4 small bay leaves
2 cups cider vinegar
2 tablespoons mixed pickling spice
½ teaspoon dry mustard
¼ teaspoon ground mace
2 teaspoons salt
½ cup olive oil, combined with ½ cup vegetable oil

Huguenot Torte

To serve 8 to 10

Preheat the oven to 400°. With a pastry brush, spread the softened butter evenly over the bottom and sides of a baking-serving dish 12 inches long, 8 inches wide and 2 to 3 inches deep. Combine the flour, baking powder and salt and sift them together onto a plate or a sheet of wax paper. Set aside.

With a wire whisk or a rotary or electric beater, beat the eggs, sugar and vanilla for 4 to 5 minutes until the mixture is thick enough to fall in a slowly dissolving ribbon when the beater is lifted from the bowl. Beat in the flour mixture. Then add the chopped apples and 1 cup of the chopped pecans and fold them into the batter gently but thoroughly with a rubber spatula.

Pour the batter into the buttered baking dish and smooth the top with the spatula. Bake in the middle of the oven for 30 to 35 minutes, or until a toothpick or cake tester inserted in the center comes out clean. Remove the torte from the oven and let it cool slightly.

Meanwhile, in a chilled bowl, beat the cream with a wire whisk or a rotary or electric beater until it is stiff enough to stand in unwavering peaks on the beater when lifted out of the bowl. Spoon the whipped cream into a serving bowl and sprinkle the top with the remaining 2 tablespoons of the chopped pecans.

Serve the Huguenot torte while it is still warm, directly from the baking dish, scooping out the portions crust side up with a serving spoon or spatula. Present the whipped cream separately.

1 tablespoon butter, softened
¼ cup flour
1 teaspoon double-acting baking powder
¼ teaspoon salt
3 eggs
1½ cups sugar
1 teaspoon vanilla extract
1 cup finely chopped peeled apples
1 cup plus 2 tablespoons finely chopped pecans
1 cup heavy cream, chilled

V

The South's Great Gift of Soul Food

W hen I was in New York getting ready to travel south for this book, I had dinner at a restaurant that specialized in soul food. The place was called West Boondock, and it offered live music and miniskirted waitresses, black and white. But the main attraction was the food: smothered pork chops, ham hocks, spareribs, ham, fried chicken, cornbread, collard greens, black-eyed peas and sweet-potato pie. I had the ham hocks, collard greens and black-eyed peas and for dessert a slice of the sweet-potato pie. It was all very rib-sticking, satisfying and entirely familiar to someone born and raised in the Deep South.

The term soul food has come into vogue only in recent years, but the cooking it stands for goes back a long way. It is a basic element of "soul" —a black life-style that disdains the hide-bound puritanical Anglo-Saxon culture and instead emphasizes directness, spontaneity and uninhibited feeling. Soul food and soul music, two of the most important manifestations of this life-style, both come from the South, the black man's first home in America. The music had its origin in the gospel singing and blues of churches, jails and the chain gangs. The food originated as the food of the black South, or, more accurately, as food of the poor South; and after the South's defeat in the Civil War it became everybody's food.

Soul food is an Afro-American invention. Contrary to popular belief, it was not brought over from Africa. What the Africans contributed was their ingenuity. Torn from their native land and thrust into the strange new environment of the Southern plantation, they were forced to make do, and they responded with remarkable resourcefulness. They took the

A steaming kettle of catfish stew, presented by Leola Spencer of the FOODS OF THE WORLD staff, typifies the appealing simplicity of soul-food cooking as it developed in the South. Everyday ingredients —catfish fillets, onions, tomatoes, potatoes, bacon—are enlivened by dashes of Worcestershire, Tabasco and pepper, and are transformed into a savory stew *(Recipe Index)*.

109

Fresh greens are a mainstay of soul-food cooking—served alone, with black-eyed peas or ham hock, or as part of a stew. Among the most popular greens are:

1. Turnip greens
2. Mustard greens
3. Dandelion greens
4. Swiss chard
5. Kale
6. Collard greens
7. Spinach
8. Kohlrabi

foods that were available to them—the greens that grew in profusion in the South, the corn and beans that had been developed by the American Indians in pre-Columbian times and the pig which had originally been brought over from Europe—and turned these unpromising foods into a highly distinctive cuisine.

All the records of the plantation South speak with high praise of the artistry of the black cooks who performed there. Sometimes the game cook came into the dining room to take a bow, and sometimes it was the pastry cook. And all the while these women were creating in their own homes something entirely different, something known today as soul food.

Soul food includes pork in all its ramifications, chicken fixed in every way and everything on earth that can be made with cornmeal. It encompasses catfish, black-eyed peas, beans, sweet potatoes and a wide variety of greens, as well as molasses and the spices originally brought over from Africa. It also includes the magic potion known as "pot likker," the rich, nourishing liquid that remains after the greens and a slab of pork have been cooked together. Yet in this entire galaxy one food stands out above all the others: pork.

The old saw that every part of the pig goes into the pot is literally true. Pig's feet are pickled or parboiled, then roasted with a gravy of vinegar and brown sugar until they are brown and crackly outside. Pig's ears are parboiled in a little water, then the water is thrown out, another small quantity of water is added along with vinegar, salt and pepper, and this mixture is simmered until there is almost no liquid left, just a small quantity of clear gravy consisting mostly of vinegar. Another indispensable part of the pig is chitterlings: the lining of the animal's stomach, which is boiled or fried golden brown. And then there are the immensely popular spareribs. A Mississippi version includes a sauce made with onions, tomatoes, vinegar, honey, orange juice, Worcestershire sauce, hot powdered mustard and heaven knows what else. This variation is called "Beautiful Soul Ribs," and the moment you eat it you understand why.

A second major soul food category is greens, which is almost as important as pork. For Southerners, whatever their race, the taste of turnip greens, collards, mustard greens—all the greens that have a slightly tonic bitterness—is the essence of home cooking. Outsiders may not have dreamed how good these can be, but only because they have never known the real thing. Southern cooks worthy of the name take extreme care not to use anything that might drown out the taste of the greens. One good cook I know simply puts in a few small cubes of fatback to point up the flavor. She browns the fatback in a big pot, adds a couple of hot red pepper pods, throws in two paper-thin slices of lemon, tosses in the greens and pours a little boiling salted water over them. She does not cook them very long; they should emerge a beautiful bottle-green in color, with the lemon and pepper mingling to make an elusive perfume and provide a nice tingle on the tongue. For anyone who likes the greens a bit hotter, she keeps a bottle of Tabasco close at hand. She saves the pot likker in which the greens were cooked—to throw it away would be a sacrilege. She serves it by itself as a soup, or ladles a small portion of it over the greens.

Pork, greens, or whatever, soul food comes close to being a religion among its devotees. People who have encountered it the way it should be cooked swear by it, no matter how many years may have passed or how far they may have wandered. I remember calling on the celebrated Mississippi-born opera star, Leontyne Price, one day in Rome. She was there for some summer recording sessions, and had taken an apartment downstairs from mine. Usually she is too busy opera-house-hopping to entertain as she loves to do, but when she decided to rent an apartment in Rome, she was determined that it have a modern kitchen. "I go dashing around the world and back," she explained, "living in hotels . . . I wake up in a room in Hotel Anonymous and think 'What city am I in today?' It could be Vienna or Milan or Berlin or wherever I'm singing. What I want is a place where I can bang around in the kitchen when I feel like it." Great artist that she is, Leontyne Price has the artist's feeling for the textures and tones of food, and she loves to cook Southern dinners for small parties of friends.

That day in Rome she was getting ready for one such dinner party, and I had promised to bring chives, dill and basil from my terrace. When I arrived, she was regally dressed in a Dior hostess gown and seated at the oval table in her dining room overlooking a court with a gently plashing fountain. The coffeepot was beside her, the score of *Salomé* was propped up before her—and she was sorting turnip greens. "This is how we do it in Laurel, Mississippi," she said. "You have to examine each leaf personally, after you've washed it. You must take the yellow part out and you must tear every bit of green leaf off the stalk, in pieces as big as postage stamps. It takes time, but this is how you have to do it. There are as many different ways to cook greens as there are to sing soprano roles. You can put in bacon fat at the beginning, or you can cook bits of fatback with the greens, or you can pour bacon fat over them after they've cooked. You put in just enough water to keep things from sticking. And I'll tell you one thing, buddy"—she assumed a mock-ferocious expression—"every drop of the pot likker is mine, all mine!"

My own experience with soul food goes back to the time when I was a boy in Mobile. I still remember the day I had my first full-fledged soul food meal, for it was one of those crazy days never lost to mind. I had been to visit a school friend whose parents summered in a rackety old white frame house on the banks of the Fish River that flows into Bon Secour Bay. It is a lazy, meandering river with innumerable branches and bayous, lush with cypresses, palmettos, thick marsh grasses, green bay trees hanging over the water and blue pickerel weed and white-flowered arrowleaf. The wild yellow American lotus and the white water lily bloom in these waters, and some of the bayous are clogged by that beautiful and prolific plant, the water hyacinth, which floats on spongy leaf pontoons and trails webby black roots. This is a sub-tropical world, and when I knew it, it was an incredibly silent one. Motorboats were not common then, and when the silence was broken, it was likely to be broken not by some mechanical annoyance but by the creaking of oarlocks. Or, in the evening the "Dutch nightingales," the frogs, would sing a deafening antiphonal chorus in voices ranging from the Butterfly McQueen treble of the tree frogs to the basso profundo of the green swamp frogs, vying like dozens of Boris Godunovs to out-boom each other.

I was to be driven home to Mobile by my uncle, who was returning from a trip to Florida, and we were supposed to meet at a filling station near the point where a car ferry crossed the river. But in good Southern fashion the time arrangements for our meeting were lackadaisical. I was obviously hours early, and I soon grew bored with waiting at the filling station. I began to eye the car ferry with more than casual interest.

The ferry was a weather-beaten wooden platform on rusted pontoons, with a cable which ran through iron hoops on the ferry rail and stretched from one side of the river to the other. Two old black men poled the ferry across, carrying two or three foot-passengers and an occasional automobile. The schedule purportedly called for a crossing every half hour, but sometimes it was four times an hour and sometimes only once, depending on the traffic. I watched the ferry creak and clank back and forth several times, and finally I could stand it no longer. By now, it was about 5 o'clock in the afternoon; the sun was bright in the sky, but the light was beginning to turn to golden dust, and the shadows were lengthening imperceptibly. I hopped on the ferry and crossed the river, intending to putter about a while, pick some blackberries, and go back on the next crossing. I knew there was a hermit who had built an earthen dome somewhere across the river, and I had heard tales of a haunted well by the site of an old French settler's burned-out house. The settler's ghost, it was claimed, spoke in French from the bottom of the well.

I did pick some ripe blackberries and eat them; I watched blue-and-green dragonflies lazily circle about, and then I opened a gate and entered a cleared field. Way over in one corner there was a huge oak and some sand pear trees, around which three white cows were moving. I started toward the great oak before I realized there was something odd about those cows. They were rearing up, striking their hooves against the tree trunks, then making strange, quirky little jumps. I stopped to look and suddenly one of them noticed me. She shook her head and tail and then she charged! The others came galumphing after her, moving in a way that I have never seen before or since, with a strange kind of playfulness that sometimes comes over matrons attending a 30th class reunion in a welter of gin and nostalgia.

I didn't pause to look further; I took off lickety-split. But the cows were heading me off from the gate, so I dashed toward the barbed-wire fence. Although it was covered with yellow jessamine and granddaddy-grey-beard vines, I managed to find an opening and barged through. But the cow that had seen me first had already reached the gate, which I had left unlatched. She butted it open and was quickly out in the lane between me and the return route to the ferry. I was beginning to panic, when I saw someone I knew coming down the road: Spinney, a handsome and jovial middle-aged black man who owned a fishing boat and took out fishing parties in these parts.

"Spinney, Spinney!" I cried. "Look out for the cows; they've gone crazy!" I was backing into a blackberry thicket with great care, sure of not being followed in there. But Spinney only ripped a big branch of callicarpa from the side of the road and rushed toward the cows, crying out "Aieeee! . . . Aiee!" in a high, urging tone. The dillypot cows looked vaguely startled, then seemed almost to giggle as they kicked up their heels and trotted back through the gate. Spinney latched it and came over to me. "Them silly fools is drunk," he explained. "That big blow we had from offen the Bay last week shook down a lot of them pears and they fomented on the ground, like makin' pear brandy. Them cows would have to go and eat 'em, so they is silly-ass drunk." He vowed he had seen gophers drunk under blackberry bushes where they had eaten windfalls.

Spinney informed me that the ferry was not running for an hour or so because the ferrymen had gone off to "tend to their fires," but he said he would send word to the filling station as to where I was, and meanwhile I should come along home with him.

The house—he shared it with his mother, a thin, straight old woman called 'Vira (Elvire)—was a silvery-gray unpainted weathered pine, shaded by two dense chinaberry trees that had been clipped into perfect globes. The front yard was grassless packed earth, divided by a walk of wooden paving blocks and edged by old soda-pop bottles turned upside down; time and sunlight had prettily discolored them in shades of blue, green and mauve. Along the fence were sunflowers and four-o'clocks. Inside, 'Vira had been baking and the house was thick with the sweet perfume of lemon extract. Everything was dark and cool, and the floors—wide pine planks smooth from long years of scouring with sand and elbow grease—were pleasant to bare feet. (In summer, everybody in that part

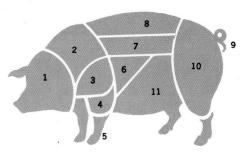

THE ALL-PURPOSE PIG
Snout to tail, the pig has long been the completely edible animal. In the South, fancy cuts such as the ham, loin and chops traditionally were rich man's fare, while blacks and the poor in general enjoyed the soul-food parts—that is, everything else except the squeal. They ate the meat, thriftily rendered the fat into lard, saved the blood for pudding and piled the scraps into the sausage grinder. In the diagram above, the various parts of pork are:
1 Hog's head, snout, ear, jowl, neck, tongue and brains
2 Shoulder roll (butt)
3 Picnic shoulder
4 Hock
5 Knuckles or feet
6 Spareribs, stomach lining (hog maw) and liver
7 Loin and kidneys
8 Fatback
9 Tail
10 Ham
11 Bacon and intestines (chitterlings)

Continued on page 120

Fixing Sunday dinner is a joint venture for Mrs. Tally Adams, her daughter Barbara, and her sister-in-law Mrs. Cornell Adams. The two Adams families live on neighboring farms outside Columbia and because their combined broods total 15 children, preparation of the prodigious quantity of food they require starts at 6 a.m. At left, Mrs. Tally Adams slices slab bacon to cook with fresh collard greens while Barbara rinses the salty bacon slices. Above, Mrs. Adams and her sister-in-law serve the youngsters at a table apart from the adults.

A Family Dinner of Classic Dishes where Soul Food Is Familiar Fare

Although soul food remained nameless until nostalgic Northern blacks christened it during the 1960s, this kind of cooking has long been familiar to Southern cooks such as Mrs. Tally Adams of Columbia, South Carolina. Soul food originated in the South; it was the handiwork of slaves who invented it out of necessity, using leftovers and just about every edible handy ingredient. Today, when Mrs. Adams prepares Sunday dinner, her menu reads like a roll call of classic soul-food dishes: cornbread, spareribs, chitterlings, pigs' feet, tails and ears, and the ubiquitous Southern fried chicken. The vegetables are black-eyed peas and collard greens that have simmered for hours with meat —a slab of bacon, salt pork (sometimes with a streak of lean), ham hocks or ham bone—and for dessert Mrs. Adams serves a rich banana pudding or sweet-potato pie. And, as the Adams family demonstrates, the indispensable ingredients of all these dishes are imagination, laughter and love.

115

Sweet-potato pies and barbecued spareribs bake in Mrs. Adams' oven *(left)* while collard greens and pork *(below)* simmer on top of the stove. The pie filling is made from boiled sieved sweet potatoes, which are mixed with eggs and milk, sweetened with sugar and spiced with cinnamon and ginger. The color and texture are not unlike that of the Thanksgiving pumpkin pie popular in New England, but Southerners prefer the sweet-potato filling for its sweeter, more delicate flavor. To bake soul-food spareribs, Mrs. Adams first lines large baking pans with foil. She moistens the pieces of meat with water, adds a little salt and pepper, then wraps the foil tightly over the ribs so that they will steam and tenderize as they bake. After they have been in the oven for an hour or so, Mrs. Adams peels the foil back to uncover the ribs and coats them with a highly seasoned barbecue mixture. She likes to use a bottled sauce, doctored with brown sugar, vinegar and hot pepper, for the final baking and glazing. (See the Recipe Index for other versions of both sweet-potato pie and barbecued spareribs.)

Collard greens are seasoned and simmered for hours with bacon and salt pork; then pigs' feet and tails are added to the pot.

Freshly picked okra, corn and tomatoes are stewed with lightly fried slab bacon slices that contribute a meaty taste.

Black-eyed peas and bacon may be flavored with molasses, as Mrs. Adams does, or red pepper, as other cooks prefer.

The hours of cooking seem time well spent when the two Adams families and their friends sit down to dinner outside on the lawn. Adults and teen-agers gather at one long table *(left)*. Tally Adams sits at the head of the table *(at bottom in the picture)* and his wife is at the far end; to her right are Cornell Adams and his wife. The younger children have a table to themselves *(above)* where they can eat at their own pace. The foods shown in the platters and bowls on the main table add up to a veritable soul-food feast. Starting from the far end down, they include barbecued spareribs; stewed okra, corn and tomatoes; sweet-potato pie; banana pudding made with layers of vanilla wafers, banana slices and custard; fried chicken; chitterlings; wedges of cornbread; spicy boiled pigs' feet, tails and ears; rice; collard greens; and black-eyed peas with bacon. The coolers behind Mrs. Tally Adams dispense gallons of fruit punch for all the family. Like most Southern children—whether black or white—the Adams flock enjoys lingering over their share of the fried chicken *(right)*.

of the world goes barefoot indoors.) The "front room," with its flowered wallpaper and mid-Victorian sofa, was in perfect order. 'Vira always kept it that way for visits from the insurance collector or the minister. But the kitchen and back porch were the live centers of the house. There was a fireplace in the kitchen, its mantel lined with shelf paper made of newspaper folded and cut into paper lace. A jam jar held neatly folded paper "spills" for lighting fires, lamps or pipes ('Vira smoked a long-stemmed old-fashioned white clay pipe). There was a scrubbed oval oak table in the middle of the room, and against a wall stood a small iron cookstove. The stovepipe went out through a window whose pane had been replaced by a sheet of zinc with an appropriate hold.

Supper was ready and 'Vira put down an extra plate for me. Catfish was the *pièce de résistance,* and 'Vira had a mysterious knowledge of these elusive creatures. She was famous for being able to vanish into the woods or marshlands and always return with a string of them. Catfish won't bite during bright daylight hours, but 'Vira knew sandy-bottomed pools which were bathed in a kind of perpetual green twilight, provided by overhanging green bay and ti-ti trees. She used anything on earth for bait—a June bug, a feather.

That was the first time I ever tasted catfish, freshly caught and fried in golden cornmeal. The meat was fine textured and the fresh-water sweetness, contrasting with the delicate crunch of the cornmeal coating, was infinitely satisfying. There was also corn on the cob, with old-fashioned crinkly hairpins stuck in each end to serve as handles, a system I have since utilized myself. There was a big pot of mixed greens with turnip dumplings in them. The pot was mostly turnip greens, but 'Vira had also thrown in a handful of mustard greens and an odd beet leaf or so. The dumplings were simplicity itself. She had beaten up an egg with a little water, salt and pepper, crumbled in some leftover yellow cornbread and added some chopped greens. Then she mixed all these together, formed dumplings by moulding them in her hands, and placed them on top of the slow-cooking greens. For Sundays and picnics, she told me, she put some chopped cooked ham or crisp crumbled bacon into the dumplings.

When Spinney told me earlier that the ferrymen were off "tending their fires," it turned out that he was speaking the gospel truth. The church across the bayou was having a barbecue on the shore that night to celebrate the pastor's fifth year with his flock. The lemon extract smell that floated through 'Vira's house was from four buttermilk pies she had baked to take along. When we had finished supper we all set out for the church—I helping to carry the pies—to inspect the progress of the barbecue, which was to take place around 10 or 11 o'clock. The church itself was clapboard, dazzlingly whitewashed outside and in. Yellow glass windows made the entire interior seem golden. The altar had a white lace cloth and huge bouquets of heavy red-purple celosia (cockscomb) with yellow coreopsis and pink and white cosmos. I still retain a definite memory of the sense of piety and elation I felt in that little church.

Two barbecue pits had been dug in a clump of pines a short way downstream from the church. One pit—the fire pit—was being tended by my friends the ferrymen. They kept it full of burning wood to supply hot embers, which they carried over to replenish the second pit; over this a pig that had been split down the back was slowly roasting. It had been killed the evening before, then hung for a while, cleaned and washed, and the roasting had begun early in the morning of the barbecue.

Every country community in the South has a Master Barbecuer, who is as greatly respected as the square-dance caller or the water-diviner with his forked stake. The barbecuer always has his own secret sauce and his own way of carrying out the ritual. At this barbecue on Fish River, the Master was a little old man with oval spectacles, who held a large dish-mop as if it were a sceptre. He had begun his labors in the morning, basting the pig very carefully with warm water that contained salt and red pepper, allowing the least possible liquid to fall into the pit. About mid-day the pig (having been turned once) had become a delicate uniform golden-brown all over, and the Master had switched to basting with a sauce. He basted slightly but more constantly as time went on, watching a trotter here or a patch of shoulder there that might be browning too quickly. At first he used small quantities of sauce but, finally, he splashed and flashed with his mop-sceptre, as though knighting the pig and mentally saying "Arise, Sir Porker!"

When the meat at last was cut and the feast began at the scrubbed trestle tables, each portion would receive a ladle of sauce. And oh, what sauce! Red hot peppers, tomatoes, black pepper, onions, a few slices of lemon, bay leaves, mace, thyme, sugar and cider vinegar. It could be duplicated in a kitchen, I think, but just as fried catfish go with supper and sunset on a bayou, barbecue goes with a scent of sun-warmed pine needles and opening four-o'clocks.

By now Spinney was hanging up the shoe-box lanterns the ladies of the congregation had fashioned by cutting stars and moons in shoe boxes and pasting colored kite paper inside them. 'Vira was arranging the pie and cake table; the watermelons were placed in big washtubs with blocks of ice, and somebody had been sent off to cut bunches of mint sprigs for the iced tea. The excitement was growing, and I tingled as I was given a small sample of the juicy roasted crackly pork. I dipped it in the sauce, and savored a marvelous blend of flavors—crisp, rich, sweet—proving indeed why Sir Porker is held in such high esteem.

I could not stay for all the festivities and fun, for the ferrymen had decided that it was now time to go back to the ferry, and they offered to take me along for the long-delayed rendezvous with my uncle.

They also took 'Vira back to her house so she could fetch a basket and bring back some ice cold Nehis from the filling station. As 'Vira and I walked down to the ferry, the sun was just going down in a dark tangle of pine and greenbay, and when we passed the orchard the cows were still running about.

"Law," said 'Vira, taking the clay pipe out of her mouth as she stared at the cows. "They's gonna be puffy-eyed and no 'count in the mornin'. And likely put out eggnog 'stead of milk."

Almost a lifetime later, on my recent journey through the South, I found myself being updated on soul food again, in rural Alabama once more, this time in a tiny community called Gee's Bend, about 35 miles

Short on eye appeal but long on flavor, catfish is a much-sought-after soul food in the South. At the Pine Point Marina on Kentucky Lake, just outside Paris, Tennessee, an angler *(above)* nets fish that almost got away, while other fishermen *(opposite page)* tote a stringful of "cats." For nonfishing soul-food lovers, catfish are raised in commercial fish-farm ponds throughout the South. They are sold alive by most fishmongers, or served already fried at the popular regional restaurants that are devoted solely to catfish.

from Selma. My mentor now was Eugene Witherspoon, pastor of the African Missionary Church, a denomination that predates the hardshell liquor-hating Baptists and serves real wine at the annual Lord's Supper. Witherspoon explained to me the mysteries of another important category of soul food: game. He showed me his freezer, crammed with turtles and other unfamiliar kinds of meat.

"That's beaver," he explained, pointing to an unidentifiable hunk. "Very dark meat, very mild and tasty. You parboil it a little, then roast it, like you'd do 'coon."

"I never tasted beaver *or* coon," I said.

"Beaver's very tasty, the meat has a good 'sistency. Some folks eat skunk. After all, meat's meat. Skunk's not the meat you go out lookin' for, but if you know how to clean it and fix it, it's good roast meat."

"How do you clean it?"

"First you have to know how to find the musks and cut 'em out clean. Then you skin it and trim it and tie a string on it and let it stay in a runnin' stream for three days. Then you parboil it with a little red pepper, and take it out and roast it."

"And 'possum?"

"Well, you take your dead 'possum and put it in the ashes, don' mind the smell of fur burnin', and you hol' his tail and turn him in those ashes.

Then you scrape all the hair off and take him out back under the china-berry tree and clean him well, you have to cut the glands out from under the arm. When 'possum is cleaned you parboil him with water and red pepper, then take him out, dry him off and put him in the turkey broiler with yams. Nothin' on earth finer.''

Mrs. Witherspoon is Church Mother of her husband's church, and although she and two friends, a Mrs. Jelson and a Mrs. Tobin, were busy preparing for an all-day singing meet, they joined in our conversation.

"Everybody wants to know 'bout Southern food,'' smiled Mrs. Jelson. "It's suddenly took holt everywhere. And, oh, it is good! People's always askin' 'how d'you make this, and how d'you make that?' Yankees always start singin' 'Mama's little baby loves shortnin' bread' when they come here, like we might wave a wand and make some shortnin' bread pop up out the ground! I don't know what they mean by shortnin' bread. It might be what my Granny made for us chillen, that we call crumbly cake. She'd take a cup of darkest brown sugar, a cup of flour and a cup of butter and bake it in her old iron stove. She'd cut it into squares and they'd crumble apart with goodness. Brown sugar and butter make a goodness!''

"What's your favorite thing to eat?'' I asked Mrs. Witherspoon.

"Well, I count it a downcast day that don't bring a sweet-potato pie to my table. I like it with everything. I'm very partial to 'possum. And fried chicken never goes off. Nothin' bad 'bout a plain old bread pie.''

"How do you make that?"

"Like the wind! Two minutes or less! You butter your dish and put in slices of bread two deep. Then you whip up milk, eggs, sugar, cinnamon and lemon extract and pour it in and bake it 'til it's nice and brown.''

The third lady, Mrs. Tobin, was rather more shy and soft-spoken. "I like fried grits and ham-onion-and-raisin hash," she finally admitted. "But the grits has to be just right. Lotta people never learn to cook grits."

"Watery grits goes with sleazy ways," sniffed Mrs. Witherspoon. "All you have to do is measure. You measure 5 cups of water, put in a nut of butter and salt as you like, then pour in the cup of grits slowly, stirrin' all the time. When it's all stirred in, you turn down the heat, put on the lid, and cook 'bout 30 to 40 minutes, stirrin' a lot. You eat it hot with butter or gravy. If you are gonna fry it, you pour the grits into a pan and let it cool and cut it in wedges or strips. You flour 'em lightly and put in a little pepper, then fry 'em in a little grease 'til they're golden brown.''

We were all getting hungrier and hungrier but couldn't stop talking about the merits of skillet-baked cornbread and how few people make cracklin' bread now, about all the combinations of cornmeal with shortening and liquid that go to make jonnycake and dodgers, hush puppies, splits and hoecake, pones and pan flats. Then we got onto peas and beans, an encyclopedia volume unto itself. And all the while, as we were talking, Mrs. Witherspoon was singing to herself:

I'm gonna do what the Spirit say do,
I'm gonna do what the Spirit say do,
If the Spirit say dance,
I'll dance, oh Lordy,
I'm gonna do what the Spirit say do.

I left Mr. Witherspoon and the ladies busy preparing for the all-day singing the next day. As I drove off, smoke was curling from farmhouse chimneys around me and the moon had emerged in a green sky.

In one guise or another, corn is a key ingredient of soul food. The dried corn is turned into the three uniquely Southern corn products shown below. At left is dried whole hominy: to make it, corn kernels are boiled in a weak lye solution, then hulled, washed and dried. The hominy grits, center, are a coarsely ground version of dried hominy. At right is the white stone-ground cornmeal that is the basic ingredient of legions of hot cornbreads.

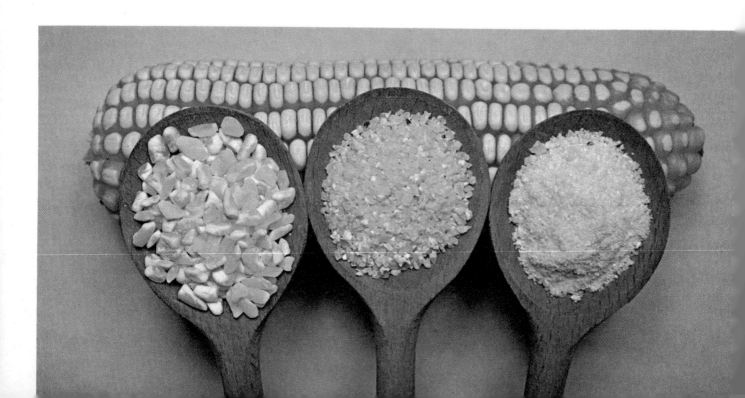

Sweet-Potato Pie

Preheat the oven to 425°. Drop the quartered sweet potatoes into enough boiling water to immerse them completely and boil briskly, uncovered, until they are tender and show no resistance when they are pierced with the point of a small skewer or knife. Drain off the water, return the pan to low heat and slide it back and forth for a minute or so to dry the potatoes completely.

Rub the sweet potatoes through a fine sieve with the back of a spoon or purée them through a food mill. Set the puréed potatoes aside to cool to room temperature.

In a deep bowl, cream the butter and brown sugar together by beating and mashing them against the sides of the bowl with the back of a wooden spoon until they are light and fluffy. Beat in the cooled puréed sweet potatoes and, when they are completely incorporated, add the eggs one at a time, beating well after each addition. Add the light corn syrup, milk, grated lemon peel, vanilla, grated nutmeg and salt and continue to beat until the filling is smooth.

Pour the sweet-potato filling into the fully baked pie shell, spreading it evenly with a rubber spatula. Bake in the middle of the oven for 10 minutes. Then reduce the oven temperature to 325° and bake the pie for 35 minutes longer, or until a knife inserted in the center comes out clean.

Serve the sweet-potato pie warm or at room temperature.

To make one 9-inch pie

4 medium-sized sweet potatoes, peeled and quartered
4 tablespoons butter, softened
¾ cup dark-brown sugar
3 eggs, lightly beaten
⅓ cup light corn syrup
⅓ cup milk
2 teaspoons finely grated fresh lemon peel
1 teaspoon vanilla extract
¼ teaspoon ground nutmeg, preferably freshly grated
½ teaspoon salt
A 9-inch short crust pastry pie shell, fully baked and cooled *(Recipe Index)*

Hush Puppies

Combine the flour, baking powder and salt and sift them together into a deep bowl. Stir in the cornmeal, unsifted, then add the eggs, one at a time, and beat vigorously with a wooden spoon until the mixture is smooth. Pour in ¾ cup of the buttermilk and stir until it is completely absorbed. If the batter seems dense, add up to ¼ cup more buttermilk by the spoonful until the batter holds its shape in a spoon. Beat in the finely chopped onions and garlic.

Preheat the oven to its lowest setting. Line a large shallow baking dish with a double thickness of paper towels and place the baking dish in the middle of the oven.

In a deep fryer or large heavy saucepan, melt enough lard to fill the pan to a depth of 2 to 3 inches, or pour in vegetable oil to a depth of 2 to 3 inches. Heat the fat until it reaches a temperature of 375° on a deep-frying thermometer.

To shape each hush puppy, scoop up a rounded tablespoon of the batter and push it into the hot fat with another spoon. Deep-fry the hush puppies 4 or 5 at a time, turning them about frequently with a slotted spoon for about 3 minutes, or until they are golden brown. Transfer them to the lined baking dish to drain and keep them warm in the low oven while you deep-fry the rest.

Serve the hush puppies hot, accompanied by butter. Traditionally hush puppies accompany fried fish.

To make 18 to 20

¼ cup flour
4 teaspoons double-acting baking powder
½ teaspoon salt
1½ cups white cornmeal, preferably water-ground
2 eggs
¾ to 1 cup buttermilk
1 tablespoon finely chopped onions
1 teaspoon finely chopped garlic
Lard or vegetable oil for deep frying

To serve 4

3 pounds catfish, porgy or
  butterfish, filleted but with skins
  left on
2 teaspoons salt
¼ teaspoon freshly ground black
  pepper
1 cup white cornmeal, preferably
  water-ground
Lard for deep frying

To serve 8 to 10

½ cup cider vinegar
⅓ cup water
2 tablespoons sugar
2 tablespoons flour
2 teaspoons dry mustard
2 teaspoons salt
½ cup heavy cream
2 tablespoons butter
4 eggs, lightly beaten
2 pounds firm white cabbage
1 cup grated scraped carrots

To serve 4 to 6

1 cup finely chopped onions
1 cup freshly made catsup *(Recipe
  Index)* or 1 cup peach preserves
  (depending on whether you
  prefer a very spicy or slightly
  sweet sauce)
¼ cup dark brown sugar
¼ cup distilled white vinegar
¼ cup Worcestershire sauce
1 teaspoon dry mustard
¼ teaspoon Tabasco
4 pounds spareribs, in 2 or 3 pieces,
  trimmed of excess fat
2 teaspoons salt
Freshly ground black pepper
2 lemons, cut crosswise into ¼-
  inch-thick slices

Southern Fried Fish

Pat the fish completely dry with paper towels. To keep the fish from curling up as they fry score the flesh side of each fillet with a small sharp knife, making three diagonal slashes about 2 inches long and ⅛ inch deep spaced an inch or so apart. Season the fillets on both sides with the salt and pepper. Then dip them in the cornmeal to coat them evenly, and gently shake off any excess meal.

In a heavy 12-inch skillet at least 2 inches deep, melt enough lard to fill the pan to a depth of about ½ inch. Heat the fat until it is very hot but not smoking, then add the fish. Fry the fillets for 4 minutes, turn them with a slotted spatula and fry for 3 or 4 minutes longer, or until they are richly and evenly browned. Arrange the fillets attractively on a heated platter and serve at once. Traditionally, Southern fried fish is accompanied by coleslaw *(below)* and hush puppies *(Recipe Index)*.

Coleslaw with Boiled Dressing

In a 2- to 3-quart saucepan, combine the vinegar, water, sugar, flour, mustard and salt and beat vigorously with a wire whisk until the mixture is smooth. Place over moderate heat and, whisking constantly, add the cream and butter and cook until the butter melts and the sauce comes to a simmer. Stir 2 or 3 tablespoonfuls of the simmering liquid into the beaten eggs and, when they are well incorporated, pour the mixture into the sauce, whisking it constantly. Reduce the heat to low and continue to whisk until the sauce thickens heavily. With a rubber spatula, scrape the contents of the saucepan into a deep bowl and cool to room temperature.

Wash the head of cabbage under cold running water, remove the tough outer leaves, and cut the cabbage into quarters. To shred the cabbage, cut out the core and slice the quarters crosswise into ⅛-inch-wide strips.

Add the shredded cabbage and the carrots to the sauce, toss together gently but thoroughly and taste for seasoning. Cover with foil or plastic wrap and refrigerate for 2 or 3 hours before serving.

Barbecued Spareribs

Preheat the oven to 400°. While it is heating, prepare the barbecue basting sauce: combine the onions, catsup or peach preserves, brown sugar, vinegar, Worcestershire, mustard and Tabasco in a 1- to 1½-quart enameled or stainless-steel saucepan. Stirring constantly with a wooden spoon, bring the sauce to a boil over high heat. Reduce the heat to low and simmer for 4 or 5 minutes until the onions are soft.

Arrange the spareribs, flesh side up, side by side on a rack set in a large shallow roasting pan and sprinkle them with the salt and a few grindings of pepper. With a pastry brush, spread about ½ cup of the basting sauce evenly over the ribs and lay the lemon slices on top. Bake uncovered in the middle of the oven for about 1½ hours, brushing the ribs 3 or 4 more times with the remaining sauce. The ribs are done if the meat shows no resistance when pierced deeply with the point of a small skewer or knife. Arrange the spareribs on a heated platter and serve at once.

Golden-fried catfish fillets, still sizzling in the skillet, are ready to join their traditional accompaniments, hush puppies and coleslaw with boiled dressing.

To serve 6 to 8

2 one-pound smoked ham hocks, or
   substitute a meaty ham bone or
   pieces of slab bacon with the rind
   on
2 cups (1 pound) dried black-eyed
   peas
1 cup coarsely chopped onions
2 medium-sized celery stalks,
   trimmed of all leaves and coarsely
   chopped
1 fresh hot red chili, about 3 inches
   long, washed, stemmed, seeded if
   desired, and coarsely chopped
   (caution: see end of recipe)
Freshly ground black pepper

To make about 2 dozen

2 cups flour
1 teaspoon baking powder
½ teaspoon salt
8 tablespoons butter, chilled and cut
   into ¼-inch bits
6 to 8 tablespoons ice water
8 medium-sized firm ripe peaches
   (about 2 pounds)
½ cup granulated sugar
¼ cup water
½ teaspoon ground cinnamon
¼ teaspoon ground nutmeg
Lard or vegetable oil for deep
   frying
½ cup confectioners' sugar

Ham Hocks and Black-eyed Peas

Place the ham hocks in a heavy 4- to 6-quart pot and add enough water to cover the meat by at least 1 inch. Bring to a boil over high heat, reduce the heat to low and simmer partially covered for 2 hours, or until the ham hocks are tender and show no resistance when pierced deeply with the point of a small skewer or sharp knife.

In a sieve or colander, wash the black-eyed peas under cold running water until the draining water is clear. Add the peas, onions, celery, chili and a few grindings of black pepper to the pot, mix well, and bring to a boil over high heat. Reduce the heat to low and simmer partially covered for 1 to 1½ hours, or until the peas are tender. Check the pot from time to time and add more boiling water if necessary. When the peas are fully cooked, they should have absorbed almost all of the pan liquid.

Taste for seasoning and serve at once from a heated platter or bowl.

NOTE: The volatile oils in fresh hot chilies may burn your skin or make your eyes smart, so clean, stem and seed them under running water. Wear rubber gloves if you can and be careful not to touch your face or eyes. Wash your hands thoroughly with soap and warm water.

Fried Peach Turnovers

Combine the flour, baking powder and salt and sift them into a deep bowl. Add the butter bits and, with your fingertips, rub the flour and fat together until they resemble flakes of coarse meal. Pour in 6 tablespoons of the ice water all at once, toss lightly and gather the dough into a ball. If the dough seems crumbly, add up to 2 tablespoons more ice water a few drops at a time until all the particles adhere. Dust the dough with flour, wrap it in wax paper and refrigerate at least 1 hour before using.

Meanwhile, drop the peaches, 3 or 4 at a time, into enough boiling water to cover them completely. Boil briskly for 2 to 3 minutes, then with a slotted spoon, transfer the peaches to a sieve or colander to drain, and peel them with a small sharp knife. Cut the peaches in half, discard the pits, and chop the fruit coarsely.

Combine the chopped peaches, granulated sugar and ¼ cup water in a 3- to 4-quart enameled or stainless-steel saucepan and bring to a boil over high heat, stirring with a wooden spoon until the sugar dissolves completely. Reduce the heat to moderate and, stirring from time to time, cook until the mixture is thick enough to hold its shape almost solidly in the spoon. With a rubber spatula, scrape the entire contents of the pan into a bowl, stir in the cinnamon and nutmeg and set the peaches aside to cool to room temperature.

On a lightly floured surface, roll the dough into a rough circle about 1/16 inch thick. With a cookie cutter or the rim of a glass, cut the dough into 4½-inch rounds. Gather the scraps into a ball, roll them out as before, and cut as many more rounds as you can.

To shape each turnover, place about 2 tablespoons of the peach mixture on the lower third of a round of dough. Moisten the edges of the round with a finger dipped in cold water, fold the round in half and press the edges tightly together to enclose the peach filling securely.

Preheat the oven to its lowest setting. Line a large shallow baking dish with a double thickness of paper towels and place it in the heated oven.

In a deep fryer or large heavy saucepan, melt enough lard to fill the pan to a depth of 2 or 3 inches, or pour in vegetable oil to a depth of 2 or 3 inches. Then heat the fat until it reaches a temperature of 375° on a deep-frying thermometer.

Deep-fry the turnovers, 3 or 4 at a time, turning them about occasionally with a slotted spoon for about 3 minutes, or until they are crisp and golden. As they brown, transfer the turnovers to the lined dish to drain and keep them warm in the oven while you deep-fry the rest.

Sprinkle the turnovers lightly with confectioners' sugar, arrange them on a heated platter and serve at once.

Catfish Stew

To serve 4

In a heavy 4- to 6-quart casserole, fry the bacon slices over moderate heat, turning them with tongs until they are crisp and brown and have rendered all their fat. Transfer them to paper towels to drain, then crumble them into small bits and set aside.

Add the onions to the fat remaining in the casserole and, stirring frequently, cook over moderate heat for about 5 minutes, until they are soft and translucent but not brown. Stir in the tomatoes, potatoes, catfish trimmings, Worcestershire, Tabasco, salt and a few grindings of pepper and bring to a boil over high heat. Reduce the heat to low, cover tightly and simmer for 30 minutes.

With tongs or a slotted spoon, remove the catfish trimmings and discard them. Add the catfish fillets and the reserved bacon and mix well. Cover the casserole tightly again and continue to simmer over low heat for 8 to 10 minutes, or until the fish flakes easily when prodded gently with a fork. Taste for seasoning and serve the stew at once, either directly from the casserole or from a large heated bowl.

5 slices lean bacon
1½ cups finely chopped onions
6 medium-sized firm ripe tomatoes, washed, cored and cut into 1½-inch pieces
2 large boiling potatoes, peeled and cut into 1-inch cubes (about 3 cups)
1 pound catfish trimmings: the head, tail and bones of the fish
2 tablespoons Worcestershire sauce
½ teaspoon Tabasco
2 teaspoons salt
Freshly ground black pepper
2 pounds catfish fillets, cut into 1½-inch pieces

Boiled Greens

To serve 6

With a sharp knife trim away any bruised or blemished spots on the greens and strip the leaves from their stems. Wash the leaves in several changes of cold running water to remove all traces of dirt or sand.

In a heavy 10- to 12-inch skillet, fry the salt pork over moderate heat, stirring the dice frequently with a slotted spoon until they are crisp and brown and have rendered all their fat. Transfer the dice and liquid fat to a bowl and pour the water into the skillet. Bring to a boil over high heat, meanwhile scraping in any brown particles that cling to the bottom and sides of the pan. Remove from the heat and set aside.

Place the greens in a heavy 4- to 6-quart pot and set over high heat. Cover tightly and cook for 3 to 4 minutes, or until the greens begin to wilt. Stir in the pork fat and dice, the skillet liquid, and the onions and sugar. Cover the pot again and continue to cook over moderate heat for about 45 minutes, or until the greens are tender.

Drain off the cooking liquid and reserve it as "pot likker" for soups, or as a dunking sauce for cornbread. Taste the boiled greens, season them with as much salt and pepper as you think they need and serve at once.

3 pounds fresh young turnip, collard or mustard greens
1½ pounds salt pork, with rind removed, cut into 1-inch dice
1½ cups water
1 cup coarsely chopped onions
1 teaspoon sugar
Salt
Freshly ground black pepper

129

VI

Deep in the Heart of Dixie

On a summer evening some years ago, two of the South's most celebrated writers, William Faulkner and Katherine Anne Porter, were dining together at a plush restaurant in Paris. Everything had been laid on to perfection; a splendid meal had been consumed, a bottle of fine Burgundy emptied, and thimble-sized glasses of an expensive liqueur drained. The maître d' and an entourage of waiters hovered close by, ready to satisfy any final whim. "Back home the butter beans are in," said Faulkner, peering into the distance, "the speckled ones." Miss Porter fiddled with her glass and stared into space. "Blackberries," she said, wistfully.

There was no need to say more. The Deep South is not just a geographical area that comprises the southernmost tier of the United States. It is an entire way of life, a state of mind, an emotional attachment that endures wherever else one may find oneself.

As you journey into this region there is a palpable difference. The landscape has an added lushness. You are moving toward the sun's home track; sunrises and sunsets are less lingering, and you can smell the steaming earth. The passionate sense of life that goes with a hot climate is evident; faces are seldom placid, but openly humorous or narrow-eyed with suspicion. All of the fascinating contradictions of an immensely complex region manifest themselves here. This is a land where the alligator dozes beneath the gentlest rose; where the uncommon coral snake idles beneath the commonplace oak.

The pace of life and the approach to life are different here. There is a kind of friendliness and civility that goes beyond ordinary manners. It is

Boiled shrimp are a much-loved delicacy in the Mobile area, where the author of this book grew up. Shrimp boats like these, tied up in Snake Bayou, go far out in the Gulf of Mexico to trawl for their catch. Brought ashore, the shrimp are boiled with onions, lemon juice, mustard and coriander seeds, hot pepper and bay leaves, and are served with mugs of ice-cold beer.

a take-your-time, sit-down-and-enjoy-yourself attitude that makes almost every encounter an experience. People are more outgoing, more amusing and more amused. This is one place where the language is still alive, where talk is still one of life's principal pleasures. And when the talk is about food, it can be utterly beguiling.

My first stop on this journey back to my own roots was at Macon, Georgia, where I had an invitation to visit an old friend, Miss Charlotte Winn. When I turned into her street, Miss Charlotte was waiting on the front porch. She had divined the moment of my arrival. The long years of our separation vanished as if they had never been. She led the way into her kitchen, a huge square room lined with large white tiles; in it were an ancient iron-and-enamel gas stove and, in the middle of the room, a gray marble-topped table. Two windows opened onto the back porch, where the family dines in warm weather, a kind of green grotto completely latticed, screened and covered with asparagus fern.

In short order our conversation turned to Miss Charlotte's favorite foods and cooking techniques. "If you're talking about Southern food—cornbread and things like that," she began, "you have to insist on the importance of iron skillets." So saying, she glanced at a row of skillets in graduated sizes hanging against the tile wall, under a shelf of pots and pans. "These are all old ones, but about five years ago one of our big ones cracked and I had to replace it. I brought the new one home and cleaned it first with alcohol to get rid of factory grease, then I scrubbed it with a brush and soap and hot water. I never use abrasives or steel wool. The idea is to get it smooth as black silk. Then I rubbed it with oil for a day or so and let it sit. After that I filled it with potato peels and water and set it in a slow oven for a morning to temper it. Then I scrubbed it again and oiled it some more. After you use a skillet, you have to wash it carefully and dry it right away, and oil it and put it away. If you take care of it, it will treat you right. Real cornbread can only be made when the skillet is greased with bacon fat and heated before you put the batter into it."

"I hope you're going to make some cornbread," I suggested. But she was already lining up other ingredients and had taken down a large skillet and was obviously setting about to make something else.

"Anybody worth two cents can make cornbread, but not everybody can make an upside-down cake," she laughed. "The name alone always brings a smile and when Yankees are joking, enviously of course, about Southern food, they say 'cawn po-un' and 'upside dow-un cay-uk' in a way we Southerners never talk!"

I watched her. This part of interior Georgia is famous cake country —the variety of cakes at fairs and church bazaars is astonishing—and Miss Charlotte is a great cakemaker. But she hates sweet icings—"cavity finders," she says darkly—and she never uses confectioners' sugar, preferring unfrosted cakes that go well with black coffee.

"This skillet . . . well, feel it . . . with time it's developed a patina . . . I only *touch* a film of butter to it. I take 1½ cups of brown sugar dotted with little pea-sized bits of butter, maybe two tablespoons of butter in all, and spread this in the bottom of my skillet. On top of the sugar I put pineapple . . . or sometimes, just as often as not, I put in thick slices of crisp apple or slices of sand-pear sliced pear-wise. Now I beat up 1½ cups of sugar and 3 eggs, and add ½ cup of water and 1½ cups of pastry flour and mix it all up. Finally I put in 1½ teaspoons of baking powder, 1 teaspoon of vanilla, the faintest pinch of allspice and a pinch of salt. I pour this batter carefully into the pan over the fruit and sugar and bake it slowly for an hour."

While we waited for the upside-down cake to bake, we sat in the green grotto and discussed the coffee that would go with it.

"Southerners like stronger, blacker coffee," Miss Charlotte said. "I can't drink those weak brews that are like dishwater; I retch if I do. Maybe it's partially because of all the substitutes we had during The War, like parched sweet-potato peel, or parched this and parched that. I like it black, and strong. Also, maybe it's because very strong coffee goes so well with our very sweet desserts. How could you get through one of those devastating, marvelous pecan pies unless you had the contrast of strong coffee?"

She went to her broom, plucked out a straw, washed it under the hot tap and stuck it into the cake in the oven. "A few minutes more, and it will be ready," she murmured.

"I learned the secret of good coffee when I went to the Sorbonne for a year. Paris was full of Brazilians in those days before they were devalued or seized by a coup or whatever, and I noticed how they always drank coffee as a sleeping draught. My friend Carlos explained how they make it in coffee country. First of all, the blacker the coffee the more that means it has been roasted and the caffein has been almost cooked away. But the secret is in scouring the pot thoroughly the minute you've used it. But thoroughly. And once a week you rub it with lemon and put it in the sun. And you leave it out, open, all the parts exposed. It's traces of yesterday's coffee that keep you awake, not freshly made well-roasted coffee."

The asparagus ferns around us reached all the way to the lattice ceiling. As we sat waiting for the cake, small light-green lizards put their heads out to peer at us.

"Lizard, Lizard, show your money-bag," said Miss Charlotte, as we had all done when we were children. The lizard she addressed obediently puffed out the bright rose-colored air sacs on each side of his head. "They hate the radio, but if I whistle 'Summertime' or 'Deep Purple' they put their heads out and wave them from side to side."

By now the kitchen was full of a spicy baking smell, and Miss Charlotte took the skillet from the oven and turned it upside down on a serving plate. The rich, dark, golden-brown cake emerged with the yellow pineapple slices glistening on top. She busied herself making coffee and we then went to work on the cake. It was a magnificent organization of sugary sogginess, pineapple sweetness and warm spiciness.

Macon itself is a kind of outlandish town, where rowdy-dowdy neon-lit drive-ins and car-hop establishments conceal what seems to be a lineup of classical temples. The Doric style of architecture sits chockablock beside Corinthian in these grandiose houses, with now and then a bit of River-boat Gothic. But all the houses are white; all have verandahs—galleries they are called locally—for placid rocking and gossip.

Atlanta, 75 miles north as the crow flies, is a very different world. The old city that used to be the sentimental as well as the geographic heart of the South is now Boomtown, U.S.A. I didn't recognize a single street corner. The place is all new skyscrapers, fountains, windways and such a-buying and a-swapping of real estate as can't be believed. Atlantans smile as they tell you about their new skyscrapers linked by glassed-in skywalks at the 23rd floor. And still there are tales of people buying land 30 miles outside the city, expecting it to be part of midtown in two years as more and more Northern businesses move South.

I went to gawk at a new wonderland hotel, with a lobby rising to misty heights, rimmed by balconies with dripping greenery that climbed all the way to the glass ceiling. In the lobby on a huge square central support, glassed-in bird-cage elevators covered with little lights moved silently up and down. It was all very improbable, like the science-fiction illustrations in magazines of the 1930s.

Still, I found two hardy survivors of an older Atlanta era. One was an unpretentious restaurant called Mary Mac's Tea-Room. The service was friendly and old-fashioned, and Mary Mac herself, with no sense of haste or fret, showed people to tables and handed out menus. She was laconic about the merits of her place. "Well . . ." she smiled, "I eat here myself three times a day. I wouldn't serve you anything I wouldn't eat. . . ." I had one of the best chicken pies I have ever tasted; there was more chicken than sauce in it, and it had a good flaky crust. And one of the many good fresh vegetables offered as a side dish intrigued me mightily. It was a baked onion, cooked with honey and tomato sauce, the perfect accompaniment to the mild flavors of the chicken pie.

I also dined at a place called Aunt Fanny's Cabin. A cynical outsider might think this establishment the biggest put-on ever, but it's for real. Every blandishment of the you-all South is evident, from singing boy waiters to spirituals around the upright piano. A wood fire snaps in the fireplace, and the smell of barbecue cooking drifts in from the back yard. (The pit there is large enough for a whole steer.) The large pots bubble with amber-colored resin, and big sweet potatoes are wrapped in parchment, tossed in, and ladled out when they float to the surface. But hot breads are the giveaway that this is not all comic opera. And there really was an Aunt Fanny Williams, a black woman born in slave times, who lived to be 100 and was a true virtuoso of the kitchen. Her biscuit recipe still produces a triumph, although it was the thin crisp corncakes accompanying the ham and resin-cooked yams that most delighted me.

After Atlanta, I dillied in Jefferson, dallied in Eatonton. I looked in vain for old ice-cream parlors. I stopped at a roadside stand to buy green-tomato-and-pepper pickles and peach preserves. Where once there were farms, now all is grazing land with beautiful herds of Charolais everywhere. On my last lap toward Alabama and home, the rain came, falling steadily and monotonously straight down through the tall pines. But the warm wind was full of spring, and the roadsides a mass of yellow jessamine. The fields were rose-red clay and emerald; the clouds ink-blue or sepia. In this part of the world nothing is gray. Not even the Spanish moss; if you squint at it, it is silver-green or silver-mauve.

Opposite: Observing a familiar Southern rite, members of the Cowan family gather for their reunion on the Salem Camp Ground, a Methodist meeting area near Conyers, Georgia. Some 125 strong, the Cowan clan assembled from as far away as Cleveland, Ohio, for this get-together. Highlight of their reunion day is the buffet-style picnic lunch. Each family contributes its food specialties—loading the tables with *(front to rear)* spongecake, chicken salad, fried chicken, pickled beets, caramel cake, chicken pie, deviled eggs, rolls, fruit salad, more fried chicken, sandwiches, potato salad and iced tea. A blessing is offered by Dr. Zach Cowan, 84-year-old patriarch of the clan, and then the lavish feast begins.

135

At last the road led onto a bluff at Spanish Fort, looking out over Mobile Bay and the maze of creeks and bayous where Alabama's river system comes together: the Alabama, the Black Warrior, the Tombigbee. And there, below me after all these years, lay my home town.

Mobile's history is a tangled skein. Spanish seamen visited the Alabama coast as early as 1505, and reported home that "the people wear hats of solid gold and life is gay and luxurious." Not until 1559 was the first attempt made to colonize the area. Tristan de Luna and 1,500 settlers arrived to lay out a city on what is now Mobile Bay, having been driven west from the Pensacola area by a hurricane that destroyed their supply ships. Things went from bad to worse with them; their food supplies ran short, the colonizers fell to quarreling among themselves, and to cap matters De Luna lost his mind.

Meanwhile the English and French were exploring this part of the world and two brothers, Frenchmen who had amassed much wealth from landholdings in Canada, appeared on the scene. The older brother, Pierre Le Moyne, Sieur d'Iberville, established a colony at Biloxi in 1699; the younger, Jean Baptiste Le Moyne, Sieur de Bienville, established Fort Louis de la Louisiane (named for King Louis XIV) in 1702. On some maps the name appears as Fort Louis de la Tribu Mauvilla, which later became Fort Louis de la Mobile and ultimately just Mobile.

Two years after its founding the colony received a particularly welcome kind of reinforcement: the ship *Pelican* arrived from France not only with soldiers and supplies, but with 23 girls who had agreed to go to the New World to marry, each receiving in return from the King a *cassette,* or trunk, that contained a dowry including, it is said, a rosary and set of sewing needles. These spirited young women soon staged a petticoat rebellion against the coarse food they had to eat in their new homes, and their adamancy was the goad that produced the first real attempts to clear land and systematically plant food crops.

For 18 years the village on Mobile Bay was the capital of the vast French territory of Louisiana, reaching from the Gulf of Mexico to Canada, from the English colonies and Spanish Florida on the Atlantic to the Rocky Mountains. But in an era of rival expansionism frontiers wriggled like water moccasins, and lands changed hands so rapidly it is hard to remember who owned what and when. Only the torrential rains and torturing mosquitoes could be counted on with certainty. In 1763, with the end of the Seven Years' War, victorious England took over all of Louisiana east of the Mississippi, including Mobile. During the American Revolution, the town changed hands again. Lending George Washington a helping hand, the Spaniards in this part of the world successfully attacked the British garrison, and Spain's flag went up over Mobile again. It was not until the War of 1812 that the United States finally annexed the District of Mobile.

This off-again, on-again history no doubt contributed heavily to the strong tendency in the Mobilian's character to enjoy each day in its own right. Parades, masquerades and balls have always been an important part of the Mobile scene, and the Carnival preceding Lent is a period of revelry unbridled.

Opposite: Mary Branch, owner and chief cook of Mary's Place at Coden, Alabama, has built her reputation on such delicacies as baked crabs. After the crabs are boiled and shelled, she mixes the meat with milk-soaked bread, raw egg, bell pepper, onion, celery, garlic, Worcestershire and Louisiana hot sauce (a milder version of Tabasco). She then spoons this spicy stuffing back into the shells, bakes them briefly and serves the crabs piping hot.

I was pondering all this when I checked in at Mobile's old Battle House Hotel, which, in its time, has been frequented by everybody on earth from General Grant to Sarah Bernhardt. The same vaulted lobby remained, the same marble columns, even a few porters whose faces I knew from two decades earlier. Looking into the dining room, I saw some waiters I remembered, and got a whiff of good food.

But walking around downtown Mobile was less reassuring. I found the streets deserted. Entire blocks were empty lots, bulldozed; and on once-busy Royal Street I passed only two or three people. Bienville Square, with its live oaks and beds of budding azaleas, was so quiet that I could hear the birds singing.

"Where is everybody?" I asked aloud in panic.

I knew my grandmother's house had been torn down years earlier, but I decided to stroll over to an old quarter in the south part of town where I had lived briefly as a child, in a delightful old house which had once been a Spanish governor's residence as well as a prison. I crossed Government Street, after a brief browse amidst the old bottles, rare coins and sagging shelves of the Haunted Bookshop, and a block farther along discovered myself on a vast terrain of fresh earth that looked like a bomb site. The southern part of town was gone, and motels and neon signs obliterated the few residences that remained.

I felt the oddest pang of mingled regret and fury as I saw, far off across this flat stretch of earth, a building I seemed to know. I plodded across the rubble and, as I approached, realized that this was the house I'd lived in, sole survivor of the fervor of destruction. There it stood, picket fence enclosing the little patch of grass, magnolia tree green, windows shining clean even if the paint on the shutters was faded.

A caretaker stood on the steps. "How is it this house is still standing, when . . . ?" I waved at the emptiness about me to finish my sentence.

"The city planners," he replied, as if the phrase explained everything. "They have their offices here. They're building a tunnel under the river."

"But we already have a tunnel under the river," I cried.

"Ah," he said, "that tunnel was too small. Now we'll have a big one alongside it."

I mumbled something and walked on. I found myself next on Conception Street, looking at the wrought-iron gallery of another house I knew. A polished brass plate on the gate bore the family name HUGER. I rang, and it was as in a tale. The door opened, and there stood Miss Ruth Huger, whom I had not seen in exactly 23 years.

"Hello, Eugene, come on in," she said, as if only a day or so had passed. Inside the house all was as before, her charming sitting room still had its many books and its mid-19th Century French air. At Miss Ruth's and all over Mobile conversations were to pick up where I'd left them years earlier, a typical Southern form of courtesy which defies separation and the passage of time.

"I have something I've been keeping for you," Miss Ruth said. "I'll run get it." She returned in a moment with a book I had long searched for: *The Gulf City Cookbook,* compiled in 1878 by the Methodist Episcopal ladies of Mobile, a kind of kitchen First Folio of our city. "It's my mother's copy, with her corrections and additions. A treasure-trove." She had not known I was coming, nor had she known I was dredging for cookery facts and secrets. It was, indeed, as in a tale.

In the old days, Mobile had been known for its oyster bars, where the famous Bon Secour oysters from the bay were opened before you on zinc counters, served on trays of chipped ice and enjoyed fresh with lemon and horseradish. You ate your first nine oysters with only lemon, the last three with a bit of horseradish. Then, if you could manage, the second dozen were eaten the same way.

On this journey of rediscovery I found only one such place, in the waterfront section, rather dim and almost empty. I questioned the white-haired man behind the counter. His hands were fantastically rough and leathery (I looked for barnacles) and he opened the oysters with a little flick of his oyster knife.

"Still good fish hereabouts?"

"Oh, the bay is 'bout fished out," he said. "Lord, we did have good fish here. Regular sideshow of fish. Down by Middle Light the little shrimp don't have any place any more to eat sea stuff, because of the aluminum factory, paperworks—all of them wastes the factories flush into the bay. But funny thing is, the current takes all that mess along the west side of the bay, and so far the oyster beds over east there to Bon Secour haven't been ruined. Best oysters in the world . . . see, because they're fatter than most others. Not so big, but fatter.

"But fish, Lord . . . I'd have to sit down and think hard to remember all the kinds I've seen in the bay in my time: croakers, spots, flounder, Spanish mackerel, king mackerel, bluefish, pompano, white trout, speckled trout." He put some oysters on my tray, delicately scratched behind an ear with one finger, and went on: "Black drum, sheepshead, mullet, tarpon, pinfish, catfish, doctor fish, squid, ribbon fish, cigarfish, yellowtail, pilot fish, kingfish—oh, and dolphins a-plenty. Tiger sharks, hammerheads, shovelnoses, sand shark and dogfish. I like the black drum best. You know that fish? It hums, it has a way of making a humming sound; you get a shoal of them humming together under the water on a moonlit night and it can do something to you. The Indians thought it was the ghosts of them was drowned. A lot of them fish don't come in the bay now, they found someplace else to go. Shrimp won't be around much longer. . . ." He stopped and made a grunting little laugh. "So let's enjoy these oysters while we can." And he plunked another down on my tray.

There was one call that I felt I had to make in Mobile for the purpose of this book and for my own edification. Mayonnaise is ultraimportant in this part of the world as a sandwich spread, dressing for salads and ingredient for stuffed crabs, and the Mobile area boasts a famous mayonnaise-maker, Mrs. John Marston of Termite Hall.

In the old days her place used to be called Halfway House because it was precisely halfway between the courthouse in downtown Mobile and the Jesuit college out in Spring Hill. But in 1940 the floor of one of the parlors "gave," as they say here in Mobile, toppling the lady of the house into a pile of jam jars and wine bottles below, and suggesting the present name of the place.

Continued on page 142

In spring, Dossy Moon travels miles to collect branches of wild sassafras before their leaves turn tough and bitter.

The Key to a Celebrated Deep Southern Dish

For 20 years Dossy Moon of Bayou La Batre, Alabama, has been supplying his neighbors with filé powder to thicken that quintessential Deep South dish called gumbo. Made with all manner of vegetables and seafood, poultry or ham, this soup is popular year round. To achieve the proper glutinous consistency, it must be thickened with gumbo filé powder or—in summer—with okra. The filé powder is an invention of the Choctaw Indians. To prepare it Moon gathers leaves of the sassafras trees that grow wild *(above)* along the Gulf of Mexico. The pulverized leaves have a delicate flavor that suggests thyme or savory. Some filé powders are doctored with other herbs, but Moon bottles the classic kind: freshly ground and unadulterated.

During the summer Dossy Moon lets the sassafras branches dry slowly in his workhouse *(left)*. As they become brittle, he strips off the leaves and stows them in burlap sacks. Then, when he is ready to prepare the filé powder, he deposits the leaves in an oversized mortar he inherited from an old-time filé maker and pulverizes them with a long pestle. He sifts out the stems, then pounds and sifts the filé two more times. Finally, he funnels the powder into glass bottles *(above)*, colored green or brown to prevent the filé from bleaching out. Tightly corked, the bottles are ready for sale locally—for 65 cents apiece.

141

Later the necessary precautions against termites were taken and restoration begun. The old hollowed oak logs which had served as water conduits were replaced by metal. But the changes were not altogether precipitate. The dark wood-paneled dining room had always been candle-lit, because the family preferred it that way, and it was not until 1969 that electricity was introduced for a wedding. An opossum still lives on the third floor or in the attic (no one is certain where) and uses the main stairs for his entrances and exits. And a grandfather's clock on the landing, otherwise silent, chimes mysteriously once or twice a year, pealing almost 40 times on the last occasion. This is a house for joyful living; a place full of children, young people, animals.

Mrs. Marston, known as Mother West Wind from a character in a favorite children's book, is a great-grandmother, and doesn't find time to cook some of the old specialties she learned from her mother. But her mayonnaise and crullers are held in such esteem in the family that she must provide them at least once a week. I asked her about the mayonnaise, and she quickly set me straight.

"Well, first of all," said Mrs. Marston, a slow-drawling, white-haired lady with a silver-headed cane in one hand and an ivory-headed cane in the other, "let's call it by its right name. It is *sauce mahonaise,* like that. When France went to war against England, and the Maréchal de Richelieu captured Fort Saint Philip at Mahon on the Island of Minorca, in 1756, his cook was hard put to find supplies; there was no butter or cream on the island. So the cook invented a new sauce made of eggs and oil: *sauce mahonaise (Recipe Index).* And in our Creole cookbooks it appears like that. It's easy to make if you're patient; big quantities are easier than small. But we'll consider enough for a modern family meal.

"Don't be chintzy in buying the olive oil: get the very best. And you have to have two fresh eggs, still warm from the yard if you can arrange that. You need mustard and you need lemon. If you're making chicken salad, you will probably want tarragon vinegar or onion vinegar. Anyway, put two egg yolks and the yolk of a hard-boiled egg in a mixing bowl placed on a wadded-up cloth to hold it steady while you're beating. Mix them well with ½ teaspoon of sharp mustard powder, 2 pinches of salt, 1 tablespoon of lemon juice and a hint of cayenne. The secret of good *mahonaise* is in adding to the oil literally a drop at a time. You can use a medicine dropper. You need about a cup and a drop more of oil. You must beat the oil drop by slow drop by slow drop into the egg mixture. Never add more oil until the last has been completely mixed in. Toward the end, you can add half a spoonful at a time. You should arrive at a very stiff glossy yellow sauce, almost like a custard.

"You can turn this into tartar sauce—wonderful with fried fish or stuffed crabs—by adding a lot of finely chopped chives, capers, parsley, dill or tarragon if you have it. Finely chopped dill pickles go well. In the south of France they make a rich *mahonaise* with tons of garlic juice in it, sometimes even chopped garlic, but I like the juice better. They call it *aïoli,* from *ail,* the French for garlic. But our cooks in the old days heard the name as High Holy *mahonaise* and we call it that, too. On a hot summer day there's no better dish than plain boiled shrimp, cold crisp cucumbers, and a big blop of High Holy. You have to peel the cucumbers and draw long runnels lengthwise down them with the tines of a fork. Then chill them in ice water heavily salted for two hours to take the meanness out. A dash of Tabasco is good in *mahonaise,* and finely scraped horseradish prepared in white wine vinegar gives a delightful flavor. Green *mahonaise* is wonderful: capers and chives and every green herb you have in your garden—including nasturtium seeds and stems—chopped fine and mixed in."

After my visit to Termite Hall, I looked up my old friends Gertrude and Robert Hunter, who asked me to save a night in Mobile for good gossip and cold cuts at their house. When I saw a number of cars parked along the road in the Spring Hill section where they live I asked somebody what was going on and was told, "Oh, there must be something at the college tonight."

I drove into the front garden (immediately noticing the absence of a great magnolia, blown down in the most recent hurricane) and around to the side entrance. I was led into a glassed-in verandah on the side, and Robert poured a whiskey for me, saying Gertrude was still primping at the mirror and would be right down. Two delightful children were brought in to be introduced. Robert's mother, Miss Caroline, appeared on the scene and we chatted. All the while, Robert kept smiling and glancing over his shoulder. Then, at last, Gertrude, who once was Queen of the Mobile Carnival, floated in, all chiffon and full of last-minute directions to the household staff.

She turned a dazzling smile on me. "Are you ready?"

"Ready for what?"

"Well," she giggled. "This is your life. . . ." And she opened a door and pushed me into the beautiful long living room with the family portraits by Sully, and now containing just about everybody I had ever known. My childhood friends, my favorite teacher, cousins of cousins, all my past. For a moment I didn't know whether to laugh or cry . . . or swing on the chandelier. I was staggered. Robert promptly shoved a double whiskey at me, and the rout took shape. We relived ancient history, I met a whole new generation, the decibel count noticeably rose. Miss Caroline and the children, sternly faithful to 8:30 dining, vanished to another verandah and began their dinner. Then Gertrude said, "Cold cuts are ready . . . but first have some hot gumbo."

In the dining room a table was laid, with all the heavy old silver gleaming in the candlelight. An enormous silver bowl full of shrimp and oyster gumbo was at one end of this table, and the smell of it almost made me faint. I had not smelled this authentic Mobile gumbo for more than two decades, but like a magic potion it sloughed off all those years in a whiff. Being the first course, it was not so chock-full of things as it would have been as a main dish. But it was a superbly flavored bisquelike liquid in which crowds of fat oysters and fat pink shrimp swam indolently. I could make out bay leaf, onion, tomato, red pepper, gumbo filé powder—the rest was a tantalizing mystery.

The "cold cuts" turned out to be an enormous baked ham, a smoked turkey, a rolled veal roast (marjoram, vermouth and bread crumbs had gone into the rolling) and a bowl of green salad. The ham was an Alabama country ham, rosy and succulent. The turkey was firm-fleshed and not overcooked, the meat impregnated with the spicy smokehouse flavor. Hot biscuits came constantly from the kitchen, and there was a beautiful dry American rosé wine.

As the evening progressed I realized that even if the city of Mobile as I knew it had vanished, my friends had not. We spoke of Carnival, of food and gardening, of larks and outings a quarter of a century ago, with all that love of the past re-evoked and retold in the Southern manner. There were so many offers of recipes, and of dishes to be tasted, that I knew that I must either settle down to an encyclopedia on Mobile cookery alone, or make my escape. I hated the thought of going; there were cousins and friends I had not seen, and the azaleas and camellias were in an outrageous riot and demonstration of color, but I had miles to go before completing my investigations for this book.

And so, all but killed with kindness and nostalgia, I turned from Mobile at last and reluctantly headed west. Mississippi was next, and I drove straight across the bottom of the state, through pine-tree and red-clay country toward the romantic old town of Natchez, high on a bluff over-looking the Mississippi River.

Originally settled by the French, then acquired by the English as a prize of war, Natchez became a kind of "fourteenth colony," Tory in character, but luxury-loving and exuberant in style. Shipping orders and bills of lading from the period include such items as "faint blue writing-paper," "otto of roses," the best white silk stockings for men, the best watered-silk ribbons for ladies, Spanish "segars" and London porter.

When cotton became the South's lifeblood in the early 19th Century, Natchez—because of its location on the lower Mississippi—quickly developed into a flourishing port. The cotton bales were shipped to England and France in exchange for manufactured goods. A new prosperity ensued. Town houses and plantation houses proliferated like mushrooms. The pillared porticoes grew taller and taller, flying stairways grander, rooms bigger. The opulence was European in origin, but the enthusiasm was unmistakably American. By 1832 town lots of Natchez had a greater value than all the rest of the land in Mississippi. Meanwhile, along the river bank flourished Natchez-under-the-Hill, a rowdy, scrabbling lot of whores, bandits, gamblers, river-pilots and gentlemen out to raise hell.

This town was a good proving ground for all that is self-consciously eccentric in the Southern nature. In one household cups of coffee were sweetened with sugared pecans. In another, silence was ordained until each member of the family had consumed the morning cup of chocolate, then a bell rang and conversation was allowed to begin. Duels were the order of the day along with "thousand-candle balls."

Natchez' fortunes were tied to cotton, and when that crop went into a decline, so did the old river port. The town was spared during The War; in fact General Ulysses Grant set up headquarters there—"right in Mama's bedroom!" as a wide-eyed old Natchez lady told me years ago. But in the long, slow, unsettled years after The War, the cotton ran out, the money ran out, the houses ran down, gardens turned to jungles and

Natchez "just plain slowed to a halt." In an effort to keep the houses together, the remnants of old families sometimes closed all but one or two rooms and lived in them, perfect illustrations of a Southern class described as "too poor to paint, too proud to whitewash."

The tide did not begin to turn until 1931, when the Mississippi State Federation of Garden Clubs held its annual meeting in Natchez. There had been a freeze that year, the gardens that had managed to survive to that point were all blighted and the customary garden tour was impossible. A tour of the old houses was hastily arranged instead, and it yielded a providential surprise. Somehow the gilt and mirrors, fine furniture and exuberant decorations were still there. A little faded perhaps, a little peeling, but it had all survived.

An irrepressible lady named Mrs. Balfour Miller pounced like a leopardess. A Natchez belle, partygoer, constant talker and idea-spinner, she had been looking for years for a channel for her great energies. Already she had restored Hope Farm, the old Spanish governor's house, reterraced and replanted the gardens. Elected president of a Natchez garden club, she pushed forward a scheme for a "pilgrimage of houses," under which all the old mansions would be open for a week and the admission charges would be used to put the houses themselves in order.

"Katherine has a whim of iron," her friends in Natchez said. They got together under her leadership and enlisted the entire population of the town, black and white, toward planning this spring tour of houses. Natchez had only one natural asset, its past, and they intended to make it pay.

When Pilgrimage Week came, the ladies of Natchez tied sun hats of fresh flowers on every lamppost, put on their hoopskirts and poured themselves double bourbons to carry them through the fray. It was the middle of the Depression, but Depression or no, the public streamed in, and the affair was a great success. Then, as the years went by, quarrels developed between rival factions of the garden club over division of money and planning of events. The dispute rose to comic-opera heights, with screaming ladies, injunctions, baffled judges, lawsuits and countersuits, and garden club members fleeing town to avoid subpoenas. After some years of rivalry, a truce was arranged by a local judge who expressed the fear that the disputants might, after all, be strangling the goose that had laid the golden egg. Formal ratification came in 1947. As Harnett Kane reported in his delightful book, *Natchez on the Mississippi,* Mrs. Melchior Beltzhoover, president of the Pilgrimage Garden Club, publicly bowed to Mrs. Homer Whittington, head of the Natchez Garden Club, who bowed back. Tears of relief flowed on every side; the Confederate Ball, the original highlight of Pilgrimage Week, was resumed, and Kane was moved to observe that it made him more hopeful that the United Nations might work.

I was in Natchez before the Pilgrimage began. But the local people were already rehearsing the polka for the Confederate Ball, where every male wears a general's uniform, and every young lady, of course, is a Southern belle. A charming guide told me there was one house I could see, because some documentary film makers were working there that day and the owner was on hand. She scribbled an address, and I went off to a

beautiful high-verandahed house with matching curved stairs ("crab claws" they are called because of their shape) that sweep dramatically up to the first floor. At the foot of one stairway stood a dazzling strawberry blonde in a pale-yellow hoopskirt and a picture hat with two long yellow ribbons hanging down to the ground. She had a puncher in hand and was punching holes in a camphor leaf.

"Hey," she said in a breathless voice. "Glad y'all could come. You have a ticket? I'm supposed to punch it."

"Only this note," I replied. "To the lady of the house."

"Oh, well," said the belle. "I reckon I'll just punch that."

I went in, found the lady of the house to be an older version of the belle outside, and commented on this resemblance. "That's my daughter Alma," the lady said. "Come on in." She showed me through a series of delightful rooms with bouquets of daffodils and camellias, pleasant colors and a mixture of furniture styles: 18th Century English "brought over first to Virginia, then brought out here," French Empire and lots of gilt ("so pretty in firelight and candlelight; those chairs look like they're *dancing*"). There were lots of pictures and unexpected gimcracks: a frontier rifle in a glass case with Sèvres porcelain, a mother-of-pearl fan signed by Jenny Lind and a rough wooden doll in a silk costume. But I wanted to ask about food and drink.

"Well," said my hostess, adjusting a lace mitt, "you have to remember that this is pecan country, the tree is native to Mississippi and Alabama, and all those Indians of the Muskogean group, the Chickasaw, the Natchez and the Choctaw all used them in every possible way. They were called pecawns, peccans, Illinois nuts, Mississippi nuts, Natchez nuts, you can find a hundred names for them. They ground them up and added them to stewed meat, or used them along with beans, or roasted them and took them along to eat on hunting trips. I tell you frankly," she smiled a secretive smile, "I wish I had a dollar for every pecan I've eaten. I'd be richer than Rockefeller."

At this point Alma was summoned and appeared shortly, tilting her hoopskirt to one side to pass through the door. "Alma will get you a drink," my hostess said, and Alma left to accomplish this mission.

"Like all the South," the lady went on, "we lived high on the hog in the old days, and were plenty glad to get collards and pones in the bad times. Now we're back up a little. We might not have the whole hog; we do have an occasional ham."

The lady spoke fondly of glazed pecans, orange-glazed pecans, pecan pie, bread made from ground pecans and no flour, fowl of all kinds stuffed with a bread-sausage-and-pecan mixture, and how one should be careful in toasting pecans in butter to take them off the fire before they are too dark, because "they go on cooking in their own fat, inside themselves." She explained that the pecans should only be salted after they have been cooked, and she added a word of warning. "You'll find you can't stop eating them," she said. "They'll make a slave of you."

Alma returned with a little tray and a bourbon highball for me. When she held it out, her mother stopped, staring, a salted pecan halfway to her lips. Suddenly she screamed. I looked behind me, but the lady was star-

Opposite: In Mobile, lawn parties fill the social calendar during the mild autumn months. Nowhere is the setting grander or more gracious than at Palmetto Hall. Built in 1846, this historic house is now privately owned—and lovingly preserved—by Mr. and Mrs. Jay P. Altmeyer. In the garden by a statue of Cupid, guests Beverly Stanky *(foreground)* and Judy Carter sample a Mobile party standby, creamed oysters in patty shells.

Continued on page 150

The South's hot summers inspire a variety of cooling dishes. This tempting luncheon comprises, from left to right, vegetable

aspic, a chicken salad, Sally Lunn buns and peppermint stick ice cream—accompanied by minted iced tea *(Recipe Index)*.

ing at Alma's hands. Alma had long fingernails, and she had carefully punched a hole in each one with her puncher.

"Alma!" gasped her mother. "Why'd you do that?"

"Oh, well," smiled Alma, looking out from under her two-foot hat brim, "I got tired of waiting. I had to punch *something.*"

All through Mississippi and north Louisiana one notes fine beef cattle and well-tended pasturage where 20 years ago there were vegetable crops or cotton. The Mississippi River is off there somewhere, but this is flat land; one must go right to the banks to see it. I wanted to have another close look at the great muddy father of waters, and so I drove through an orchard of tall pecan trees, then through marshy flatlands to arrive at a bank littered with dead branches deposited by the current. I thought of the old river steamers and races such as the one between the *Morning Star* and the *Queen of the West* (immortalized in the famous Currier & Ives print). The captain of the winning *Morning Star* credited his success to the fact that he had left ashore all excess weight, including his kid gloves and the gilded ornaments on the stackbrace. The riverboats had famous dining rooms; their hot biscuits and inky coffee were legend. The captain was a real friend for the people in the river towns to cultivate: he could be counted on to bring from New Orleans a basket of oranges, a case of fine rum, a cashmere shawl or a wedding ring—whatever was needed. In the early years he brought white flour to river landings where only cornmeal was known.

The wildly romantic South of bygone days that took its pitch from Walter Scott's chivalrous romances can easily be conjured here when you come upon four huge Corinthian columns rising from brick rubble at the end of a long weed-choked carriage drive. Close by, in the middle of a deserted cotton field, stand two very high chimneys, with weeds springing from their tops.

The Spanish moss is everywhere on the east side of the river, and then, suddenly, when you cross into Arkansas, it is nowhere to be seen. Arkansas was the surprise of my safari, the unknown state. It is three or four worlds in one. The part bordering on Louisiana is all deepest Deep South. This is true even though some of the plantations are only two generations old, diesel tractors have replaced the mules, and overhead small planes belch noxious clouds of boll-weevil poison. In the western part of Arkansas you suddenly see ten-gallon hats and rancher's boots and the beginning of those endless miles of plains that go on forever. But in the northwestern part of the state the apple orchards and wheat fields make one think of the Middle West. And the greatest surprise of all for me was Hot Springs, a world apart from the rest of the state, a wild operetta fantasy of a town, recalling both Italian mineral spas and American country clubs of the 1920s. The bathhouses are in an Italianate style, with formal gardens and parks, perhaps the influence of the Chicago gangsters who frequented the town.

In the last half-century Arkansas has become an important poultry-farming center, supplying enormous amounts of broilers and eggs for distant markets, and a major producer of fruits and vegetables. Peaches and apples, white and sweet potatoes, vast acres of spinach and tomatoes grow here. Every farm has melons, but Hempstead County leads the way; a watermelon weighing 195 pounds has been reported. And, of course, Arkansas means rice, a crop that grows in the swampy lowlands southeast of Little Rock, between the Arkansas and Mississippi Rivers.

Arkansas also means fishing and hunting. Its spectacular lakes and winding streams abound in black bass and catfish. The hills that rise gently from the east, reaching blue heights as one goes farther west, still teem with game and wildfowl.

All through the South people had spoken to me of Stuttgart, Arkansas, and the region around there as a duck-hunter's paradise. I had met men in the Carolinas and on the Gulf Coast who went regularly to Arkansas for duck shooting.

Not surprisingly, I ran into all sorts of theories as to how this delicious bird should be prepared. One hunter I encountered said he simply picks off the feathers, splits the duck down the back, cleans it, then rubs it with salt, pepper, a mixture of bacon fat and butter and cooks it over a hot fire 3½ minutes on one side and the same time on the other.

A housewife in Little Rock suggested a completely different way of preparing the bird. She informed me that the way to get rid of the duck's gamy taste—if you object to it—is to clean the bird, then soak it in salt water for an hour before cooking it. After that she rubs it with salt, pepper and a little powdered ginger. She stuffs the bird with a slice of apple, a small onion stuck with six or eight cloves and a blade of mace. Then she covers it with strips of bacon and bastes it with a mixture of red wine, hot water and blackberry or currant jam, and cooks it in the oven.

A doctor in Pascagoula, Mississippi, told me most emphatically that "the game should not have fancy stuffings, and should have very few spices or such. It is the duck's own flavor that counts, and whatever you add should only be to point up that flavor. This applies especially to the canvasback, which feeds on wild celery, and is the most delicately flavored of all wildfowl." Normally this man does not stuff his ducks, but bastes them with bacon fat, muscadine, port or sherry. He does, though, make a concession for ducks that have a fishy flavor or are gamy. He rubs the inside of these birds with fresh sage leaves, and puts lemon or orange slices in them along with a handful of blanched cranberries. The worst sin, according to the doctor, is to cook the duck until it is dry. The right way, he explained, is to cook it "just until the blood will not run when you stick a fork into the flesh."

In Arkansas I might have gone on talking about ducks indefinitely, but I was hurrying to a rendezvous with friends in Stuttgart who had promised me some catfish. To a Deep Southerner, black or white, the very word catfish sets up a chain reaction of associations, all pleasurable. It brings to mind whichever pond or stream or bayou or "crik" or branch or reservoir was the scene of one's first encounter with this ugly but irresistible monster —lacking in scales but equipped with feline whiskers (barbels, really) that can pierce a man's hand.

The time to catch catfish is that moment of intense stillness after sunset, with the rosy afterglow not yet gone and the very woods seeming to hold their breath. Later a little breeze breaks the spell, accenting the smell of the wood fire which has been built to cook the catfish and their faithful Southern equerries, the hush puppies. Then comes the sweet white flesh of a channel catfish in its light golden casing of water-ground cornmeal . . . ah, me!

Catfish are always skinned before cooking. It's not hard to do, but you have to be careful not to get stuck by one of the "whiskers." Once the head is severed the skin can be pulled right off. Then the fish is fried, whole, filleted or sliced into steaks (Recipe Index); or it is cut into chunks to make a catfish stew (Recipe Index). The tastiest of the catfish tribe, the channel catfish, prefers clear running water, a gravel-bottomed river or a large lake with clear pools and currents. The bullhead cat thrives in any water, even sluggish ponds and bayous.

In the last few years people on both sides of the Mississippi, with its vast network of tributaries, have begun to be nervous about eating catfish, in view of the increasing pollution of waters, the scavenging habits of the catfish, and the incident a few years ago when the lower Mississippi was clogged with the bodies of catfish that had died from ingesting minute quantities of an insecticide called endrin. So now there is a new wrinkle —catfish farms. Fingerling catfish are brought in from untainted lakes and put into sweet-water ponds where they are fed on high-protein commercial feeds. One of the pioneer catfish farmers is Edgar ("Chip") Farmer of Dumas, Arkansas, in the delta country near the junction of the Mississippi and Arkansas Rivers. He began 12 years ago with a dozen or so channel catfish in some ponds he had created in his rice fields on a 3,000-acre plantation. Those cats became his brood stock for one of the largest catfish operations in the United States. He made $55,000 his first year, selling ready-to-eat catfish to the catfish restaurants that have sprung up in the mid-South, as well as live fingerlings to stock fresh-water lakes in Missouri and other parts of the country. Now his annual income is over $400,000.

Other catfish farms have been established and the market is expanding. Japan, France and Latin American countries have placed orders for live fingerlings, and Little Rock is the headquarters of a newly formed Association of Catfish Farmers of America (they number over 500), which expects the catfish market to build in little time to a scale now enjoyed by trout and shrimp.

Impressive statistics these, but as I went to my friends' house in Stuttgart I had more immediate considerations in mind. I had not tasted fried catfish since I left Alabama many years ago. I rang the doorbell, the door opened, and a well-remembered aroma enchanted me.

I managed to get through a bourbon and water and tried not to seem hungry, but I was ready to stampede to the dinner table. We took our seats and a platter of golden trophies appeared. I dived in, starting with two small fish and I don't dare say how many hush puppies. I took a sip of cold white wine, and I lifted the first forkful of sweet white meat to my mouth. There was that authentic, unlike-any-other-fish taste. My hosts looked at me, awaiting some word.

"I will need," I said through a hush puppy, "a drooling-bib and a tear bottle here and now, and stretcher service afterwards."

Opposite: "Take two and butter them while they're hot" is the catch phrase with which hospitable Southerners introduce the hot biscuits appearing on their tables. These classic baking-powder biscuits are quick and easy to make (Recipe Index). Crisp on the outside and feathery light inside, they are a welcome addition to any meal.

CHAPTER VI RECIPES

To make one 10-inch loaf

¼ cup lukewarm water (110° to 115°)
1 package active dry yeast
1 tablespoon plus ¼ cup sugar
4 to 4½ cups flour
2 teaspoons salt
¾ cup lukewarm milk (110° to 115°)
3 eggs
12 tablespoons butter, softened and cut into ½-inch bits, plus 2 tablespoons butter, softened

Sally Lunn

Pour the lukewarm water into a small bowl and sprinkle the yeast and 1 tablespoon of the sugar over it. Let the mixture rest for 3 minutes, then mix. Set the bowl in a warm, draft-free place (such as an unlighted oven) for 10 minutes, or until the mixture almost doubles in volume.

Combine 4 cups of the flour, the remaining ¼ cup of sugar and the salt and sift them together into a deep bowl. Make a well in the center and into it pour the yeast, lukewarm milk and eggs. With a wooden spoon, gradually incorporate the dry ingredients into the liquid ones and stir until smooth. Beat in the 12 tablespoons of butter bits, a little at a time, and beat until the dough can be gathered into a compact ball. Place the dough on a lightly floured surface and knead by pushing it down with the heels of your hands, pressing it forward and folding it back on itself. As you knead, work in up to ½ cup more flour, sprinkling it over the dough and adding only enough to make a firm dough. Knead for about 15 minutes, or until the dough is smooth, shiny and elastic.

With a pastry brush, spread 1 tablespoon of softened butter over the inside of a large bowl. Drop in the dough and turn it about to butter the entire surface. Drape the bowl with a kitchen towel and place it in the draft-free place for about 30 minutes, or until it doubles in volume.

Brush the remaining tablespoon of softened butter over the bottom and sides of a 10-inch Turk's-head mold. Punch the dough down with a single blow of your fist. Then shape it into a ball and place it in the buttered mold. Drape with a towel and set aside in the draft-free place for about 1 hour, or until the loaf doubles in bulk.

Preheat the oven to 350°. Bake in the middle of the oven for 45 to 50 minutes, or until the bread is golden brown. Turn the bread out of the mold and rap the bottom with your fingertips. If it does not sound hollow, return it to the mold and bake for 5 to 10 minutes longer. Turn the bread out on a wire cake rack and serve warm or at room temperature.

NOTE: If you prefer, Sally Lunn may be baked in muffin tins. Prepare the dough as described above and let it rise once. Brush 1 tablespoon of butter evenly over the inside surfaces of 16 three-inch muffin tin cups. Then punch the dough down, divide it into 16 equal portions and shape each of these into a small ball. Place the balls in the buttered muffin cups, drape with a towel and set them aside in a draft-free place for about 45 minutes, or until they double in bulk. Bake in the middle of a preheated 350° oven for 40 to 45 minutes, or until golden brown. Turn the buns out on a wire cake rack and serve warm or at room temperature.

To make 1½ quarts

6 ounces peppermint stick candy, 3 ounces pulverized in a blender or finely crushed with a rolling pin and 3 ounces finely chopped
½ cup sugar
1 quart heavy cream
1½ teaspoons vanilla extract

Peppermint Stick Candy Ice Cream

Combine the pulverized peppermint stick candy, the sugar and 1 cup of the cream in a heavy 1½- to 2-quart saucepan. Then set the pan over low heat and stir until the sugar dissolves completely. Remove the pan from the heat and stir in the vanilla extract and the remaining 3 cups of cream. Refrigerate the cream mixture until it is thoroughly chilled.

Pack a 2-quart ice-cream freezer with layers of finely crushed or cracked ice and coarse rock salt in the proportions recommended by the manufacturers, adding cold water if the directions call for it.

If you have a hand ice-cream maker, fill it with the ice-cream mixture, and let it stand for 3 or 4 minutes. Then turn the handle, starting slowly at first, and crank continuously for a few minutes. Add the chopped peppermint stick candy and continue to crank for 10 minutes longer. Do not stop turning or the ice cream may be lumpy. When the handle can barely be moved, the ice cream is ready to serve. If you wish to keep it for an hour or two, remove the lid and dasher. Scrape the ice cream off the dasher and pack it firmly in the container. Cover securely, pour off any water in the bucket and repack the ice and salt solidly around it.

If you have an electric ice-cream maker, fill the can with the ice-cream mixture, cover the can, turn it on and let it churn for about 5 minutes. Add the chopped candy, cover again and continue to churn for 10 minutes longer, or until the motor slows or actually stops. Serve the ice cream immediately or follow the procedure above to keep it for an hour or two.

Lacking an ice-cream maker, pour the ice-cream mixture and chopped candy into 2 ice-cube trays without their dividers, spreading it evenly. Freeze for about 6 hours, stirring every 30 minutes or so and scraping into it the ice particles that form around the edges of the tray.

Tightly covered, the ice cream may safely be kept in the freezer for several weeks. Before serving, place it in the refrigerator for 20 or 30 minutes to let it soften slightly so that it can be easily served.

Summertime Vegetable Aspic

Combine the tomatoes, onions, celery leaves, parsley sprigs, bay leaf and ¼ cup of cold water in a 3- to 4-quart enameled or stainless-steel saucepan and bring to a boil over high heat, stirring from time to time. Reduce the heat to low and simmer partially covered for 30 minutes, or until the vegetables are very soft. Strain the contents of the pan through a fine sieve set over a bowl, pressing down on the vegetables and herbs with the back of a spoon to extract their juices before discarding them.

Meanwhile, pour the remaining ¼ cup of cold water into a small heatproof bowl and sprinkle the gelatin over it. When the gelatin has softened for 2 or 3 minutes, set the bowl in a skillet of simmering water and cook over low heat, stirring constantly, until the gelatin dissolves completely.

Stir the dissolved gelatin into the vegetable juices, add the lemon juice, salt and a few grindings of black pepper, and taste for seasoning. Refrigerate until the mixture begins to thicken and is syrupy. Then stir in the cabbage, celery, green pepper, carrot, parsley and pimiento.

Rinse a 3-cup mold under cold running water and invert it to drain. Pour the vegetable aspic mixture into the mold, cover with foil or plastic wrap and refrigerate for at least 4 hours, or until firm to the touch.

To unmold and serve the aspic, run a thin-bladed knife around the edges of the mold to loosen the sides and dip the bottom briefly in hot water. Place an inverted serving plate over the mold and, grasping plate and mold together firmly, turn them over. Rap the plate sharply on a table and the vegetable aspic should slide out easily.

To serve 4 to 6

9 medium-sized firm ripe tomatoes (about 3 pounds), washed, cored and coarsely chopped
2 medium-sized onions, peeled and coarsely chopped
½ cup coarsely chopped celery leaves
2 fresh parsley sprigs
1 small bay leaf
½ cup cold water
4 teaspoons unflavored gelatin
1 tablespoon strained fresh lemon juice
2 teaspoons salt
Freshly ground black pepper
1 cup finely shredded cabbage
½ cup coarsely chopped celery
⅓ cup finely chopped green pepper
1 medium-sized carrot, scraped and cut crosswise into ⅛-inch-thick slices
2 tablespoons finely chopped fresh parsley
1 tablespoon finely chopped pimiento

Flaunting their fillings are five open-faced, single-crust pies favored in the South. From top left clockwise: black bottom pie, named for its base of chocolate custard under layers of rum custard and whipped cream; sweet-potato pie; orange meringue pie; pecan pie and peach pie. For recipes, see the Recipe Index.

To serve 6 to 8

A 4-pound fresh beef tongue
2 cups distilled white vinegar
1 cup dry red wine
1 cup dark brown sugar
2 medium-sized onions, peeled and
  cut into ¼-inch-thick slices
1 medium-sized garlic clove, peeled
  and cut crosswise into ⅛-inch-
  thick slices
1 tablespoon dry mustard
1 teaspoon crumbled dried thyme
1 tablespoon salt

To serve 6 to 8

CHICKEN SALAD
Two 3- to 3½-pound chickens,
  each cut into 6 to 8 pieces
1 small onion, peeled and cut into
  ¼-inch-thick slices
1 medium-sized carrot, scraped and
  cut into ¼-inch-thick slices
½ cup coarsely chopped celery
  leaves
3 sprigs fresh parsley
2 tablespoons salt
10 whole black peppercorns
4 hard-cooked eggs, finely chopped
1 cup finely chopped celery
½ cup finely chopped scallions,
  including 3 inches of the green
  tops
¼ cup strained fresh lemon juice

BOILED DRESSING
3 tablespoons sugar
1 tablespoon flour
1 teaspoon dry mustard
1 teaspoon salt
½ cup distilled white vinegar
½ cup water
1 tablespoon butter
2 eggs, lightly beaten

Mobile Thyme Tongue

With a small sharp skewer, pierce completely through the beef tongue in at least a dozen places. Then set the tongue aside in an enameled casserole just large enough to hold it comfortably.

Combine the vinegar, wine, sugar, onions, garlic, mustard, thyme and salt in a 2-quart saucepan. Bring to a boil over high heat, stirring until the sugar and mustard dissolve. Immediately pour over the tongue and turn the meat about to moisten it evenly. Refrigerate uncovered and when the marinade is cool, cover the casserole with its lid. Let the tongue marinate in the refrigerator for 24 hours, turning it over two or three times.

Preheat the oven to 300°. Bring to a boil, then cover the casserole with a double thickness of foil and set its lid in place. Bake the tongue in the middle of the oven for 2½ to 3 hours, or until it shows no resistance when pierced deeply with a fork. While it is still hot, skin the tongue and cut away the fat, bone and gristle at its base.

If you plan to serve the tongue hot, transfer it to a heated platter. Skim and discard as much fat as possible from the surface of the cooking liquid, then strain the liquid through a fine sieve into a small bowl. Taste for seasoning, and present the sauce in a sauceboat with the tongue.

If you plan to serve the tongue cold, let it cool to room temperature in the cooking liquid; refrigerate until ready to serve. Carve the tongue and arrange the slices on a chilled platter. Skim and strain the cooking liquid and serve it separately. Mobile thyme tongue is frequently accompanied by watermelon-rind pickles *(Recipe Index)*.

Southern Chicken Salad with Boiled Dressing

Combine the chicken, onion, carrot, celery leaves, parsley, 2 tablespoons of salt and the peppercorns in a heavy 4- to 5-quart casserole and pour in enough water to immerse the chicken completely. Bring to a boil over high heat, reduce the heat to low and simmer partially covered for 30 to 40 minutes, or until the chicken is tender but not falling apart.

With tongs or a slotted spoon, transfer the chicken to a platter or cutting board. (Strain the cooking liquid through a fine sieve, pressing down hard on the vegetables with the back of a spoon before discarding them. Reserve the stock for another use.) Remove the skin and bones from the chicken and discard them. Cut the meat into 1-inch pieces and place them in a serving bowl. Add the eggs, celery, scallions and lemon juice and with a wooden spoon toss together gently but thoroughly. Cover with foil or plastic wrap and refrigerate until ready to serve.

Meanwhile, prepare the boiled dressing in the following fashion: In a small enameled or stainless-steel saucepan, mix the sugar, flour, mustard and 1 teaspoon of salt together. With a wire whisk, stir in the vinegar, water and butter and cook over moderate heat, whisking constantly until the mixture comes to a boil and thickens lightly. Stir 1 or 2 tablespoonfuls of the simmering liquid into the beaten eggs, then pour the heated eggs into the saucepan and whisk until smooth. With a rubber spatula, transfer the dressing to a bowl and let it cool to room temperature.

Just before serving, pour the boiled dressing over the chicken mixture and stir until all the pieces of chicken and vegetables are evenly moistened.

Black Bottom Pie

Preheat the oven to 375°. To prepare the crust, combine the pulverized gingersnaps and melted butter in a 9-inch pie tin and stir until all the crumbs are moistened. Spread the crumb mixture in the bottom of the tin. Place another 9-inch pie tin over the crumbs and press it down firmly to spread the crust mixture evenly in the bottom and sides of the first tin. Remove the second tin and smooth the top edges of the crust with your fingers. Bake in the middle of the oven for 8 to 10 minutes, or until the crust is delicately colored. Set aside and cool to room temperature.

Meanwhile, prepare the custard and chocolate layer in the following fashion: Pour the cold water into a small heatproof bowl and sprinkle the gelatin over it. When the gelatin has softened for 2 or 3 minutes, set the bowl in a skillet of simmering water and, stirring constantly, cook over low heat until the gelatin dissolves completely. Remove the skillet from the heat, but leave the bowl in the water to keep the gelatin fluid.

In a heavy 2- to 3-quart saucepan, heat the milk until small bubbles begin to form around the edges of the pan. Remove from the heat and cover to keep warm. With a wire whisk or a rotary or electric beater, beat the egg yolks, ½ cup of sugar, cornstarch and a pinch of salt for 3 to 4 minutes, or until the yolks thicken slightly. Beating constantly, pour in the hot milk in a thin stream, then pour the mixture into the saucepan.

Place the pan over low heat and, stirring constantly and deeply with a wooden spoon, simmer for 10 to 12 minutes, or until the custard is thick enough to coat the spoon lightly. Do not allow the mixture to come anywhere near the boiling point or it may curdle. Remove the pan from the heat and stir in the dissolved gelatin.

Melt the 3 ounces of chocolate in a small heavy pan over low heat, stirring constantly. Measure 1 cup of the custard into a bowl and set the rest aside. Stirring the custard in the bowl constantly, slowly pour in the melted chocolate and, when it is completely incorporated, add the vanilla. Pour the chocolate-layer mixture into the cooled pie shell, spreading it and smoothing the top with a rubber spatula. Refrigerate for at least 1 hour, or until the chocolate layer is firm to the touch.

With a whisk or beater, beat the egg whites and cream of tartar together until they begin to thicken. Add the sugar and continue to beat until the whites are stiff enough to form unwavering peaks on the beater when it is lifted out of the bowl. Set the reserved custard into a larger pan half filled with ice and cold water. Stir it with a metal spoon until it thickens enough to flow sluggishly off the spoon. Remove from the ice. With a rubber spatula, stir the rum and 2 or 3 tablespoons of the egg whites into the custard. Scoop the remaining egg whites over the custard and, with the spatula, fold them together gently but thoroughly. Pour the mixture gently into the pie, and smooth with the spatula. Refrigerate for 2 hours, or until the top layer is firm to the touch.

Just before serving, prepare the topping. In a chilled bowl, whip the heavy cream with a wire whisk or a rotary or electric beater until firm enough to stand in unwavering peaks on the beater when it is lifted from the bowl. Beat in the confectioners' sugar, then spread over the top of the pie with a rubber spatula. Using the finest side of a hand-grater, grate the remaining chocolate evenly over the cream. Serve at once.

To make one 9-inch pie

CRUST
24 ginger snaps, pulverized in a blender or wrapped in a towel and finely crushed with a rolling pin (about 1⅓ cups)
4 tablespoons butter, melted

CUSTARD
¼ cup cold water
1 tablespoon unflavored gelatin
1¾ cups milk
4 egg yolks
½ cup sugar
1 tablespoon cornstarch
A pinch of salt

CHOCOLATE LAYER
3 one-ounce squares semisweet chocolate
1 teaspoon vanilla extract

RUM LAYER
4 egg whites
⅛ teaspoon cream of tartar
⅓ cup sugar
1 tablespoon rum

TOPPING
1 cup heavy cream, chilled
2 tablespoons confectioners' sugar
¼ ounce semisweet chocolate

VII

Juleps, Jiggers and Jillions of Colas

The South attempts to sate its insatiable thirst with potables ranging from iced tea to fruit punch, mint juleps and straight bourbon whiskey. In true Southern style, Mrs. John Marston, on the porch of Termite Hall in Mobile, attends to some mending while keeping a comfortable pitcherful of minted iced tea close at hand.

The South has an unquenchable thirst. Hot weather is an inescapable fact of life in this part of the world, and the heat is the muggy, steam-bath kind that drives man and beast to cover and leaves everybody limp. Harper Lee's novel *To Kill a Mockingbird* describes this heat in her home state of Alabama: "A black dog suffered on a summer's day. . . . Men's stiff collars wilted by nine in the morning. Ladies bathed before noon, after their three o'clock naps, and by nightfall were like soft teacakes with frostings of sweat and sweet talcum."

Southerners respond to the suffocating, enervating heat by quaffing an almost endless assortment of beverages. They sip such familiar standbys as minted iced tea and lemonade. They guzzle a whole color spectrum of quick pickups: Coca-Cola, Pepsi Cola, Royal Crown Cola, Dr. Pepper and Nehi. And the variety of alcoholic beverages they consume is literally staggering: moonshine, Southern Comfort, bourbon and branch water, and that quintessential Southern concoction, the mint julep.

The Southern craving for soft drinks amounts almost to an addiction. The inhabitants of the region are likely to be seen with a drink in hand anytime from sunup to well after sundown. Even the wheels of justice stop grinding while the South attempts to slake its thirst. A friend of mine attended a murder trial in Mississippi. It was one of those airless August days in the delta and the courtroom was stifling, with hundreds of people jam-packed together. In the middle of the proceedings, the judge declared a recess, and everybody—His Honor, the accused, counsel, jurors, witnesses and spectators—drank Coca-Colas.

Among the soft drinks favored by the South, Coke is king, and the story of its rise to fame and fortune is a tale in itself. Back in 1886 an Atlanta druggist named John Pemberton, who was seeking a remedy for headaches, mixed some extract of coca leaves and cola nuts in a three-legged iron pot in his backyard and stirred the mixture with an oar. He called it Coca-Cola, and within a year his drugstore had dispensed 25 gallons of this concoction for a total profit of $50. That same year another Atlanta druggist accidentally mixed some carbonated water with Coca-Cola, thus hitting upon the fateful combination that gave the drink its zest. But it was a third Atlanta druggist who really launched Coca-Cola on its way around the world. In 1891 Asa Candler purchased all rights to the Pemberton formula for $2,000. In time he sold the bottling rights to a pair of Chattanooga lawyers for $1. They never did pay him the dollar, but he and Coca-Cola still prospered mightily as a result of their enterprise, for it was the bottling of the drink (with his secret syrup in it) that made possible its worldwide distribution.

Today Coca-Cola does a business of more than one billion dollars a year. It is sold in 130 lands, and is so successful overseas that in some quarters it has come to be regarded as a symbol of intrusive American culture.

The precise composition of this ubiquitous drink remains a closely guarded secret. All the company will say is that it is "prepared with sugar and water, phosphoric acid, caffein, extractives from coca leaves (cocaine removed) and cola nuts, and other flavoring materials; colored with caramel." The "other flavoring materials" make up a mystery ingredient known as 7X. The formula for their elixir is kept in a safe-deposit box in the Trust Company of Georgia in Atlanta, and is known only to two company chemists. From time to time one of them will disappear into a laboratory at Coca-Cola headquarters in Atlanta and produce a batch of 7X. This is shipped to bottling plants around the world, with exact instructions to the bottlers as to how much of it to add to other Coca-Cola ingredients. The 7X formula alone is valued by its guardians at a cool $42 million, not that they would sell it at any price.

When it comes to alcoholic beverages, the South has been equally enterprising. Most of America's hard liquor—the best and the worst—comes from this section of the country. The worst, or at least the roughest, is moonshine, that bone-shattering, unaged, illicit variety of corn whiskey also known as corn likker, or white lightning. Its familiars drink this powerful brew without batting an eye. You will see one of them turn a jug up to his lips, take a big pull from it and wipe off his mouth with the back of his hand, and you will think there could hardly be anything in that jug stronger than tea. But then you take a swig yourself, and it knocks off the top of your head. Tears come to your eyes; your vocal cords seem to be paralyzed; you gasp for breath and your insides feel as though they are on fire.

For the most part, moonshine is the product of the mountain areas—the southern highlands of the Appalachian Range, extending down through West Virginia, Kentucky and Tennessee and the Ozarks in southern Missouri and Arkansas. The farms that dot the ridges are not easily accessible, and the people like it that way.

Served ice cold in a silver mug, the mint julep symbolizes Southern hospitality yet stirs many an ardent debate. In Louisville, where it is an indispensable part of Kentucky Derby festivities, the julep is always made of bourbon, sweetened with a syrup of crushed mint and sugar. Southerners elsewhere prefer a base of rye, rum or brandy. And while Kentuckians mash the mint in preparing the syrup, some enthusiasts fervently insist that the mint be left unbruised.

There is a good economic reason why moonshine comes from the mountains. It is made with corn, and the little patches of corn that grow in the high fastnesses are too small and too remote for their tiny yields to be hauled to distant marketplaces. Instead, the corn is converted into cheap crude whiskey. What its makers do not drink themselves they sell to customers whose innards are made of iron.

The mountains have proved a boon to moonshiners for another eminently practical reason. Because moonshine does not conform to government specifications, moonshiners are tax dodgers, constantly engaged in a game of hide-and-seek with federal alcohol tax agents, who are popularly known as "revenooers." In the mountains it is much easier for moonshiners to conceal their illegal operations, and from my firsthand observation they seemed to be coming along very well. One rangy Ozark mountaineer told me, "We pretty nigh got them fellows foxed now," meaning, of course, the revenue agents. "We burn butane in our stills," he explained. "And it don't make no smoke. They used to jes' set in their cars on some ridge and wait to see the smoke curlin' up from outa the pines in the valley, then come chargin'. Now . . ."—he stamped his foot and laughed a kind of billy-goat laugh—"they can't see doodley-squat."

The best Southern whiskey, and for that matter the best indigenous American whiskey, is bourbon. This beverage is carefully defined by law: it must be distilled from a fermented mash of not less than 51 per cent

Continued on page 168

The Derby: A Racing Classic amid a Whirl of Parties

An annual institution since 1875, the Kentucky Derby is America's favorite horse race and the high point of Kentucky social life. Starting on Thursday and stretching through Sunday, Derby weekend is an unending round of revels. For the past 20 years, one of the most lavish parties has been the pre-Derby breakfast *(above)* given by Louisville *Courier-Journal* publisher Barry Bingham and his wife. The buffet, which rarely varies, is shown at left: salad, batter cakes, Jerusalem artichoke pickles, hot rolls, Kentucky ham, bacon, fried apples and scrambled eggs. Fresh strawberries and cream follow. Thus regaled, the Binghams' 300 guests repair to Churchill Downs to watch the Derby. The 1970 winner was Dust Commander, shown at right with jockey Mike Manganello.

The Kentucky Derby—off and running above—is the ninth race in a program of 10, held at Churchill Downs every year on the first Saturday of May. More than 100,000 people are on hand to see the famous "run for the roses."

People go to the Kentucky Derby to root home a winner, of course, but no matter which horse wins, places, shows or finishes out of the money there is plenty of good cheer around. Most of it takes the form of mint juleps. Vendors such as Gerald Mark *(left)* hawk juleps in special commemorative glasses at $1.50 apiece. Each glass bears an emblem of the Derby and a list of all previous winners. The juleps are made with sugar syrup and one ounce of bourbon. Spectators like them well enough to purchase 50,000 on Derby day—but for hard-drinking horseplayers, the juleps leave about an ounce or more of bourbon to be desired. And so visitors to the track often carry their own flasks to fortify their spirits.

corn grain. Once the fermented mash has been distilled, it is aged for at least two years (four years is usual). When bottled, the whiskey must be not less than 80 proof, meaning that it must contain at least 40 per cent alcohol. Nothing but distilled water may be added to adjust the proof.

The spirit takes its name from Bourbon County, Kentucky, where it was first manufactured. Originally a very large county covering all the north-central part of the state, it was later sliced up into several smaller counties; oddly, the present Bourbon County contains no distilleries.

Before Kentucky was settled in the 18th Century, whiskey usually was made with barley or rye mash, but the new territory proved to be good corn-growing country, and there was another felicitous turn of events as well: an infusion of Irish and Scottish settlers, both skilled at whiskey-making and endowed with a prodigious thirst. The abundance everywhere in the region of clean, cold water from limestone springs made distilling here seem almost predestined. Apart from the fact that water filtered through layers of limestone resulted in an iron-free, superior taste, the coldness of the water made it usable for cooling and condensing the vapor from the still. The identity of the first manufacturer of bourbon has long been disputed, but nowadays credit for this blessed event is generally given to a Baptist minister named Elijah Craig, and 1789 is set as the date of his inspiration. And I for one find spiritual comfort in the fact that this fine whiskey was invented not by the devil but by the clergy.

How the tradition of using charred barrels came into being is shrouded in regional myth. One story tells of a careless cooper who drowsed while some dampened staves were steaming by the fire. The staves burned but he made the barrels with them anyway, and a new flavor was imparted to the contents. Another tarrydiddle would have it that a thrifty cooper, intending to resell some barrels in which salted fish had been shipped, carefully burned out the interiors to get rid of every trace of fishiness. My own favorite explanation holds that a Kentucky farmer buried several barrels of whiskey under his barn to age. Lightning struck the barn, it burned down and a few years later, digging there, the farmer rediscovered the barrels, charred black but with the honey-red liquid unharmed, and noticeably better than any other whiskey he had made. Whatever the truth of these tales, the law requires bourbon to be aged in charred new white oak barrels that must never be re-used.

Whenever the conversation turns to bourbon, you are likely to hear a lot about "sour mash" whiskeys, and most of what you hear is nonsense. Almost all bourbons are sour mash whiskeys. In preparing bourbon, the mash of corn, barley and wheat or rye is mixed with pure water and cooked in a pot. Fresh yeast is then combined with a part of the previous day's mash, which has soured overnight. This mixture, known as sour mash, is added to the new bourbon mash and the whole brew allowed to ferment. Whiskey-makers say sour mash gives their liquor "continuity" and assures a uniformity of flavor. Some whiskey-makers, such as the famous Jack Daniel's distillers in Tennessee, put the words "sour mash" on the bottle, but most bourbon manufacturers shy away from the term because they feel the word "sour" might turn some of their customers off.

Besides its consumption straight, on the rocks or combined with branch water (meaning water dipped from a clear, pure stream), bourbon is used as the base of all sorts of drinks: in old-fashioneds, sours, even—heaven help us—with Coke or with ginger ale. Many of its aficionados assert that a cupful, tablespoonful or simple splash does wonders for all manner of foods—whether in such confections as bourbon balls (Recipe Index), cake frostings or in cakes themselves. A Kentucky recipe for black cake, in reality a kind of fruit cake, uses bourbon along with sour cream, hickory nuts, raisins, dates and blackberry or loganberry jam. And one young man in Fayette County told me that when he cooks thickish steak fillets, he sears them first by turning them in blazing bourbon.

But beyond question the way to enjoy bourbon at its best is in a mint julep. This is the South's great drink, ideal balm for hot weather and indeed for all the world's woes. The proper preparation of the mint julep is an even more emotion-ridden subject than the proper preparation of fried chicken. Some people make their juleps with bourbon, while others insist on rye, brandy or rum. Some people pour in one ounce of whiskey, and others say you'll never be able to taste it unless you put in a lot more. The Greenbrier Hotel, for example, that posh hostelry at White Sulphur Springs, West Virginia, uses three ounces of Jack Daniel's whiskey in its juleps, making them potent and mighty fine.

Most people use tap water in their juleps, but others claim that only water from the purest spring will do. Some misguided souls put a cherry on top of the julep, and include a slice of fruit in the drink—things that no Southerner in his right mind would do. As for the container in which the julep is to be served, there is a silver mug school of thought and one that insists on glasses. Finally, there is the matter of the mint. Some people say you must crush it, while others argue vehemently that bruising it is a sacrilege, like snoring during a church service or being caught in a mosque with your shoes on.

So with all these hotly contested points in mind, we will now pick our way through a mine field by telling you how *we* think a mint julep should be made, no doubt setting off explosions as we go.

You begin by taking some confectioners' sugar or superfine sugar—either one will dissolve more readily than ordinary granulated sugar—and put it in a silver mint julep mug. (An aluminum one, or a tall glass, will do nicely if you do not have a silver mug.) Then you put about a tablespoon of water on the sugar and add several sprigs of fresh mint, preferably mint just picked from the garden. Next you take a muddler or a spoon and crush the mint so that the juice comes out and makes a fine syrup with the dissolved sugar and water. Don't be afraid to bruise the mint; the glory of a julep is the mingling of fresh mint and bourbon flavors and unless you crush the mint, you will never know that glory.

Once you have made your syrup, you crush some ice very, very fine—this is the hardest part of the job—then pack the mug to the top with the crushed ice. After that, you simply pour good bourbon over the ice until it reaches the brim of the mug.

Finally, you put a sprig of mint in the top of the julep, and set the mug in the refrigerator until a beautiful frost covers it. You must not touch the mug with your fingers. Hold it with a napkin, or the natural

Tennessee: Where Breakfast Is a Bash

Breakfast is a big meal in Tennessee, a carryover from the days when people worked in the fields and needed lots of energy for an early start on the day. In the summertime breakfast still is likely to include fried chicken, eggs, tomatoes, potatoes, corn, biscuits and sorghum molasses. Ham is often substituted for the fried chicken in winter, Tennessee being famous for its country hams. At other meals, baked sweet potatoes are broken open and served with lots of butter, and sweet-potato pie is a favorite dessert. Spiced beef is a Nashville specialty; it is marinated in vinegar, brown sugar, salt and pepper, then simmered in water with brown sugar and sliced paper-thin. The Hotel Peabody, a Tennessee landmark in Memphis, serves excellent vanilla muffins, spoon bread and hot biscuits. Jackson, also in the western part of the state, boasts an outstanding restaurant called Georgia's. The menu there features Tennessee ham steak, steaming boiled grits, homemade peach preserves and—if one has room—generous portions of fried catfish.

Continued on page 172

The Making of a Good Bourbon

Leading makers of bourbon whiskey pride themselves on preparing their product carefully so that each bottle of a brand tastes exactly like all the rest. Large distillers hire chemists to achieve this precision, but as the sign at left indicates, the family-owned Old Fitzgerald distillery in Louisville, Kentucky, takes such stock in its own expertise that the services of chemists are disdained. Old Fitzgerald is prepared by cooking a mash of corn, wheat (most distillers use rye) and barley malt in pure iron-free water from limestone springs. Federal law requires that the bourbon mash be at least 51 per cent corn, but the Old Fitzgerald mixture is 70 per cent corn. The cooked mash is mixed with part of the previous day's batch—known as "spent beer." Yeast is then added and the mash ferments in tubs for 3 to 4 days. To the left of the glass of bourbon on the opposite page is a container of ground hops blossoms, used in making the yeast culture. The fermented mixture is distilled twice to ensure purity. The distilled liquor is aged in charred new white oak barrels (below) to impart bourbon's distinctive mellow flavor and amber color. The law also requires that bourbon be aged at least two years, but Old Fitzgerald is aged for six years.

After aging in barrels, the whiskey is poured off, diluted with distilled water to 86.8 or 90 or 100 proof, and then bottled.

oils from your hand will leave marks on the mug and it will not frost properly. To avoid this dire outcome one Kentucky lady used to put on white gloves before mixing juleps.

When you take the julep from the refrigerator, try a touch learned from another Southern lady. There may be a little ice water at the top of the julep. Put a tablespoon of bourbon on top of the ice to make the first sip good and strong. Now you are all set, with a triple threat in your hands: a drink that looks beautiful, exudes fragrance and tastes like a nectar of the gods.

A word of warning to the unwary drinker is in order at this point: A mint julep packs a wallop. It is really little more than straight bourbon whiskey, until the ice begins to melt and dilute it. Irvin S. Cobb, the late humorist and first citizen of Paducah, Kentucky, once wrote a recipe for a mint julep and with it he included this cautionary note: "The first Kentucky julep an alien drinks is a sensation, the second is a rhythmic benefaction, but the third is a grievous error."

There is another even more devastating way to mix mint juleps, one that has led, no doubt, to many a grievous error. My Southern friends tell me the custom has faded nowadays, but in the era before World War II, on hot summer nights, college students would take a gallon-sized Mason jar, put about half a cup of sugar in it, then add a lot of mint and fill the jar with cracked ice. After that they would pour bourbon in the jar until it came up to the brim. Next, a towel would be wrapped around the jar and tied in place with a string. Then about six or eight people would sit cross-legged in a circle and pass the jar around; every time it came your way you were supposed to take a big swig. It was a fine way to see how much julep you could hold, but usually when the jar came around about the sixth time, you were lucky to be able to hold that.

Taken more temperately, a mint julep is a splendid overture to Southern summer food. In Kentucky there is a marvelous meat-and-vegetable stew called a burgoo. The official father of burgoo was a famous Lexington chef named Gus Jaubert, who cooked a huge mess of it for the Confederate General John Hunt Morgan and his cavalrymen during The War, and later showed his impartiality by preparing 6,000 gallons for a Grand Army of the Republic reunion at Louisville in 1895. The burgoo calls for three kinds of meat: beef, chicken and squirrel or almost any kind of game. Corn, tomatoes, potatoes, okra, carrots, green peppers, turnips, onions—just about any combination of fresh vegetables may be included. Cream is added in some places, and some Kentucky cooks toss in a few splashes of bourbon.

You can prepare burgoo in your own kitchen *(Recipe Index)* and with a mint julep or two as a starter, you will have a memorable meal. Better yet, head for Louisville on the first Saturday in May, Kentucky Derby Day. People will be handing you juleps as fast as you can drink them, and if you happen to be invited to a house like Barry Bingham's *(pages 164-165)*, you will really be in luck. By 5 o'clock in the afternoon, when the horses come out of the paddock at Churchill Downs and the band strikes up "My Old Kentucky Home," you'll think there's nothing like the Southland, its juleps, its food and its people.

CHAPTER **VII** RECIPES

Mint Julep

Mint juleps are made many ways and Southerners have countless firmly held opinions about which method is right, or best. Though the classic Kentucky whiskey base is bourbon, Georgians often substitute half cognac and half peach brandy; in Louisiana some bartenders use rum, in Maryland they use rye and in Virginia they sometimes add a little cognac to the bourbon. The oldest recipes do not suggest bruising the mint, and you may keep the leaves intact if you do not want the julep to have a pronounced flavor of mint. The following recipe is one version of the classic Kentucky-style mint julep.

To make 1 drink

6 small fresh mint leaves plus 1
    sprig fresh mint
1½ teaspoons confectioners' or
    superfine sugar
1 tablespoon cold water
Shaved or finely crushed ice
4 ounces Kentucky bourbon

Place the mint leaves, sugar and water in an 8-ounce highball glass or, more traditionally, a silver mint-julep mug. With a bar muddler, crush the mint, then stir until the sugar dissolves. Pack the glass tightly almost to the top with shaved or crushed ice and pour in the bourbon. With a long-handled bar spoon, use a chopping motion to mix the ice and whiskey together. Dry the outside of the glass or mug and chill the julep in the refrigerator for at least 1 hour or in the freezer for about 30 minutes, until the outside of the glass or mug is covered with frost.

To serve, remove the mint julep from the refrigerator with paper napkins or towels, taking care not to wipe off the frost. Garnish the drink by planting the sprig of mint in the ice. Insert a straw and serve at once.

Syllabub

Syllabub was originally an English drink, closely related to egg nog. Its name is reputedly derived from wine that came from Sillery, in the Champagne region of France, and from "bub," which was Elizabethan English slang for a bubbly drink. Always made with wine, syllabub was considered by 18th- and 19th-Century American men to be a ladies' Christmas drink; they preferred the whiskey-based egg nog. In recent years syllabub has been served more frequently as a dessert, as described below. It may also be beaten very thick and used as a topping for fruits or cakes.

To serve 8

½ cup brandy
½ cup pale dry sherry
½ cup superfine sugar
¼ cup strained, fresh lemon juice
1 tablespoon finely grated fresh
    lemon peel
1 cup heavy cream

Combine the brandy, sherry, sugar, lemon juice and lemon peel in a large bowl. Mix well and set aside at room temperature for 15 to 20 minutes. Then stir in the cream and set aside for 15 minutes longer.

With a large wire whisk or a rotary beater, whip the mixture vigorously for about 1 minute until it begins to foam heavily on top. With a fine wire-mesh skimmer or slotted spoon, scoop the foam from the surface and place it gently in a wine or champagne glass. Beat the cream mixture for another minute or so, skim it as before and add the foam to the glass. Repeat until the glass is full; refrigerate it at once. Following this procedure, fill and immediately refrigerate 7 more glasses.

You may serve the syllabub at once or keep it in the refrigerator for as long as 12 hours. If you prefer to prepare this dessert well in advance, the glasses of syllabub can safely be kept in the freezer for 2 days.

Syllabub is a frothy Southern sweet adapted from a 16th Century English tipple. In the old recipe, a cow was milked directly into a bowl of wine to create a bubbly drink. In the modern version, brandy and sherry are flavored with sugar and lemon, then thickened with heavy cream and beaten briefly. The froth that forms is scooped into a glass with a skimmer *(above)*. To keep the froth coming, the cream is whipped and skimmed repeatedly. Accompanied by pecans and raisins, syllabub is served in glasses and eaten with spoons *(right)*.

Bourbon Balls

In a small heavy skillet, melt the chocolate over low heat, stirring almost constantly to prevent the bottom from scorching. Remove the pan from the heat and let the chocolate cool to lukewarm.

Combine the pulverized vanilla wafers, pecans and ⅔ cup of sugar in a deep bowl. Pour in the chocolate, bourbon and corn syrup and stir vigorously with a wooden spoon until the ingredients are well combined.

To shape each bourbon ball, scoop up about a tablespoon of the mixture and pat it into a ball about 1 inch in diameter. Roll the balls in the remaining cup of sugar and, when they are lightly coated on all sides, place them in a wide-mouthed 1-quart jar equipped with a securely fitting lid. Cut two rounds from a double thickness of paper towels to fit inside the lid of the jar. Moisten the paper rounds with a little additional bourbon and press them tightly into the lid.

Seal the jar with the paper-lined lid and set the bourbon balls aside at room temperature for 3 or 4 days before serving. Tightly covered, the bourbon balls can safely be kept for 3 to 4 weeks.

To make about 60 one-inch candies

8 one-ounce squares semisweet chocolate, coarsely chopped
60 vanilla wafers, pulverized in a blender or wrapped in a towel and finely crushed with a rolling pin (about 3 cups)
1 cup finely chopped pecans
1⅔ cups sugar
½ cup bourbon
¼ cup light corn syrup

White Fruit Cake

Preheat the oven to 250°. With a pastry brush, spread 1 tablespoon of the softened butter over the bottom and sides of a 9-by-3-inch springform tube cake pan. Coat two strips of wax paper with another tablespoon of the butter and fit the strips around the tube and the sides of the pan, with the greased surfaces toward the center. Set aside.

Combine the flour, baking powder, nutmeg and salt and sift them together into a deep bowl. Add the raisins, lemon peel, orange peel, pineapple and citron, and toss the fruit about with a spoon until the pieces are evenly coated.

In another deep bowl, cream the remaining 12 tablespoons of butter and the sugar together, beating and mashing them against the sides of the bowl with the back of a large wooden spoon until the mixture is light and fluffy. Stir in the flour-and-fruit mixture a cup or so at a time. Then add ¾ cup of the bourbon and, when it is completely incorporated, stir in the slivered almonds.

With a wire whisk or a rotary or electric beater, beat the egg whites until they are stiff enough to stand in unwavering peaks on the beater when it is lifted from the bowl. Scoop the egg whites over the batter and, with a rubber spatula, fold them together gently but thoroughly.

Pour the batter into the paper-lined pan, filling it about three quarters full, and smooth the top with the spatula. Bake in the middle of the oven for 2½ to 3 hours, or until a toothpick or cake tester inserted in the center of the cake comes out clean.

Let the cake cool overnight before removing the sides of the springform. Then slip it off the bottom of the pan and carefully peel away the paper. Place the cake on a serving plate and sprinkle it evenly with the remaining ½ cup of bourbon. Wrap in cheesecloth and set the cake aside at room temperature for at least 24 hours before serving. Securely wrapped in foil or plastic, it can be kept for several months, and its flavor will improve with age.

To make one 6-pound cake

14 tablespoons butter, softened
3 cups flour
2 teaspoons double-acting baking powder
½ teaspoon ground nutmeg, preferably freshly grated
¾ teaspoon salt
2 cups golden raisins
¾ cup finely slivered candied lemon peel (about 6 ounces)
¾ cup finely slivered candied orange peel (about 6 ounces)
¾ cup finely slivered candied pineapple (about 6 ounces)
¾ cup finely chopped candied citron (about 6 ounces)
1 cup sugar
1¼ cups bourbon
1½ cups slivered blanched almonds (about 6 ounces)
8 egg whites

Christmas in the South means a creamy bowl of rum-and-bourbon-based eggnog *(bottom left)* and a rich array of cakes and candies: coconut cake *(top left)*; white fruitcake *(top right)*; bourbon ball candies *(bottom right)*; and *(center)* sugary divinity candies topped with pecans. *(Recipe Index.)*

VIII

Florida: The Never-Never Land

Everyone who noses his car down toward Florida sets out with a ready-made image in mind: a picture of palm trees, sunny beaches and blue-green water, of pelicans and alligators, of tourists by the tons. Hardly anyone goes to Florida simply to sample the local dishes, and yet the state is full of culinary surprises and delights.

My first stop in Florida was Pensacola, the oldest community on the Gulf Coast. Its superb natural harbor attracted Tristan de Luna and his company of 1,500 would-be settlers as early as 1559. A hurricane routed the Spaniards almost as soon as they arrived, but even so Pensacola claims, on the strength of Tristan's ill-fated effort, to be the site of the country's earliest settlement by white men, and in 1959 pridefully celebrated "America's first quadricentennial."

During its checkered history Pensacola changed its flag no fewer than 13 times before finally becoming a part of the United States. One of my favorite characters in Gulf Coast chronicles perfectly personifies the mix that went into the making of the area. His name was Alexander McGillivray and, improbable as it may seem, he was chief of the Creek Indians in these parts back in Revolutionary days. His father was Scottish, his mother French-Indian; he was educated in Charleston and esteemed by George Washington and other contemporaries, despite the fact that he served simultaneously as an officer in the British, Spanish and American armies when these powers were contending for control of Pensacola.

Nowadays the city is full of live oaks and oleanders, a hammock-and-ho-hum atmosphere. Some 30,000 men trained at the Naval Air Station

Rising like Proteus from the sea, Miami scuba diver Paul Damman emerges with live conchs from the ocean depths and heaps them safely in a basket supported by an inner tube. Later, as shown on the next page, Damman will prepare conch chowder. In Florida the sweet, clamlike conchs are also chopped up for fritters or marinated in Key lime juice to make a fine salad.

A city fireman by trade, Paul Damman likes to prepare conch chowder for James McKinnell (*above*) and other members of his hook and ladder company. To make the chowder, Damman extracts the conchs from their shells and grinds the meat into a kettle. He cooks it with onions, tomatoes, tomato juice, Worcestershire sauce, bay leaves and oregano, and adds crisp-fried chunks of salt pork before serving.

here during World War II, and this is still very much a Navy town. Even though the military services and good food rarely go hand in hand, there is excellent eating in Pensacola. Red snappers, those well-fleshed, 50- and 60-pound beauties, are a particular favorite. The steaks or fillets are baked. A bit of orange juice and grated orange rind usually goes into the cooking, pointing up the fish flavor admirably (*Recipe Index*).

All along the northern Florida coast, on past Panama City and Port St. Joe, Apalachicola and Cedar Key, that rather special fish, the pompano, is also much in evidence. The pompano is flat and bright blue and silver in color, with a slim "waist" between its tail and body; the head is smallish for the body, with a big eye and sour-mouth expression that give the fish a mean look. But its prime distinction is gastronomic: even people who normally dislike fish will feast on pompano and go back for more. To savor its flavor fully you must eat it within an hour after it is pulled from the water. Broiled immediately, the firm flesh with its sweetish sea taste is unbeatable. Another way of preparing pompano is *en papillote* (sealed in a paper bag or folded in cooking parchment and cooked with various seasonings such as cayenne and thyme). This dish is much acclaimed along the Gulf Coast, although there are also fierce adherents of pompano stuffed with fresh Gulf shrimp and scallions moistened with sherry and baked with butter (*Recipe Index*).

Florida, of course, is our leading producer of citrus fruits, responsible for more than 80 per cent of all the oranges grown in the United States as well as most of the grapefruit and tangerines. The citrus belt extends roughly from Ocala down to just north of Lake Okeechobee, and when you drive down through Orlando toward Lakeland you come upon it like an explosion. A sweetness in the air suddenly hits you: the oranges are in bloom, and in the warm sun the scent is downright intoxicating.

In the backwoods near Lakeland, I went to call on Benton McClintock, who owns an orange grove at the end of a long, straight, flat road. A cousin in Pensacola had urged that I sample Mr. McClintock's orange wine, which he makes not for sale but only for home use, although he does produce limited quantities of pickled oranges for public consumption. He turned out to be a white-haired, blue-eyed, tanned gentleman just under 90 who informed me that daily draughts of orange wine were his simple recipe for longevity. We sat in wicker rockers on his long front verandah, and his servant, Sam, as old and good-humored as Mr. McClintock, brought out two glasses and a dark bottle beaded with pearls of moisture. When opened, the bottle gave off a marvelous perfume: something compounded of the ghosts of orange leaves, the smell of drying clover, the dry fruitiness of certain Chablis or *blancs de blancs*. But the liquid Sam poured into our glasses was unmistakably orange and pale golden.

"Actually," Mr. McClintock told me, "my Grandma taught us how to make orange wine. She was English, from Jamaica, and her family had always made it. Her family in England, that is, before they were in Jamaica. The secret is that the oranges must be past ripe, even better if they're moldy. I reckon in the old days when England brought in oranges from Spain they musta had a lot of moldy ones to contend with and it was natural to invent a wine from them."

"How do you make it?" I asked, finishing a second glass.

"You need about 12 pounds of oranges; I pick up some off the ground, or find moldy ones in the bottom of a basket, you know. I slice 'em up in a big vat and pour 3 gallons of boiling water over 'em and stir 'em all up good, and put a cloth tight over 'em. I leave 'em three weeks without touching 'em. If the oranges were good and moldy you've now got a crust of mold on the vat. You have to get that crust off without breaking it, if you can manage. Then you strain the liquid carefully into another vat, put in 9 pounds of sugar and go on stirring until it is dissolved, then cover the bowl real tight with the cloth and leave it there for four days. Every morning about 10 o'clock I uncover it and stir it up real good. After four days you're ready to put it into bottles. After a month you taste it. Every batch will come out slightly different; you might have to put a little sugar in each bottle. But if it tastes sweet when you try it after a month, then leave it alone. After about a year and a half you've got as fine a wine as ever was . . . and strong, too. Nothing sissy about it!"

After protesting over and again that I should stay, Mr. McClintock finally accepted the idea that my time was limited, pressed a bottle of the orange wine into my hands and extracted from me a promise to return. The wine had done its work and I found a curious weightlessness in my step as I stumbled through the blossoming orange grove. By some in-

Cold boiled stone crab claws are served to Jerrie Cobb and Ken Savard, guests at the Coconut Grove Sailing Club on Miami's Biscayne Bay. Only the claws of the Florida stone crab are eaten, but these are oversized and the meat is rich and sweet. To preserve the species, Florida fishermen remove one claw from each stone crab they catch, then return the crab alive to the ocean; the claw is regenerated in two seasons. Boiled in their heavy shells, the claws are served hot or cold, with plain or garlic butter.

explicable association of ideas I began to think how strongly entrenched Florida is in the European imagination, and how such Romantic poets as Wordsworth and Coleridge and various other literary lights had been influenced by a book we scarcely hear of any more in the United States. The great American naturalist William Bartram wrote this book in 1791, and it was an eye-opener in its day, in spite of its slightly daunting title of *Travels through North & South Carolina, Georgia, East & West Florida, the Cherokee Country, the Extensive Territories of the Muscogulges, or Creek Confederacy, and the Country of the Chactaws; containing an Account of the Soil and Natural Productions of those Regions, together with Observations on the Manners of the Indians.*

Throughout his Florida journey Bartram remained wide-eyed with awe. Ostensibly interested only in plants and trees, he noted everything. He would write at night when the mosquitoes made sleep impossible, then would catch a few hours' rest before he was awakened again by "wild turkey-cocks saluting each other from the sun-brightened tops of the lofty cypresses and magnolias." Describing the crowing, he reported that the turkey cocks "begin at early dawn and continue until sunrise from March . . . to April . . . the watch word being caught and repeated from one to another for hundreds of miles around; the whole country is for an hour or more in a universal shout." Bartram also observed the Indians making

182

"hiccory milk," and carefully noted the process. They pounded bushels of hickory nuts and cast them into boiling water, then strained the water very fine and skimmed from the top of the mixture a thick oil, "rich and sweet as cream," which they used in cooking, especially for such dishes as hominy and corn cakes.

The impression Bartram's account gives of the lush richness of Florida is borne out after almost two centuries, with now and then a touch more exotic than even Bartram would have bargained for. One wonders how he would have reacted, for example, to the sight of Tarpon Springs, one of the most Greek of Greek communities in America, home of the sponge fishers. After all the weathered blond Anglo-Saxon types I had encountered in Florida thus far, the people of Tarpon Springs were suddenly staggeringly Mediterranean, with much rolling of black eyes, and flashing of white teeth contrasted with black mustaches. The boats of the sponge fishers are broad-built and decorated in bright colors; they bear names like *Aphrodite, Pericles, Hercules*. I was two months late for the annual blessing of the sponge fleet, or rather for the blessing of the waters the fleet will work. On the day of Epiphany the Greek Orthodox Archbishop of North and South America and other clergy, in crimson, gold and white, march in procession to the harbor. There a white dove, representing the Holy Spirit, is released; then a gold cross, symbolic of the Baptism of Christ, is thrown into the waters of the Gulf by the Archbishop. All the sponge fishers dive for it; the lucky man who brings up the cross will be, so the belief goes, under special divine protection for a year.

All this I learned from a local restaurateur, John Haganis, as we sat under a warm sun and drank ouzo. With this anise-flavored liqueur—beloved of Greeks wherever they may settle—we ate very salty black olives and a pale-gray spread which we scooped up with crackers. "You know," Haganis told me, "the Greeks almost were destined to come to Tarpon Springs. Everything they like best in the world is here: fish, shrimp and other shellfish, and their basics, eggplant, okra and tomatoes." He entertained me with a tale about the town's most colorful character of the last century, the Duke of Sutherland, Queen Victoria's cousin, who always disembarked from his yacht to the music of four bagpipers in swaying kilts. The Duke was in disgrace with Cousin Vickie because he was traveling with a lady who happened not to be his wife. When his wife died in England he married his ladylove in the Episcopal church at Dunedin, not far from Tarpon Springs. The Floridians liked him and were not overly concerned with moral dilemmas.

I was interested in the Duke, but just as much so in the dip. It was both smooth and piquant in taste, and seemed to have little granules of pearl gray in it; the more I ate of it the more I wondered what was in it.

"This dip is all over the Middle East, the Balkans, Greece," Haganis explained. "We call it poor man's caviar."

"But what is it? How do you make it?"

He chuckled. "It's so simple-minded I'm ashamed to tell you. You roast whole unpeeled eggplants over a charcoal fire until the skin is black and charred. You can do it in the oven but it makes a mess, and the taste

At Islamorada, in the Florida Keys, 13-year-old Danny Borden hitches a ride on a green sea turtle. These turtles are netted off the Florida coast and in the West Indies, and shipped alive to commercial pens (called crawls or kraals) around Key West to await butchering. Part of the turtle meat is sliced into steaks and marketed fresh; most of it is canned in turtle soup.

isn't really quite as good. When the eggplants are good and scorched you peel them and mash up the flesh with a potato masher, adding a little salt and lemon juice as you go along. Then when I'm making it, I add black pepper and cayenne pepper. Mama likes it bland, I like it hot; so I try to hit a halfway mark. Now comes one of life's gravest decisions: you have to decide whether you want to add garlic or onion. Whichever, it should be the juice, or should be so finely pounded into the flesh that you don't know it's there. Then you add oil, a little at a time. When the mix has absorbed as much oil as it will, but not one drop more, then it's ready. It's better if you leave it overnight in the icebox.''

Eggplant, which is also called *melanzane* locally, turns up in many forms: fried, marinated, in various pies and casseroles. But it is only one of Tarpon Springs' culinary temptations. At the Louis Pappas Restaurant they make a salad that is downright MGM Technicolor and Ziegfeld Follies combined. To achieve this masterpiece they must have recourse to the riches of Ruskin, a community farther down the Gulf Coast that is known as the "salad bowl of the nation." And, as a matter of fact, an impressive amount of America's salad vegetables in the winter months does come from Ruskin. Just north of the Little Manatee River, it bears no resemblance whatever to any other farming community I have known. Each field is shielded on four sides by tall, dark Australian pines to protect the

tender plants from a possible chill wind. From these "secret gardens" come mild, sweet onions to be munched like Jonathan apples, radishes, every sort of green, corn, small cherry tomatoes in bunches like grapes, enormous beefsteak tomatoes one expects to be flavorless but that have all the sun-insinuated richness one could wish.

Louis Pappas' restaurant knows how to cope with this vast wealth. A little hill of potato salad is arranged on lettuce leaves. On this are deployed, with theatrical artifice, wedges of ripe tomato, sprigs of watercress, cucumber, avocado, *feta* (Greek goat cheese), green pepper, beets, shrimp, radishes and fillets of anchovy. This fantasy is dressed with oil and vinegar, oregano is sprinkled over it and garlic bread accompanies it. The freshness, the crispness of the whole fanciful creation enchanted my palate and gave me a wonderful sense of well-being. I looked in vain for a staircase with Follies girls descending.

St. Petersburg, about 35 miles down the coast from Tarpon Springs, is another world. About a century ago it was all marshland and tropical vegetation. Then the son of the first mayor of Detroit came down and bought 1,700 acres, envisioning a city. John Constantine Williams was his name; he was grand in manner and had a beard halfway to his knees. He dreamed of a railroad. He met Piotr Alexeitch Dementieff-Iverskoy, an exiled Imperial Guards officer from the Russian court, who was much in trouble

Seafood fancier A. J. (Al) McClane of Palm Beach is fishing editor of *Field and Stream* and a weekend chef. He likes to prepare *tortue aux cerises,* or turtle with cherries. Enjoyed here by McClane and his wife Patty, the turtle meat is cooked with cherries, mushrooms, chicken broth, Madeira and kirsch, then garnished with prosciutto, chopped eggs and smoked salmon.

Continued on page 188

A Cabbage from a Palm Tree

The epitome of Florida's exotic fare is heart of palm, sometimes less glamorously called swamp cabbage. Eaten raw in salads or boiled as a vegetable, the heart is the "bud," or core, of the trunk of the young *Sabal palmetto*. To harvest the heart, the tree must be cut down; at left Seminole Indians Joe and Reuben Billie ax a palm on the Brighton Indian Reservation near Lake Okeechobee. Then the outer layers are stripped away and a salad is prepared, as shown in the sequence on these pages. Lest conservationists take alarm, it should be noted that these trees are plentiful and besides, cutting them and preparing the salad with fresh hearts of palm is so much trouble that most cooks use canned hearts of palm from Brazil.

After the palm is felled, its fronds are stripped off and the bulblike end chopped from the trunk.

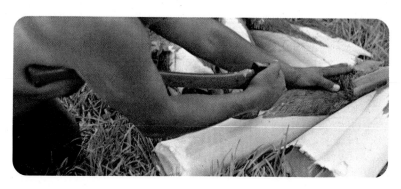

To reach the palm heart, layer after layer of tough sheathing must be slit and peeled away one at a time.

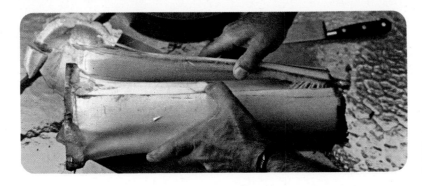

Just before serving, the last few protective layers of fibrous sheathing are cut and slipped off.

Properly trimmed, the heart of palm emerges as a slim stalk that is easy to slice and break into segments.

Fresh hearts of palm make an epicurean salad when combined with pimiento strips, lemon slices, green olives and parsley, then tossed with vinaigrette dressing. The raw hearts have a toothsome crunch and a mild flavor reminiscent of asparagus. Boiled or canned, the hearts lose crispness but not their delicacy and are a festive vegetable that may be served hot or cold.

Florida's spiny lobsters, or sea crayfish, lack the pincer claws of their Maine cousins, but their tails are meaty and succulent. For a beach party at Islamorada, in the Florida Keys, the spiny lobsters are split, filled with a stuffing of chopped fish and Key lime juice *(above),* and grilled over hot coals.

for his liberal opinions. Dementieff (he changed his name to Peter Demens) had started up a lumber-milling business in Florida and had already built a short rail line. In return for a nice hunk of land, he agreed to lay out more ambitious tracks and put Williams' imaginary town on the map. What could they call it? The two men tossed a coin, Demens won the toss and so did his nostalgia for his home town in Russia: the American St. Petersburg was born.

Nowadays the city is populated almost entirely by what are called senior citizens. Not that you'd know it. They're a lively bunch, busy beyond belief in the Florida sunshine. The parks have shuffleboard alleys that are constantly in use; there are picnics, card parties, dances, heaven knows how many clubs based on mutual interests or experiences, stamp clubs, garden clubs, French clubs, Scandinavian clubs, a poetry league. There have been free public concerts for over 70 years, and an open forum where everything can be discussed—except religion and politics. In the early 1900s a local real estate dealer was worried that there were too few places to rest one's feet in downtown St. Petersburg. He put benches on the sidewalk with his business slogan: MITCHELL, THE SAND MAN. THE HONEST REAL ESTATE DEALER. HE NEVER SLEEPS. The publicity aspect vanished in time, but the benches remained and multiplied and are now civic-owned. You can sit down anywhere in St. Petersburg. And you can go to a "drive-in" church where 1,300 to 1,400 automobiles are lined up for the sermon on the amplifier.

Friends in St. Petersburg advised me to be sure not to miss nearby

Rum and coconut juice is the featured drink at the Islamorada beach party. To prepare the drink, Bill Kissim frees a coconut *(left)*. Then he lops off the top, spikes the clear, sweet coconut juice with rum and sips the finished drink with a pretty guest, Linda Shoemaker.

Plant City. "They have strawberries this big," I was told with gestures of both thumbs and forefingers indicating a huge circle.

"Sure, big as duck eggs!" I scoffed.

Still, my friends were right. Plant City has the biggest damn strawberries I ever saw. And thanks to Florida's rich soil, the inflated size does not mean a cotton-wadding flavor. This holds true of all the jumbo fruits grown around the state: they are as delicious as normal-sized fruits. There are guavas, tamarinds, sapodillas, papayas and carambolas—the five-star apples that look like a cross between an apricot and an orange, and are shaped like a perfect star when you cut through them to expose a cross section. Small wonder that Floridians are blessed with excellent sherbets, chutneys, mousses, cakes and pies of fresh fruit. I also had a marvelous plain clear gelatin made of sweet orange and lemon juice with a bit of honey as well as sugar in it. I hate the poisonous frozen neon red and green salads that turn up in countless public eateries across the country, but I love the Gulf Coast's salads and molds and mousses that look and are so fresh and cool. Florida cookery glories in these specialties, and the variety of gelatin dishes to be found there would provide material for a thick encyclopedia volume.

In the galaxy of richly colorful communities that dot Florida's West Coast, the grandest attraction is Tampa. The broad well-protected natural harbor here used to be a haven for a few fishermen, an excellent refuge for pirates. Notable among the latter was José Gaspar, the city's rascally patron who ravaged the coastal waters for more than 30 years, *Continued on page 193*

A Sampler of Florida's Strange Fruits

Florida offers a year-round orgy for fruit fanciers. The oranges and grapefruit are juicy, the pineapples plump, and there are all sorts of strange fruits rarely found elsewhere in the U.S. Though some originated in Asia, most came from the West Indies and Latin America.

1. Barbados cherry
2. Sweet carambola
3. Green mango
4. Longan
5. Red mango
6. Tangelo
7. Sapodilla, or naseberry
8. Akee

9. Guava
10. Mango
11. Mild carambola
12. Eggfruit, or Ti-Es
13. Mexican avocado
14. Sugar apple,
    sweetsop, or
    cherimoya
15. Ceriman, or
    Monstera deliciosa
16. Sweequassa

The Dual Surprise of Florida's Key Lime Pie

Deceptively mild in appearance, the delicate filling of Florida's renowned Key lime pie has an unexpected edge of tartness. The rich pie is at its creamy best served ice cold, and since a traditional pastry crust tends to become soggy when refrigerated, many cooks prefer to make the crust with graham cracker crumbs, as seen in the pie below the server. The Key lime itself, which is prized for its juiciness and distinctive flavor, is also deceptive in appearance. When fully ripe its skin is lemon-colored, but the lime is green inside.

192

and whose depredations are celebrated every year by a carnival in which a band of latter-day pirates "recapture" the city. Half a century after Gaspar's death, the city became a snug retreat for Confederate blockade runners during The War. Still, Tampa might have remained largely the haunt of mosquitoes and alligators, with a few sagging piers, but for two big-time Yankee operators whose fierce rivalry in the late 1890s literally created Florida as we know it.

Henry Plant and Henry Flagler were both up from nothing and down from Connecticut. Both could spot a dollar 10 miles off by moonlight, and both had their eyes on the trade potential of Central and South American markets. Both built rail lines in Florida, and both constructed fantasy towns at the termini of their lines. Flagler sent architects to Spain when planning his Ponce de Leon Inn at St. Augustine, and the resulting exuberance of mixed Spanish-Italian-Victorian-exotic marked the debut of the "Florida baroque" style of hotel architecture. Plant's town was Tampa; he chose it for its harbor, pushing his rail lines right to the water and wiring Flagler that he had done so.

"Where is Tampa?" Flagler replied.

"Just follow the crowds," Plant sniffed, and set out to prove his point by building the Tampa Bay Hotel. The opening night, in 1891, was by all accounts a bash. Two thousand guests came to guzzle champagne while opera singers and string quartets performed by the wicked glitter of that wondrous new form of illumination, the bare electric bulb. The building, which now houses Tampa University, is straight out of the Arabian Nights, with four chunky minarets rising above a pile of Moorish domes and arches, thickets of columns and vast courts. The original furnishings for the old hotel included huge Spanish mahogany doors, sofas from the Tuileries in Paris, Japanese bric-a-brac, and busts of Queen Elizabeth and Queen Mary of Scotland.

Tampa is every bit as eclectic when it comes to food. It boasts Italian and Chinese restaurants of no mean accomplishment, and restaurants such as Las Novedades that combine Spanish food, Moorish arches and a wrought-iron decor. The soups here are all special and splendid, from the classic Spanish tradition, with interesting New World changes or additions. I tried one soup called *verzada,* which included beans, a bit of ham hock, potatoes, onion, green pepper, chunks of *morcilla* sausage, a hint of bacon and bay leaf, and a lot of collard greens. It was thick and satisfying, and did not encourage one to sample other courses, but I could not restrain myself when I spotted some large pale-pink shrimp.

While most Gulf ports lament the decline of shrimp fishing, Tampa rejoices that in recent years its sizable shrimp fleet happened upon a hitherto unknown bank of large shrimp. The city's restaurants serve these fat and sassy creatures in dozens of ways; at Novedades I ate them plain with green rice. Then I consumed a lime ice *(Recipe Index)* for dessert and decided I might never eat again. But after a nap and a look at the interior of the Tampa Bay Hotel-turned-university (where the students habitually scribble notices of elections and dances on the marble bottoms of Venus and Apollo), I found myself ready for another meal. I dined at a restaurant where I sipped sherry and ate an enslaving appetizer called *bollitos,* black-eyed peas and garlic made into a paste and deep-fried in tiny balls. Then, with renewed appetite, I went on to a fine sautéed shrimp and green pepper.

Both Tampa and neighboring Ybor City have large Cuban populations. The next morning, scouting the courts and alleys of Ybor City, I found a fiery deviled crab being sold in the street, and watched an expert make "Cuban sandwiches," not unlike the Poor Boy sandwiches found elsewhere on the Gulf. In this case, the excellent locally baked Cuban bread was sliced in half and spread with butter on one half, mustard on the other. Slices of sausage, ham, barbecued pork, Gruyère cheese (paper-thin) and dill pickles were loaded in. My experience of this robust concoction made me vow to return to the Tampa area someday and to eat my way through every restaurant and every street stall.

I had intended to give Miami Beach a wide berth, because the food there is really neither Southern nor representative of Florida but a costlier form of New York-Continental fare. But a friend had told me of one place that I must not miss, and so I drove southwest from Tampa. En route the black, black earth seemed like wet coal dust, and in the Immokalee region, not far from Fort Myers, there again were unbelievable vegetable fields—contrasting greens, silvery-blue cabbages, golden mustard flowers. Near the Tamiami Trail the sudden surprise of pineapple acres looked like pure screen-musical fantasy—only the hula girls were lacking—and then I sped down toward Miami along a curving highway where there were more sky and water than land, giving one the impression of roller-skating on a whale's back.

In Miami Beach I found myself incongruously wandering among that city's pretentious pleasure palaces looking for a restaurant that goes by the modest name of Joe's. The search proved eminently worthwhile, for the specialty at Joe's is a great Florida delicacy, stone crabs. With their flat, oval shells and large, black-tipped claws, these crabs look bulkier than Maryland blue crabs, although they actually measure only about five inches from tip to tip when fully grown. They are abundant in the waters around southern Florida, but their habit of burrowing deep in the sand and mud, and their powerful claws—which can bite very hard—make them difficult to capture. Stone crabs are valued for the excellent meat in their claws; once a crab has been caught and subdued, one of these jumbo claws is broken off and the crab is tossed back into the water, where in due course it will grow a replacement claw.

The claws are boiled and then cracked with a hammer or stones before being brought to the table. At Joe's I used a small two-tined fork to pick out the sweet and delicate meat, which tasted much like lobster. The crab was served with melted garlic butter—a mustard sauce was also offered—and I drank a small bottle of 1966 Pouilly-Fuissé, which went perfectly with the sweetness of the crabmeat. Joe's reputation as a haven for stone-crab mavens was easy for me to believe.

From Miami Beach to Key West is a distance of 160 miles. Key West is the end of the line, the southernmost city in the United States, lying at the far edge of the Florida Keys. There are 25 major islands in this archipelago, which stretches out in a wide arc pointing southwest from the tip of mainland Florida, and there used to be a railroad—built by the indefatigable Henry Flagler—running all the way across from Miami to Key West. But a hurricane—the worst in memory of old-time residents—destroyed the railroad in 1935.

The Overseas Highway, which was built on the battered railroad bed, and opened in 1938, is unquestionably one of the most beautiful highways in all the world. It runs right down the length of the archipelago, linking the coral islands like beads on a string. For long stretches—the longest is the Seven Mile Bridge—the road runs right out over the sea, and there is nothing but sun, sky and sparkling blue-green water all around. Pirates, smugglers and adventurers frequented these waters when the Keys belonged to Spain. Nowadays the entire area is a fisherman's paradise. Anglers are lured here in droves by the long-bodied snook, the acrobatic tarpon that can leap 10 feet out of the water; the chameleonlike dolphin that changes its color from blue to green to yellow after it is caught; and the sailfish, with its massive dorsal fin knifing through the water. And there are bonefish, permit, red drum, spotted sea trout, ladyfish, barracuda, snapper, kingfish and amberjack, enough unusual varieties to satisfy the most avid trophy-hunter.

Key West, which lies between the Atlantic Ocean and the Gulf of Mexico, is an island four miles long and less than two miles wide. This too is a Navy town, and the island's chief industry is the Boca Chica Naval Base, where President Harry Truman liked to spend his vacations as Chief Executive, lolling about in wildly colored sport shirts. The town itself is kind of shabby, crowded with motels and marinas, but the streets are bright with poinciana and coconut palms, and the vegetation reflects the early history of the Keys. Many of the plants found here—sapodilla, banyan, tamarind, East Indian palm, frangipani, night-blooming cereus—grew from seed brought by seafarers from all over the world.

There is much exotic food in Key West. The Cuban influence is strongly felt, a legacy of the years when the traffic to and from nearby Havana was quick and easy. Such dishes as *bolichi* roast (beef stuffed with hard-boiled eggs), *alcaporado* (beef stew with raisins and olives) and *arroz con pollo* (chicken with rice) are regulars on Key West menus.

Another Key West specialty is green-turtle steak. The turtles come mostly from remote areas of the Caribbean, as far as Costa Rica, and are kept in pens called kraals. The meat is tough—"you have to pound the hell out of it," a Floridian told me. The steaks are pan-fried in a batter or drenched with flour and sautéed, and served with rice pilaf.

There are two kinds of limes here: the Persian lime and the Key lime. Key West cooks like to "hot up" a dish with Old Sour, a fermented lime juice which can curl the straightest hair if not taken with caution. Key limes, which local folk deem essential to the making of their great specialty, Key lime pie, are juicier, smaller, tarter and more acid than ordinary limes. Their skins are yellow, but they are green inside. The pie *(Recipe Index)* has a conventional or graham-cracker crust and a creamy topping, and it is delicious.

Perhaps the most exotic of all Key West dishes is conch chowder, made with the mollusk that inhabits the surrounding coral reefs. (The

Spanish word for it, *conchas,* is in fact a term for Key Westers themselves.) The shell in which this creature dwells is universally admired; it is the large spiral shell that you see decorating mantelpieces and coffee tables or that sometimes fulfills the role of a doorstop. On Southern plantations it was used as a horn to summon field hands from afar, and through the ages countless children have held it up to their ears to hear the ocean's roar.

When first plucked from the water, the shell is bright pink, but the color tends to fade rapidly. The creature inside is strong and muscular, with sharp eyes and a keen sense of smell. It can stick out its foot and propel itself about by clumsy leaps and bounds; a family of conch, washed up on the beach, has been likened to a herd of miniature elephants as they lumbered about trying to get back into the water. But if you approach one, the conch will quickly pop back into its shell.

Conch meat is tough, and must be pounded and chopped before cooking. Key West cooks use it in a variety of ways. They make fritters by frying the chopped conch in a batter of flour and eggs, and serve the fritters with wedges of Key lime and a hot tomato seafood sauce. They also prepare a salad of diced conch meat and onion marinated in lime juice.

But the best way to eat this shellfish is in conch chowder *(Recipe Index)*. The conch is ground, mixed with fried salt-pork bits, tomatoes, potatoes, rice and bay leaves, and cooked over low heat for about an hour. During the last few minutes of cooking, evaporated milk is stirred in. The conch meat, which tastes somewhat like clams, is firmly textured, sweet and redolent of the sea. A steaming bowl of this fine chowder climaxed my long journey through the South.

By now, I was having trouble with waist buttons, surfeit and nostalgia. I had been endlessly amused and delighted by everything consciously, self-consciously or unconsciously deep-dyed Southern. In some ways my travels had saddened me. I regretted seeing how much had been destroyed willfully and fruitlessly in the name of Progress, that quaint 19th Century concept so little in accord with the facts of life, which clots, swarms, flows, quivers, but never did and never will move in anything like a march from one point to another. I had been made painfully aware of paradox: in a region of overwhelming natural riches, there was poverty unseemly in this country and this day and age. And oh, I was infinitely bored with all those old shibboleths and jingoistic prejudices that keep the human and natural resources from being realized.

But, even amid the tugs and hesitancies of Southern history there is reason to rejoice that all Southerners of whatever pigmentation or persuasion have retained an appreciation of the table as something more than just the place where one eats. It is a kind of precious fount of talk and affection, and it reflects an alert awareness of colors and flavors. The immediate impact of Southern cookery in general, and in particular of the soul food prepared in the South, is one of great pleasure, but by implication its message is much more profound.

And now having returned to my apartment in Rome, I await the ring of the postman delivering Calloway grits from Georgia and sassafras root from Arkansas. For, in a sense, I've never left home.

Key Lime Pie

Originally Key lime pie was made with a pastry crust—and traditional cooks insist it should still be. (For this version, use the fully baked short-crust pastry pie shell described in the Recipe Booklet.) Inasmuch as the pie is at its best when refrigerated and served very cold, a graham-cracker crust—which survives chilling nicely—has been popular, even in Key West, since the mid-19th Century.

Combine the graham-cracker crumbs and the melted butter in a 9-inch pie tin and rub them between your fingers until the crumbs are evenly moistened. Spread the crumbs loosely, place a second 9-inch pie tin on top and press down firmly to distribute the crumbs evenly over the bottom and sides of the lower tin. Remove the second pan and, with your fingers, smooth the top edges of the crust. Refrigerate until ready to fill.

In a deep bowl, beat the egg yolks with a wire whisk or a rotary or electric beater for 4 or 5 minutes, or until they are very thick. Beat in the sweetened condensed milk and the lime juice. Pour the mixture into the pie shell and smooth the top with a rubber spatula. Cover with foil or plastic wrap and refrigerate the pie for at least 4 hours, or until the filling is firm to the touch.

Just before serving, whip the cream with a wire whisk or a rotary or electric beater until it is stiff enough to stand in unwavering peaks on the beater when it is lifted from the bowl. Spread the cream over the pie, smoothing it and creating decorative swirls on the top with a small metal spatula. Serve at once.

To make one 9-inch pie

CRUST
6 ounces graham crackers, pulverized in a blender or wrapped in a towel and finely crushed with a rolling pin (¾ cup)
6 tablespoons unsalted butter, melted

PIE
6 egg yolks
Two 14-ounce cans sweetened condensed milk
1 cup strained fresh Key lime juice, or substitute other fresh lime juice
1 cup heavy cream, chilled

Lime Sherbet

Pour the 2 tablespoons of cold water into a small bowl and sprinkle the gelatin over it to soften.

Combine the remaining 2 cups of water and the sugar in a small heavy saucepan and boil over high heat for about 5 minutes, stirring until the sugar dissolves and the syrup becomes completely clear. Thoroughly stir in the gelatin, remove the pan from the heat, and add the lime juice, salt and food coloring. Pour into a bowl and cool to room temperature. Then pour the mixture into 2 ice-cube trays from which the dividers have been removed. Freeze for 1 to 1½ hours, or until solid particles begin to form on the bottom and sides of the tray. Beat the sherbet briskly with the flat of a fork and return it to the freezer for 1 to 1½ hours more.

With a wire whisk or a rotary or electric beater, beat the egg whites until stiff enough to stand in unwavering peaks on the beater when lifted from the bowl. With a rubber spatula, scrape the sherbet into a deep bowl. Scoop the egg whites over the sherbet and fold them together thoroughly, return the lime sherbet to the ice-cube trays, smooth the tops with a spatula and freeze for 2 or 3 hours longer until the finished sherbet has a fine snowy texture.

To serve, spoon the sherbet into parfait glasses or dessert dishes.

To make about 1 pint

2 tablespoons plus 2 cups cold water
1 teaspoon unflavored gelatin
2 cups sugar
2 cups strained fresh lime juice
¼ teaspoon salt
2 drops green food coloring
2 egg whites

To make one 9-inch 4-layer cake

CAKE

2 tablespoons butter, softened
2 tablespoons plus 2 cups flour,
    sifted before measuring
1 teaspoon double-acting baking
    powder
⅛ teaspoon salt
8 egg yolks
2 cups sugar
¼ cup strained fresh lemon juice
2 teaspoons finely grated
    fresh lemon peel
8 egg whites

FILLING

1½ cups sugar
¼ cup cornstarch
⅛ teaspoon salt
2 eggs, lightly beaten
2 tablespoons butter, cut into
    ¼-inch bits
2 tablespoons finely grated fresh
    lemon peel
⅔ cup strained fresh lemon juice
1 cup water

ICING

4 egg whites
½ cup confectioners' sugar
1 teaspoon vanilla extract
1½ cups white corn syrup
2 cups freshly grated, peeled
    coconut meat

Coconut Cake with Lemon Filling

Preheat the oven to 350°. With a pastry brush, spread the 2 tablespoons of softened butter over the bottom and sides of two 9-inch layer-cake pans. Add 1 tablespoon of flour to each pan and, one at a time, tip the pans from side to side to distribute the flour evenly. Then invert each pan and rap it sharply to remove the excess flour.

Combine the 2 cups of sifted flour, the teaspoon of baking powder and ⅛ teaspoon of salt and sift them together on a plate or on a sheet of wax paper. Set aside.

In a deep bowl, beat the egg yolks and 2 cups of sugar with a wire whisk or a rotary or electric beater for 4 to 5 minutes, or until the mixture is thick enough to fall back on itself in a slowly dissolving ribbon when the beater is lifted from the bowl. Beat in the ¼ cup lemon juice and 2 teaspoons lemon peel. Then add the flour mixture, about ½ cup at a time, beating well after each addition.

With a whisk or a rotary or electric beater, beat the 8 egg whites in another bowl until they are stiff enough to stand in unwavering peaks on the beater when it is lifted up out of the bowl. Scoop the egg whites over the batter and, with a rubber spatula, fold them gently but thoroughly together until no trace of white shows.

Pour the batter into the buttered and floured pans, dividing it equally between them and smoothing the tops with the spatula. Bake in the middle of the oven for about 20 minutes, or until a toothpick or cake tester inserted in the center of the cake comes out clean and dry. Let the cakes cool in the pans for about 5 minutes, then turn them out on wire racks to cool to room temperature.

Meanwhile, prepare the filling in the following fashion: Combine the 1½ cups sugar, the cornstarch, ⅛ teaspoon salt and the 2 beaten eggs in a heavy 1½- to 2-quart saucepan and mix well with a wire whisk or wooden spoon. Stir in the butter bits, 2 tablespoons lemon peel, ⅔ cup lemon juice and 1 cup water and, when all the ingredients are well blended, set the pan over high heat.

Stirring the filling mixture constantly, bring to a boil over high heat. Immediately reduce the heat to low and continue to stir until the filling is smooth and thick enough to coat the spoon heavily. Scrape the filling into a bowl with a rubber spatula, and let it cool to room temperature.

When the cake and filling are cool, prepare the icing: With a wire whisk or a rotary or electric beater, beat the 4 egg whites until they are stiff enough to stand in soft peaks on the uplifted beater. Sprinkle them with the confectioners' sugar and vanilla and continue to beat until the egg whites are stiff and glossy.

In a small saucepan, bring the corn syrup to a boil over high heat and cook briskly until it reaches a temperature of 239° on a candy thermometer, or until a drop spooned into ice water immediately forms a soft ball. Beating the egg white mixture constantly with a wooden spoon, pour in the corn syrup in a slow, thin stream and continue to beat until the icing is smooth, thick and cool.

To assemble, cut each cake in half horizontally, thus creating four thin layers. Place one layer, cut side up, on an inverted cake or pie tin and, with a small metal spatula, spread about ⅓ of the lemon filling over it.

Put another cake layer on top, spread with filling, and cover it with the third layer. Spread this layer with the remaining filling, and place the fourth layer on top.

Smooth the icing over the top and sides of the cake with the spatula. Then sprinkle the coconut generously on the top and, with your fingers, pat it into the sides of the cake. Carefully transfer the coconut cake to a serving plate and serve at once. If the cake must wait, drape waxed paper around the top and sides to keep the icing moist.

In Key West and other parts of the Deep South coconut cake is traditionally served at Christmastime.

Red Snapper Citrus

To serve 4

½ cup finely chopped onions
¼ cup strained fresh orange juice
2 teaspoons finely grated fresh orange peel
1 teaspoon salt
Four 8- to 10-ounce red snapper fillets, with the skin left on
A pinch of ground nutmeg, preferably freshly grated
Freshly ground black pepper

Mix the onions, orange juice, orange peel and salt together in a shallow baking-serving dish large enough to hold the red snapper fillets in one layer. Add the fillets, turn them about in the orange mixture to moisten them evenly, then place them skin side up and set aside to marinate at room temperature for about 30 minutes.

Preheat the oven to 400°. Turn the fillets flesh side up and sprinkle them with a pinch of nutmeg and a few grindings of pepper. Basting the fish with the marinade from time to time, bake in the middle of the oven for 10 to 12 minutes, or until the fillets flake easily when prodded gently with a fork. Do not overcook. Serve the fish at once directly from the baking dish.

NOTE: Red snapper citrus can also be served chilled. If you prefer to present the fish cold, add 1 more teaspoon of salt to the marinade ingredients and follow the directions above for marinating and baking the fillets. Then cool them to room temperature, cover the dish tightly with foil or plastic wrap and refrigerate for 5 to 6 hours. The marinade will become a delicate jelly when it is chilled.

Conch Chowder

To serve 6 to 8

2½ pounds cooked conch meat, thoroughly defrosted if frozen
½ pound lean salt pork or bacon, finely chopped
2 medium-sized onions, peeled and cut crosswise into ¼-inch-thick slices
1½ teaspoons finely chopped garlic
4 medium-sized firm ripe tomatoes, washed, cored and coarsely chopped
1 large boiling potato, peeled and cut into ½-inch cubes
1 tablespoon uncooked long-grain white rice
3 medium-sized bay leaves
1 quart water
A 13-ounce can evaporated milk

Put the conch meat through the finest blade of a food grinder and set aside in a small bowl.

In a heavy 5- to 6-quart casserole, fry the salt pork or bacon over moderate heat, stirring frequently, until the bits are crisp and brown and have rendered all their fat. Add the sliced onions and chopped garlic and, stirring frequently, cook for about 5 minutes until the onions are soft and translucent but not brown.

Stir in the conch meat, tomatoes, potato, rice, bay leaves and water, and bring to a boil over high heat. Reduce the heat to low and simmer partially covered for 1 hour. Pour in the evaporated milk and stir until the chowder is heated through, but do not allow it to come to a boil.

Taste for seasoning and serve at once from a heated tureen or in individual soup plates.

NOTE: Evaporated milk is a traditional ingredient in conch chowder. Introduced about 1885, evaporated milk required no refrigeration and quickly became a popular product in Florida as well as other Deep-South states. Even today it is widely used in Southern cooking.

To make about 2 cups

A 4-pound firm ripe pineapple,
  stemmed, peeled, cored and
  coarsely chopped
2 cups sugar
1½ cups tarragon vinegar
2 two-inch pieces stick cinnamon,
  coarsely crushed with a mallet or
  the side of a cleaver and
  wrapped in cheesecloth together
  with 2 teaspoons whole cloves

To make about 3 pints

9 medium-sized oranges
1 medium-sized grapefruit
4 lemons
5 to 6 cups sugar

To make about 3 quarts

4 pounds firm, slightly underripe
  mangoes, peeled, pitted and the
  flesh cut into 1½-inch chunks
3 cups cider vinegar
2 cups dark-brown sugar
2 cups seedless raisins
1 cup dried currants
2 cups finely chopped onions
4 large garlic cloves, peeled, finely
  chopped and crushed with a
  mortar and pestle or with the side
  of a cleaver or heavy knife
A 3-inch piece fresh ginger root,
  scraped and cut into ⅛-inch
  slices
1½ teaspoons ground mace
1½ teaspoons ground cloves
1 teaspoon crushed dried hot red
  pepper

Palm Beach Pineapple Relish

Combine the pineapple, sugar, vinegar and bag of spices in a heavy 2- to 3-quart enameled casserole and bring to a boil over high heat, stirring with a wooden spoon to dissolve the sugar. Reduce the heat to moderate and, stirring from time to time, cook uncovered for about 30 minutes, or until the pineapple pieces are translucent and the mixture is thick enough to hold its shape almost solidly in the spoon. Remove and discard the cheesecloth bag of spices.

Ladle the relish immediately into hot sterilized jars, filling them to within ⅛ inch of the top and following the directions for canning and sealing in the Recipe Booklet. Pineapple relish is served with cold meats.

Citrus Marmalade

Wash the oranges, grapefruit and lemons and pat them dry with paper towels. With a swivel-bladed vegetable parer, remove the peel without cutting into the bitter white pith and cut it into strips one inch long and ⅛ inch wide. Cut away the white outer pith of the fruit.

Slice the fruit in half crosswise. Wrap the halves one at a time in a double thickness of damp cheesecloth and twist the cloth to squeeze all of the juice into a bowl. Wrap all the squeezed pulp into the cloth and tie the cloth securely into a bag. Measure the juice; then add enough cold water to make 3½ quarts of liquid. Drop in the bag of pulp and the strips of peel and set aside at room temperature for at least 12 hours.

Pour the contents of the bowl—the juice and water, peel and bag of pulp—into an 8- to 10-quart enameled casserole and bring to a boil over high heat. Reduce the heat to low and, stirring frequently, simmer uncovered for 2 hours. Remove the pulp bag and extract its liquid by pressing it against the side of the casserole with the back of a spoon. Now measure the mixture and add 1 cup of sugar for each cup of the mixture. Bring to a boil, stirring constantly. When the sugar has dissolved, increase the heat to high and boil briskly for 20 to 30 minutes undisturbed, until the marmalade reaches a temperature of 220° on a jelly, candy or deep-frying thermometer.

Remove from the heat. With a large spoon skim off the surface foam. Ladle the marmalade into hot sterilized jars or jelly glasses following the instructions in the Recipe Booklet. To prevent the peel from floating to the top gently shake the jars occasionally as they cool.

Mango Chutney

Place the mango chunks in a 6- to 8-quart enameled or stainless-steel pot and stir in the vinegar, sugar, raisins, currants, onions, garlic, ginger root, mace, cloves and red pepper. Bring to a boil over high heat, stirring until the sugar dissolves. Then reduce the heat to low and, stirring from time to time, simmer uncovered for 30 to 40 minutes, or until the mango chunks are tender but still intact.

Ladle the chutney immediately into hot sterilized jars, filling them to within about ⅛ inch of the top and following the directions for canning and sealing in the Recipe Booklet.

Apple-Mint Jelly

Combine the apples and water in a heavy 5- to 6-quart enameled or stainless-steel saucepan and bring to a boil over high heat. Reduce the heat to low, cover tightly and simmer for 20 to 25 minutes, or until the apples are tender and can be mashed easily against the side of the pan with the back of a spoon.

Line a large colander or sieve with 4 layers of dampened cheesecloth and place it over a large enameled pot. The bottom of the colander or sieve should be suspended above the pot by at least 3 or 4 inches. Pour in the apple mixture and allow the juice to drain through undisturbed for 3 to 4 hours. (Do not squeeze the cloth or stir the juice or the finished jelly will be cloudy.)

When the juice has drained through completely, measure and return it to the enameled pot. Discard the apple pulp. Add 1 cup of sugar for each cup of juice and bring to a boil over high heat, stirring until the sugar dissolves. Cook briskly, uncovered and undisturbed, until the jelly reaches a temperature of 200° on a jelly, candy or deep-frying thermometer. Stir in the mint and continue to cook uncovered until the thermometer registers 220° (or 8° above the boiling point of water in your locality).

Remove the pot from the heat and carefully skim off the surface foam with a large spoon. Ladle the jelly into hot sterilized jars or jelly glasses, filling them to within ⅛ inch of the tops and following the directions for canning and sealing in the Recipe Booklet.

To make about 4 cups

9 or 10 medium-sized tart cooking apples (3 pounds), about ¾ of the apples fully ripened and ¼ underripe, unpeeled but cored and coarsely chopped
3 cups water
4 to 5 cups sugar
2 tablespoons coarsely cut fresh mint leaves

Orange Meringue Pie

In a small heavy saucepan, heat the evaporated milk until bubbles begin to appear around the edges of the pan. Remove from the heat and cover to keep the milk warm.

In a deep bowl, beat the egg yolks with a wire whisk or rotary or electric beater for about a minute. Slowly add ½ cup of the sugar and the gelatin, and continue beating for 4 to 5 minutes until the mixture is thick enough to fall back on itself in a slowly dissolving ribbon when the beater is lifted out of the bowl.

Beating constantly, pour in the warm milk in a slow thin stream. Then pour the custard mixture back into the saucepan and, stirring constantly with a wooden spoon, cook over low heat for about 5 minutes. Do not let it come anywhere near a boil or the custard will curdle. When the custard is thick enough to coat the spoon lightly, remove the pan from the heat and stir in the orange liqueur and orange peel. Transfer the custard to a bowl and let it cool to room temperature.

Preheat the oven to 350°. With a wire whisk or a rotary or electric beater, beat the egg whites to a froth. Add the remaining ¼ cup of sugar and continue to beat until the meringue is stiff enough to stand in unwavering peaks on the beater when it is lifted from the bowl.

Pour the cooled custard into the pie shell and smooth the top with a rubber spatula. Then spread the meringue on top, mounding it slightly in the center and creating decorative swirls with the spatula. Bake in the upper third of the oven for about 15 minutes, or until the meringue is firm and a delicate brown. Cool to room temperature before serving.

To make one 9-inch pie

1½ cups evaporated milk
4 egg yolks
¾ cup sugar
2 teaspoons unflavored gelatin
⅓ cup Grand Marnier or other orange-flavored liqueur such as Cointreau, Triple Sec or Curaçao
2 tablespoons finely grated fresh orange peel
4 egg whites
A 9-inch short-crust pastry pie shell, fully baked and cooled (Recipe Index)

Recipe Index

NOTE: An R preceding a page refers to the Recipe Booklet. Size, weight and material are specified for pans in the recipes because they affect cooking results. A pan should be just large enough to hold its contents comfortably. Heavy pans heat slowly and cook food at a constant rate. Aluminum and cast iron conduct heat well but may discolor foods that are made with egg yolks, wine, vinegar or lemon. Enamelware is a fairly poor conductor of heat. Many recipes recommend stainless steel or enameled cast iron, which do not have these faults.

INGREDIENTS: Most of the ingredients called for in this book's recipes can be found at any grocery or supermarket. Few recipes include products that are not widely available. Live terrapin and conch are rarely found outside the southern Atlantic coast, but frozen or canned terrapin meat and frozen conch meat often can be ordered through your local fish store. Fresh soft-shell blue crabs are available only in the late spring and summer months along the Atlantic and parts of the Gulf Coasts. A small amount of soft-shell crab is available frozen. Stone- or water-ground cornmeal and whole hominy are available through some supermarkets, gourmet shops and health food stores. Two mail-order sources are Byrd Mill Company, P.O. Box 5167, Richmond, Virginia 23220, and Great Valley Mills, Quakertown, Pennsylvania 18951. Smithfield and country-style hams can be ordered through gourmet shops and local butchers.

Credits and Acknowledgments

The sources for the illustrations that appear in this book are shown below. Credits for the pictures from left to right are separated by commas, from top to bottom by dashes.

Cover—Richard Jeffery. Photographs by Mark Kauffman—12, 20, 21, 26, 30, 31, 43, 46, 47, 48, 49, 72, 73, 75, 78, 79, 80, 94, 104, 105, 106, 108, 110, 127, 148, 149, 153, 156, 157, 163, 174, 176, 177, 192. Enrico Ferorelli—9, 15, 34, 35, 50, 51, 130, 137, 140, 141, 146, 160. Other photographs: page 4—Velio Cioni, Henry Groskinsky—Richard Henry, Walter Daran. 6—Map by Gloria duBouchet and Lothar Roth. 10—Culver Pictures. 17—Bruce Roberts from Rapho Guillumette. 38 through 41—Bud Lee. 52 —Richard Jeffery. 56, 57—Brian Seed. 60—Richard Jeffery—Eric Schaal © by the White House Historical Association, portrait by Rembrandt Peale. 61 through 67—Richard Jeffery. 89 through 93 —Bruce Roberts from Rapho Guillumette. 96, 97—Tessa Traeger. 98 through 101—Costa Manos from Magnum. 114 through 119 —John Dominis for LIFE. 122, 123—Bruce Roberts from Rapho Guillumette. 124—Richard Jeffery. 134—Jay Leviton. 164—Fred Schnell. 165—Fred Schnell—Neil Leifer for SPORTS ILLUSTRATED. 166, 167—George Silk for LIFE—Fred Schnell (2). 170, 171 —Anthony Blake. 178 through 189—Arie deZanger. 190, 191 —John Dominis.

For help and advice in the production of this book, editors and staff extend their thanks to the following:
in Alabama: Mr. and Mrs. Jay P. Altmayer; Mrs. Mary Branch; Miss Judy Carter; Mr. Caldwell Delaney; Mrs. A. A. Hory Jr.: Miss Ruth Huger; Mr. and Mrs. Robert Hunter; Mr. and Mrs. James L. Jackson; Mr. Stewart Leblanc; Mrs. John Marston; Mr. and Mrs. Dossy Moon; Miss Charlotte Robinson; Mr. William P. Sartor; Mrs. E. S. Sledge; Mrs. William Spratly-Burks; Miss Beverly Stanky; Mr. and Mrs. W. E. Tillman; Mr. and Mrs. E. M. Trigg; Mr. and Mrs. Peter Trigg; Miss Anne Louise Walter; The Rev. Francis X. Walter; Mr. and Mrs. Edwin Zelnicker; *in Delaware:* Mr. J. Frank Gordy, Executive Director, and Ann Nesbitt, Delmarva Poultry Industry, Inc.; *in Florida:* Greater Ruskin Chamber of Commerce; Mr. John Haganis; Dr. William F. Knight; Mr. Wallace E. Manis; Mr. Ed Mazzer; Mr. and Mrs. A. J. McClane; Mr. Lucas Pappas; Mrs. Thomas Kenneth Young; *in Georgia:* Mr. and Mrs. Hugh Armstrong Jr.; Mr. and Mrs. Lawrence M. Austin; Masters James and Lawrence Austin; The Coca-Cola Company; Mr. and Mrs. J. Walter Cowart; Mr. and Mrs. Christopher Frame; Miss Isabelle Harrison; Mr. and Mrs. Joseph Harrison; Mr. Joseph Harrison Jr.; Mr. and Mrs. Leonard Hendrix; Miss Barbara Huger; Mr. Beekman Huger; Mrs. Anna Hunter; Mr. and Mrs. Moultrie Lee; Levy's of Savannah; Mrs. Flora Undercofler; Mr. George Williams; Mrs. C. L. Winn; *in Illinois:* Mr. Fred J. Reudy, Funk Bros. Seed Company; *in Indiana:* Mary Scott Buntin, The Ball Corporation; *in Iowa:* Mr. William Schapaugh, Asgrow Seed Co.; *in Kentucky:* Mr. and Mrs. Barry Bingham; Col. Anna Friedman Goldman, Kentucky Colonels; Mr. Victor Korfhage; Mr. J. M. Maier, Louisville Cooperage Company; Mr. Julian P. Van Winkle, President, Mr. Donald Hynes, and Mr. Richard Parrish, Old Fitzgerald Distillery; Mr. and Mrs. W. Gavin Whitsett; *in Maryland:* Mr. Gary Black Jr.; Mrs. Ann Blevins Dear; Mr. and Mrs. Daniel Dickman; Mr. Edward B. Freeman; Mr. and Mrs. Dave Gordon; Mr. William James Price III; Mr. William James Price IV; Mr. Thomas Schweizer; Mrs. J. Millard Tawes; Mr. Philip Wagner; Mr. Henry Wheelwright; Mr. and Mrs. Bruce P. Wilson; Mr. Jay M. Wilson; Mrs. Janet E. C. Wurtzburger; *in Mississippi:* Professor G. R. Ammerman, Mississippi State University; Mr. and Mrs. Tommy Buckles; Mrs. Stanley Burkley; Mr. and Mrs. Leslie Carpenter; Mrs. William Feltus III; Mrs. Gordon Gulman; Mrs. J. Balfour Miller; Mrs. George Prince; Mrs. Thomas J. Reed; Mrs. Marian Smith; Mrs. Irene Tyree; Mrs. Robert Y. Wood Jr.; *in New York:* Mr. C. Edmonds Allen III; Mr. Mario Dubsky; Mr. Albert Durante, Vice President, The Bourbon Institute; Mrs. Eileen Hughes; Mrs. David H. Wallace; *in North Carolina:* Miss Daphne Athas; Mr. John Ayers; Mrs. Craig English; Mr. Eckart Murphy; Miss Page Shamburger; *in South Carolina:* Mr. and Mrs. Charles H. P. Duell; Mrs. Frances R. Edmunds; Mr. Peter Manigault; Mr. and Mrs. Emmett Robinson; Mr. and Mrs. Norman Stevenson; Dr. James A. Timmerman; Mrs. Henry P. Walker; Mrs. J. I. Waring; *in Tennessee:* Mr. John Nichios, Georgia's Restaurant; Mrs. Yvonne Phiefer; Mrs. Trent Sexton, *in Texas:* Mr. James Beals, Quaker Oats Co.; *in Virginia:* Anne Woods Antiques; Mr. James A. Bear Jr., Curator, Monticello; Mr. Stuart S. Burford; Mr. Benny Daisey; Mr. Parke Griffin; Mr. Alton Gwaltney, Mr. Mac Leach, and Mr. James C. Sprigg Jr. of Smithfield Ham and Products; Miss Edith Healy; Mr. R. L. Herrmann, V. W. Joyner & Co.: Miss Jill King; Professor Frederick Nickols; Mr. W. G. Redd, Gwaltney, Inc.; The Thomas Jefferson Memorial Foundation; Mr. and Mrs. Russell Thompson; Mr. Robert Lacy and Mr. A. C. Young III, E. M. Todd Co., Inc.; Mrs. Milfred Williams; *in Washington, D.C.:* Mrs. Helen D. Bullock, National Trust for Historic Preservation; Mr. Gordon Webb, U.S. Department of Agriculture; *in Paris:* Princesse Hélène de Julac-Verny; *in Rome:* Miss Margaret Aubrey-Smith.

The following shops and firms in New York City supplied antiques, tableware and other objects used in the studio photography in this book: Ann-Morris, Antiques; Belgravia House; Berry's Antiques; Bob Pryor Antiques; Ceralène China; Fireside Antiques; James Robinson, Inc.; John-Lewis Antiques; Judith Amdur, Antique Silver; La Cuisinière, Inc.; Mayhew; Obelisk; S. Wyler, Inc.; Samuel H. Straus, Old Sterling Silver; Spode Inc.; Tablerie, Inc.; 1066 A.D. Antiques; The 18th Century Shop; Thibaut Wallpapers; Tiffany & Co.

Sources consulted in the production of this book include: *The Standard Cyclopedia of Horticulture* by L. H. Bailey; material quoted from *Thomas Jefferson's Garden Book,* pp. 68-69, with permission from the American Philosophical Society, Philadelphia; *A Treasury of Southern Folklore,* edited by B. A. Botkin; *The Southern Cookbook* by Marion Brown; *The Williamsburg Art of Cookery* by Helen Bullock; *Colonial Virginia Cookery* by Jane Carson; *Gulf Coast Country* by Hodding Carter and Anthony Ragusin; *Southern Interiors* by Samuel Chamberlain; *Tar Heels* by Jonathan Daniels; *The Head and the Heart of Thomas Jefferson* by John Dos Passos; *The Virginia Dynasties* by Clifford Dowdey; *Thomas Jefferson* by Edward Dumbauld; *The Growth of Southern Civilization* by Clement Easton; The American Guide Series: *Alabama, Arkansas, Delaware, Florida, Georgia, Maryland, North Carolina, South Carolina,* Federal Writers' Project; *Explorers and Settlers,* edited by Robert G. Ferris; *The Man from Monticello* by Thomas Fleming; *Arkansas* by John Gould Fletcher; *Out of Kentucky Kitchens* by Marion Flexner; *Stalking the Wild Asparagus,* Euell Gibbons; *Maryland's Way,* published by the Hammond-Howard House Association; *Soul Food Cookbook* by Jim Harwood and Ed Callahan; *Charleston Receipts,* compiled by the Junior League of Charleston, S.C.; *The Plantation South* by Katharine M. Jones; *Natchez on the Mississippi* by Harnett Kane; *Thomas Jefferson's Cook Book* by Marie Kimball; *McClane's Standard Fishing Encyclopedia,* edited by A. J. McClane; *Principles of Field Crop Production* by John H. Martin and Warren H. Leonard; *Jefferson Himself* by Bernard Mayo; *Virginians At Home* by Edmund S. Morgan; *The Growth of the American Republic —Vol. 1* by Samuel Eliot Morison and Henry Steele Commager; *Robert Carty of Nomini Hall* by Louis Morton; *A Jefferson Profile* by Saul H. Padover; *Southern Accent* by William T. Polk; *Princess Pamela's Soul Food Cook Book; The Domestic Life of Thomas Jefferson* by Sarah N. Randolph; *Sojourn in Savannah* by Betty Rauers and Franklin Traub; *Cross Creek Cookery* by Majorie Kinnan Rawlings; *Ozark Country* by O. E. Rayburn; *The Carolina Housewife,* edited by Anna Wells Rutledge; *Sketches* by Nannie H. Savage; *Gumbo Ya-Ya* by Lyle Saxon, Edward Dreyer and Robert Tallant; *The World of Soul* by Arnold Shaw; *South Carolina Cook Book* by the South Carolina Council of Farm Women; *Marine Products of Commerce* by Donald K. Tressler; *The Shaping of Colonial Virginia* by Thomas J. Wertenbaker; material quoted from *Look Homeward, Angel* by Thomas Wolfe with permission of Charles Scribner's Sons, New York; *Everyday Life in Colonial America* by Louis B. Wright; *Dishes and Beverages of the Old South* by Martha McCulloch Williams. Recipe for beaten biscuits *(page 91, Recipe Booklet)* adapted from *My Favorite Maryland Recipes* by Avalynne Tawes © 1964 by Helen Avalynne Tawes, reprinted by permission of Random House, Inc.

XX Printed in U.S.A.